Angel Answers

This book belongs to
Jessie Knox.

Also by Diana Cooper

Angel Inspiration
A Little Light on the Spiritual Laws
Silent Stones
The Codes of Power
The Web of Light
Discover Atlantis (with Shaaron Hutton)
(published by Hodder Mobius)

New Light on Ascension
A Little Light on Angels
(published by Findhorn Press)

Light Up Your Life
A Time for Transformation
Transform Your Life
The Power of Inner Peace
(published by Piatkus)

Angel
Answers

DIANA COOPER

HODDER
MOBIUS

First published in Great Britain in 2007 by Mobius
An imprint of Hodder & Stoughton
An Hachette Livre UK company

First published in paperback in 2008

10

A CIP catalogue record for this title is available from the British Library

ISBN 978 0 340 93550 7

Typeset in Berkeley Book by Palimpsest Book Production Limited,
Grangemouth, Stirlingshire

Printed and bound by CPI Group (UK) Ltd, Croydon, CR0 4YY

Hodder & Stoughton policy is to use papers that are natural, renewable
and recyclable products and made from wood grown in sustainable forests.
The logging and manufacturing processes are expected to conform to the
environmental regulations of the country of origin.

Hodder & Stoughton Ltd
A division of Hodder Headline
338 Euston Road
London NW1 3BH

www.hodder.co.uk

I dedicate this book to my special grandson, Finn, with much love.

Acknowledgements

I would like to thank all those who have shared their stories and experiences with me. A special thanks to Mary Robinson and Heather Agnew for their unfailing support and help in so many ways. Greg Suart has enabled me to write by taking so many other responsibilities from my shoulders and has always been at the other end of the telephone with wise counsel. Again and again Roger Kirby has dropped everything to sort out my computer systems with unfailing patience and warm humour. And I want to acknowledge Helen Coyle, my editor, for her gentle yet perceptive comments.

Of course, my gratitude as always to the angels, unicorns and great Masters for their guidance, responses, constant encouragement and flow of energy.

Contents

Introduction

When I was forty-two and in the depths of despair at my pending divorce, an angel came to me. This luminous six-foot being showed me a glimpse of my future, in which I was standing on a platform talking to a hall full of people about spiritual matters. They all had rainbow-coloured auras, which the angel indicated signified that they were spiritually open and evolved.

This precious moment of illumination returned hope and meaning to my life. Up to that time I knew nothing about angels and had given them no thought. Nor had I any knowledge of religion or spirituality. I hugged this secret to myself for some time, but when I at last dared to tell people, they said, 'Why you? It's not fair. You weren't even spiritual!' So I meditated for an answer and was told that everyone is given a vision at some time in their lives, but most dismiss these flashes as imagination. I held on to mine and made it reality.

However, it was another ten years before I started to work with angels. On this occasion they asked me to tell people about them. In some horror, I declined. Who was I to do such a thing? Surely everyone would think I was weird! But they repeated the request and questioned whether it was my ego or my Higher Self doing my work. So I agreed to do it. I remember well walking downstairs in my dressing gown to tell my daughter that I was going to be teaching about angels in future. We looked at each other in complete shock. But it changed my life and I have communicated with them ever since, travelling worldwide to spread their light. After that I also wrote *A Little Light on Angels* and *Angel Inspiration* at their specific instruction.

A few years later they invited me to bring information about Atlantis forward. It began with a dream in which I was, tantalisingly enough, given

1

the first part of a spiritual novel in which a young man called Marcus is given a scroll from Atlantis by a Tibetan monk and told to get it translated and spread the knowledge. That set me on a seek-and-search, and eventually I wrote a trilogy of novels, The Silent Stones. The Codes of Power and The Web of Light, all threaded with spiritual information, especially that from Atlantis.

And then the angels of Atlantis, the high-frequency beings who hold the wisdom and knowledge of Atlantis, impressed on me that they were returning now to help humanity. They asked me to write about the Golden Times of Atlantis, a fifteen-hundred-year period when heaven reigned on Earth and when the citizens had gifts and powers beyond our current comprehension. It was an awesome task, but they worked with me and my friend Shaaron Hutton, who is an amazing channel, and together we wrote *Discover Atlantis*.

After that I had a year off from writing! However, wherever I went I was asked not just about angels but about the spiritual world and the puzzling reality humans have created for themselves. It seems everyone is waking up and starting to ask questions, so in this book the angels answer some of those most commonly asked by people who are seeking an understanding of life, such as: Why does God let earthquakes happen? Where was the angel when that child died? If there was a God surely He wouldn't let all these bad things happen? What caused 9/11? Where was Atlantis and why did it fall? I hope it will bring you a sense of peace and clarity as you come to comprehend the great divine order of things.

YOUR GUARDIAN ANGEL

Everyone has their own personal guardian angel, so you too have one who is designated to help you. Even though you may not be aware of it, you can feel your angel's presence. While you may have many angels near you who can answer your questions, it will be easier for you to receive answers from your own familiar guardian angel.

You can connect with the angels for personal or cosmic answers. Here are some methods you might like to try for yourself. If the feeling you have is not loving and peaceful, it is not an angel of light, for an angel of light will always enfold you in peace and give you a loving answer. Simply imagine a blue cloak of protection being placed over you and open your eyes.

To get in touch with your guardian angel
1. Sit comfortably where it is quiet and you will be undisturbed.
2. If possible light a candle and dedicate it to your connection with your angel.
3. Breathe comfortably. On the in-breath focus on love and on the out-breath, peace.
4. When you feel relaxed, breathe in love and breathe out the colour gold until you are in a golden cocoon.
5. Imagine, sense or think that your guardian angel is in front of you. You may sense a touch or smell a perfume, or nothing may happen. Trust that your angel is close, drawn in by you thinking about it.
6. Clearly formulate your question for your angel.
7. Sit quietly, for a few minutes focusing on relaxing your body.
8. You may receive a reply during this time, but you may have to wait, for answers are often dropped in later when you are least expecting them.
9. You have opened up during this exercise, so imagine you are pulling your aura in, like a cloak, and place a symbol of protection, such as a cross or an ankh, in front, behind, to either side, below and above you. You may also like to put a circle of golden light around yourself.
10. Then open your eyes.
11. Be patient! Repeat this exercise daily until you receive your answers.

As you get more used to communicating with your angel, ask your questions when you have a quiet moment, perhaps when you are going for a walk, driving the car or when you are out in the garden. But remember to let your mind stop whirling for long enough to hear the reply. You can also ask for elucidation last thing at night before you go to sleep. The response may come in a dream or as a realisation during the next few days.

Answers do not necessarily come in the way you expect. You may have a sudden thought or awareness, but you are more likely to hear a friend say something which encapsulates the response. You may hear it on the radio or read it in a book. The angels will make sure it is presented to you in some way. Your task is to remain alert and listening.

Connecting with angels changed and inspired my life. It can do the same for yours. I am a most curious person and have asked the angels many questions over the years – and have always received an answer. Sometimes it is that I am not yet ready to understand their reply! However, here are the angelic responses I received to some of life's conundrums, and I hope you find them comforting, helpful and inspiring. Remember that for every problem there is a solution at a higher level, and the angels can help you find it. All you have to do is ask.

SPIRITUAL
QUESTIONS

Angels

What are angels?

Angels are high spiritual beings who come from the heart of God and do His bidding. They live in the seventh heaven, which is another way of describing the seventh dimension. Their frequency is so light and high that they are usually invisible to humans.

Do they have free will?

Angels of light do not have freedom of choice. They must do the will of God and always act for the highest good, spreading love and light.

Are they male or female?

They are androgynous and beyond sexuality.

What is their purpose?

Their purpose is to serve the Source of All That Is. Guardian angels act as messengers and intermediaries between the human kingdoms and God. Higher angels have an infinite range of responsibilities to perform.

Why are angels being talked about everywhere now?

Because the frequency on the planet is rising, more humans are sensing their presence. Although this is often unconscious, people are starting to ask questions about them. And, also, more of you are truly connecting to the angelic realms and sharing the wisdom they bring to you.

Are there more angels on Earth now and if so why?

There are currently more angels on your planet than there have ever been. One reason is because there are more souls who have incarnated and each is looked after by a guardian angel. The second is that by divine decree your planet is to rise in frequency through two dimensions, which is a monumental shift. In order to facilitate this, millions of angels are being directed to Earth. They are helping to bring lightworkers together, co-ordinating plans for the good of the planet, comforting those whose loved ones are passing, steadying people as the light levels rise and shining light wherever they can.

If angels are beings of love, why don't they always save people from death, harm or injury?

Your Higher Self makes certain choices for your growth and experience. If this involves an accident as a wake-up call to force you on to a different path or to teach a quality such as patience, no angel of light is allowed to countermand such a decision. If your soul makes a divine contract to die at a particular time, your guardian angel cannot use its will to force you to remain in a physical body.

All is divinely perfect, including death, which is the gateway to freedom, love and light.

Are there angels in the angel clouds?

If an angel pauses for a while in the sky above you, when climatic conditions are right, condensation forms round its vibration and creates a cloud of that shape. The angelic form may have moved away, but you can be sure one was there.

It was a glorious sunny afternoon and a friend and I were walking by the sea. We looked up to see thousands of perfectly formed angel clouds over us. The blue sky resembled the dome of a cathedral painted with white winged beings, row upon row of them. They remained like that for half an hour before starting to break up and drift away. I have seen many beautiful angel clouds, but that was the most awesome.

Are the pathways of cloud that I sometimes see angel stairways?

Yes, a host of angels has passed that way leaving a trail of vapour, like a path or stairs, behind them.

Margaret told me, 'I have often seen angels, but on this occasion I looked up to see a great gathering of angels crossing the sky. They were moving very quickly as if on a mission. After they disappeared, a wide trail of cloud formed where they had passed.'

GUARDIAN ANGELS

When does the guardian angel connect to a newborn baby?

The child's guardian angel is present at the birth and connects to its charge immediately afterwards. In most cases it has watched over the baby throughout pregnancy.

Does the same guardian angel stay with you through your life?

Yes.

Does the same guardian angel stay with you throughout all your lives?

A guardian angel is allocated to you for each lifetime, depending on your level of spiritual growth. Because your angel evolves as you do, you may have the same familiar being to watch over you in several consecutive lives.

What do guardian angels do?

They hold the divine blueprint for your life, which contains your highest possible potential. They constantly remind you of it. In addition they comfort you when you are sad, sing to you when you need solace, make sure you meet the right people at the appropriate time and save you if it is not your time to die. They take your prayers up to God and act as intermediaries between you and God when this is necessary.

Must I ask for help?

Oh yes. Because you have free will, your guardian angel cannot help unless you ask for it. They can whisper to you and hope you take their guidance, but they cannot step in to assist you without your permission.

Should I say thank you?

Of course. As above, so below. Angels love to be appreciated just as you do, and thanks which are sincerely offered open the gates of abundance. Just send out a little thank you when you realise they have helped you. It is even more powerful to thank them when you ask for something because it demonstrates your faith that help is forthcoming.

How can your guardian angel help you?

Your guardian angel can meet you in your dreams and offer you guidance that is easier to hear than in your waking state! You probably will not consciously remember these meetings, but the messages will have registered. If you are open and ready it can give you spirit healing or can direct you to the perfect healer. It can take messages from you to someone else's guardian angel, with the aim of ameliorating a relationship or situation. Your angel constantly brings you comfort and enfolds you in love. It can protect you from harm and, if it is not your time to die, save you from an untimely end.

Does it help if I tell the angels what is wrong?

No. When you focus on what is wrong, the angels can do nothing to help. You are picturing what you do not want and the universe interprets this as an instruction. It is most helpful to create a vision of your desired outcome and describe it to the angels. Always add the prayerful proviso that you only want that which is for the highest good. This statement allows the angels to disregard your request if there is something better envisaged for you.

Can your guardian angel bring you love?

If you ask and, more important, if you are truly ready, your guardian angel will arrange for you to meet the love of your life.

Can your guardian angel physically save your life?

Yes. Many a person has been physically saved through the intervention of their angel. The being of light can also synchronise events so that the doctor you need is present at the moment of crisis, a passerby has a first-aid kit or you are thrown clear of an accident and land softly. It can help you in a million other ways.

Molly was cycling down the road when a car sped round the corner and hit her bike. The impact threw her high into the air. Suddenly she found herself floating down in slow motion. She landed so softly that there was not even a bruise. She was completely unhurt and none of the witnesses to the accident could believe what they saw. Molly is convinced her guardian angel held and protected her.

What if I don't listen to my guardian angel?

If you do not listen, you may miss the opportunities available to you or let your life go off at a tangent. It is when you are quiet and still that your guardian angel can drop guidance into your mind. It comes as a thought or idea, so take time for contemplation and rest so that it can come through.

Do guardian angels get angry with their charges?

Guardian angels have infinite patience and radiate only love. Anger is a human emotion.

Do people have just one guardian angel?

Yes, you have only one guardian angel, though other angels often work with you. You also have guides and helpers.

Do other angels also surround you?

When you start to work with the angels, more than one may be attracted to your energy. Then, as you direct the angels to help someone in need, you become the bridge of light through which they can enter the other person's energy field. Some people are surrounded by hundreds of angels.

Where do angels come from?

They come from the heart of God.

Have angels ever been humans?

Angels are pure spirit and have not had a physical incarnation. The only beings of the angelic hierarchy who do their spiritual work in a body are some of the dolphins. A very few ineffably evolved, heart-centred beings like Mother Mary belong to the angelic as well as the human realms.

ARCHANGELS

What are archangels?

Archangels are very-high-frequency angels who oversee the guardian angels. There are many thousands of archangels, but until recent years very few worked with humanity. However, there are now hundreds who are directly connecting to those individuals and groups who can channel their light and spread it.

What do archangels do?

Archangels direct the guardian angels. They also undertake large projects to help you on Earth. They pass ideas and information up to the mighty Principalities and Powers who are even higher-frequency beings. Some archangels, like Archangel Michael or Archangel Gabriel, have very specific roles to help humanity.

Who is Archangel Michael?

Archangel Michael is often depicted holding a shield and sword of truth. This is because his energy will protect you, give you courage and set you free from your own lower self. He will place a deep blue cloak of protection around you to keep you safe from harmful energies or cut any cords that hold you back. Remember to ask! His name means 'Who is like God'.

Who is Archangel Gabriel?

Archangel Gabriel is seen in a pure white ray of light as he brings purification to situations around you and helps you find clarity. His energy also helps you transmute negative emotions and lower thoughts. His name means 'God is my strength'.

Archangel Uriel

Archangel Uriel is often depicted in a ruby-coloured cloak, symbolising the gold of wisdom and purple of majesty. He literally brings you wisdom and helps you dissolve your fears. Uriel is in charge of the angels of peace, those who enfold troubled people and situations. His name means 'Fire of God'.

Archangel Raphael

Archangel Raphael is the healing archangel. You can ask him for help during meditation or sleep and he will assist you in any way that is karmically allowed. He will enable you to open your third eye, developing both your clairvoyance and your ability to soothe your own and other people's troubled minds. Raphael is also the Angel of Abundance and can unlock doors to prosperity, happiness, love or your heart's desire. He will even protect you on your travels. His name means 'God has healed'.

Who are the angels of Atlantis?

The people in Golden Atlantis, a distant time of high spiritual attainment, were much more highly evolved than humans currently are. Each individual was attended by a guardian angel, of the same frequency as your archangels are now. As the vibration of the planet is now rising and it is time for the energy of heaven to return to Earth, the angels of Atlantis are returning. They seek people with whom they can work to help bring back the wisdom of Atlantis. If you feel you would like to do this, meditate and offer to work with them. You will know if your offer has been accepted because you will find yourself in situations where you can talk of spiritual matters or spread the light in some other way.

> ~ **Meditation to meet the angels of Atlantis** ~
>
> ~ Sit quietly where you will be undisturbed.
> ~ Breathe in and out evenly until you feel relaxed.
> ~ Picture a beautiful, calm blue sea.
> ~ A dolphin approaches you and playfully touches you.
> ~ As you reach out your hand to touch it, a blue-white light flows into your heart.

> — You find yourself smiling and glowing as the dolphin disappears and a pure white angel stands in front of you.
> — Thank the angel of Atlantis for appearing.
> — Ask if you may work with and for it.
> — Sit quietly so that guidance can start to come to you.

You may need to do this several times before you feel a genuine connection.

Who are the angels above the archangels?

The Principalities vibrate at a higher frequency than the archangels. They are in charge of towns, huge companies, government buildings, big schools, hospitals, countries or large projects. Like all angels, they cannot interfere with human free will and can only help your world through human invitation. So if you wish to assist your community or country, visualise the perfection that you desire. Of course, in the eyes of God, the divine perfection already is. The Principalities can take the energy of your vision to raise the lower situation to the highest possible outcome.

Who are the Lords of Karma?

They are highly evolved angels, called Powers, higher in frequency than the Principalities, and they are in charge of individual, family, ancestral, country and world karma. They oversee the universal akashic records, which is a register of all human actions, a cosmic balance sheet.

Who are the angels of birth and death?

These are also from the realms of the Powers. They watch over births to ensure that babies are born at the right time and in a perfect way for their karma, which is not necessarily the way humans would like it to be. And they supervise the death process to check that a person's spirit passes at the optimum moment for his soul's progress.

Who are the higher angels?

Virtues are currently focused on Earth, sending beams of light into the minds and hearts of humanity to facilitate changes in consciousness.

Dominions are known as angels of mercy for they spread love and compassion. They are helping humanity move in a more spiritual direction.

Thrones receive divine wisdom directly from Source and download it in a way that humanity can understand. They look after the planets. Lady Gaia, who is in charge of Earth, is a throne.

Cherubim are called angels of wisdom and they are the guardians of the stars and the heavens.

Seraphim surround the Godhead, singing the praises of the Creator. In so doing they maintain the vibration of creation. Then, through the power of their love, they direct the energy which emanates from Source into the universes.

SPIRIT GUIDES AND HELPERS

What are spirit guides?

Spirit guides are those who have generally experienced an incarnation. Then, after death, they have trained in the inner planes to guide and help people from the spirit world. Some of the senior ones are very highly evolved. There are also a few special guides who have never lived on Earth, but they usually connect with their charges for a specific mission.

What is the difference between a spirit guide and an angel?

Angels are pure spiritual beings who have never experienced life in a physical body, nor do they have free will. Their will is the

16

divine will. Furthermore, your guardian angel is allocated to you at birth and stays with you throughout your incarnation, evolving as you do.

Usually a spirit guide has lived life in a human body and therefore understands the limitations, as well as the temptations, of free will. They may not stay with you for a lifetime, as guides are attracted to you according to your level of light at any given period. A particular one may work with you for a short while and then move on. You may have several with you at once, each offering guidance about a different aspect of your life. For example, you may have a guide who is a healer, a second who is a nun, a third a wise teacher and another an expert who offers business advice. In addition, you may have one who gives you courage and strength. Each or all approach you when you need their expertise.

Spirit guides evolve through service, so their spiritual growth is not dependent on yours.

I feel my grandmother around me. Is she my guide?

This is possible but unlikely, as guides have specific training for their role. It is more likely she is a helper, for you have loved ones in spirit who wish to remain near you and assist you from the other side. There are many who aid humans from the spirit side of life.

When I talk of my grandmother, who is in spirit, the lights flash on and off. Is this my imagination?

When they die your loved ones still feel close to you. Often, without the veils of illusion between you, they love you even more. They try to draw your attention to their presence and the flashing of a light is one way to do this. Switching an appliance on or off is another favourite way of indicating their proximity, while some tap on doors and others may waft a curtain.

Jill was feeling very low after her husband died. On the first anniversary of his passing she was in the kitchen when the radio turned itself on and their favourite tune was playing. 'I know he came back to cheer me up and it felt so good!' she told me.

My uncle loved to bet on the horses. He died two years ago and I often feel him around me when I pass the betting shop. Once I'm sure he gave me the name of a horse and I was tempted to put some money on it. Luckily I didn't as it lost. Am I imagining this?

If your uncle's spirit is earthbound in his old haunts, you may well sense his presence when you are there. He may still be experiencing the thrill of gambling vicariously through you. Alternatively, he may visit you from the spirit world in a place that is familiar because he loves you. Regarding the betting: if you did not trust his wisdom in life, do not do so just because he is in spirit!

Does everyone have a spirit guide?

Most people have at least one. Remember that not all spirit guides are highly evolved.

What do spirit guides do?

They help the angels. They also arrange for you to be in the right place at the appropriate time for certain meetings and events, offer guidance and help with projects such as the writing of a book or a creative plan. They beam energy to you and sometimes download teaching or information to you.

Who are the ascended masters?

They are those who have learned and mastered the lessons of Earth and ascended to a higher frequency. Working with the archangels, they oversee the incarnations of evolved souls on your planet. The most advanced are known as the Illumined Ones.

Who is Kumeka?

Kumeka is a lord of light, who has graciously agreed to work with your planet during the changes ahead as the Master of the Eighth Ray. He comes from another universe and has never incarnated in a physical body. You may call on him for higher transmutation and deep inner cleansing.

DARK ANGELS

Are there dark angels?

There are dark angels on Earth because it is a plane of duality. This means that everything in the light has its counterpart in the dark, for shadow helps to accentuate the light.

What is the purpose of dark angels?

Dark angels ultimately serve the Godhead by placing temptation in your way and testing you. However, if you listen and respond to their inducements, you will find yourself off your spiritual path. Then you will flounder in the world of illusion and glamour until you turn to embrace the light once more. Always exercise your powers of discernment, discrimination, common sense, selflessness and your own sense of right and wrong.

Does everyone have a dark angel?

No! Only people who close their hearts and allow ego to dominate attract dark angels, who whisper to them of personal power, riches and glory.

How do I ensure no dark angel comes near me?

Keep your heart open, be compassionate, kind and loving. Act for the highest good and never from selfish desire. Watch that your thoughts are positive and wholesome. Then no dark angel will touch you.

Why doesn't my guardian angel protect me from dark angels?

Those who listen to dark angels have invited them in with their thoughts of power, self-aggrandisement and lower desires. They have free will to do this. However, if someone calls in a dark one, their guardian angel must step aside. Each of you is the Creator in your own personal world, and if a human wishes to exclude the Divine that is their prerogative.

Do dark angels have free will?

Yes. Like humans, they are not subject to divine will, which is why they try to lead weak or egotistical souls astray.

Do politicians who opt for war listen to dark angels?

Yes, dark angels impress on those with huge egos thoughts of war and power. Angels of light whisper only of peace, conciliation and co-operation.

Could a dark angel talk to a religious leader?

Oh yes. Where that leader preaches from ego rather than integrity, a dark angel can approach with thoughts of separation, revenge or hatred. Angels of light only spread oneness, togetherness, harmony and love.

Atlantis

Did Atlantis really exist?

Atlantis existed as terra firma. The extraordinary powers of the people and their advanced spiritual technology have been interpreted as myths or legends by later civilisations to whom the Atlantean achievements are beyond explanation.

What was it?

Atlantis was a controlled experiment designed to see if humans could fully enter a physical body, experience emotion and sexuality, and still maintain their divinity. It failed five times as humanity resorted to control and cruelty and finally the continent was submerged by a great flood. However, it did produce an extraordinary period when the energy on the planet was the highest it has ever been.

Where was it?

At first Atlantis was a physical continent extending over the Atlantic Ocean. However, each time Atlantis was destroyed, less of the land remained. Finally there were only five islands left and a few mountain tips are the only reminders of the great civilisation.

When was it?

The experiment lasted 240,000 years and was finally abandoned in 10,000 BC.

Why was Atlantis so important?

It was the longest lasting civilisation, so almost everyone currently incarnate experienced a life there. The final attempt was fully controlled as Atlantis was protected by a dome so that nothing could enter and leave. At no other time have people developed such advanced spiritual technology, and, most important of all, Oneness was achieved for several centuries by the masses. During that period they maintained the frequency of heaven on Earth.

How long did Golden Atlantis last?

Fifteen hundred years.

How did the people maintain their high frequency?

There was no ownership, for they regarded themselves collectively as wise caretakers of the land and everything on it.

They realised that everything is divine, rocks, plants and animals as well as humans, so they honoured and respected the God In All Things.

They understood the power of gratitude and this kept abundance flowing to them.

They had no personal ambition but lived relaxed and contemplative lives.

They had no negative thoughts or words. Everything was positive, which produced outcomes for the highest good of all.

They had no tenses for past or future, so they lived in the eternal contented present, which automatically created a happy tomorrow.

They abided by the precept, do unto others as you would have them do unto you.

They practised co-operation and sharing.

They never received without giving or gave without receiving, so they kept their karma balanced at all times, reflecting in good health and blessed lives.

They constantly expressed their creativity in art, music, sport, games and simple fun.

They did what they loved to do most and this was encouraged by their families and the community.

What spiritual and psychic gifts did they have?

All were clairvoyant and could see energies round people, animals and plants, so they were able to empathise with all life forms. Because everything was transparent, there was total honesty and trust. They could transmit pictures long distance into someone else's third eye.

They were clairaudient, able to send and receive verbal messages over distances, from people as well as the angels. Because they were all heart-centred and empathetic, clairsentience was natural to them. They could feel the feelings of others as well as the emotions and impressions left in objects, so they could 'read' them.

All were healers, and some were trained in advanced healing.

Many developed and practised gifts such as teleportation, mind control, telekinesis and levitation. The Initiates learned to master gravity and manifestation.

What was the Temple of Poseidon?

Sometimes known as the Cathedral of the Sacred Heights, this was the great temple built on one of seven peaks overlooking the plains of Atlantis. It was the home of the High Priests and Priestesses and housed the Great Crystal, the Sphinx of Atlantis and advanced initiation chambers.

What was the Great Crystal?

It was a giant quartz crystal made from pure Source energy, which acted as a power generator, a mainframe computer and an inter-dimensional portal. Through it the High Priests and Priestesses controlled the weather, activated the dome over the continent and downloaded spiritual teachings and new technology into smaller crystals.

Is it true that the Great Crystal lies at the bottom of the ocean in the centre of the Bermuda Triangle?

Yes. When the Illumined Ones now need to use the portal, the Great Crystal is activated and everything within the Bermuda Triangle goes through a rapid interdimensional shift, disappearing into a higher frequency. Of course, the souls of all those affected have agreed to partake in this experience.

How many High Priests and Priestesses were there?

At any given time there were twelve High Priests and Priestesses collectively known as the Alta. Those that were in place at the start of the final experiment, the era of Golden Atlantis, chose the 84,000 volunteers who seeded the continent. Each High Priest or Priestess was in charge of the development of a region, bringing their own individuality to their area. As Golden Atlantis rose in frequency, they were replaced by other Great Ones. However, at the end of Atlantis, the original twelve were brought back to take the survivors of their regions out into the world.

Did a High Priest or High Priestess ever marry during Golden Atlantis?

No. All their energy was dedicated to serving their people for the highest good.

If life in Golden Atlantis was so wonderful, why did it fall?

Life on Earth is cyclical. The people could no longer maintain the purity of the frequency of this time. Everything was done for the common good, until one of the highly trained Magi thought he could use some of the power for his own ego satisfaction. Then Atlantis started to devolve.

What human qualities caused Atlantis to fall?

Desire for personal power, control and arrogance were the over-riding characteristics.

Is it true that we on Earth are following in the footsteps of the fall of Atlantis?

Yes and no. In their arrogance, the late Atlanteans thought they could harness and manipulate nature. Thus they were trying to change God. They genetically modified plants, experimented with and cloned creatures, implanted control boxes or chips into humans and animals, and condoned slavery. You too have sunk to these practices. The leaders received repeated warnings but chose to ignore them. This was what decided the Illumined Ones that the experiment must be terminated.

As more of you focus on the light and the good, it is possible for you to avert the fate of Atlantis. Every single decision you choose, as an individual and collectively, makes a difference.

Are those who caused the fall of Atlantis in incarnation now?

The vast majority have returned to try to put right what went wrong then.

What technology did they have?

Their advanced technology was based on crystal power and mind control. Much of it was so awesome it is beyond your current comprehension.

They powered huge flying craft which travelled silently at vast speeds.

They dematerialised objects and rematerialised them elsewhere, moving great stones and building huge 'futuristic' cities in this way.

They reached into other planets to access their minerals and metals, then moulded them into use with mind power.

Their computer network was incredible. Your present one is in an infant stage in comparison.

They had superior medical and surgical techniques, as well as telecommunication systems.

They could control the weather, locally and across the continent.

THE CRYSTAL SKULLS

What were the crystal skulls?

In the golden times the High Priest or Priestess created twelve crystal skulls, one for each region. The skulls were all fashioned from their own individual solid piece of quartz. They were formed by mind control and thought power, which is why your scientists cannot find any evidence of tools being used. They were advanced computers.

What did they look like?

They were the size and shape of a human skull. They had a jaw that moved and were able to speak and sing. Within the quartz was a network of prisms and lenses, which lit up the face and eyes, so that each radiated a unique beauty.

Why was this shape chosen?

The skull was considered to contain the expression of human consciousness. Using this part of the body as a computer also suggested the ability of the spirit and soul to travel in time and space.

What was the purpose of the crystals skulls?

They were record keepers, highly advanced computers, one for each of the twelve tribes of Atlantis. Into these the High Priests and Priestesses programmed knowledge of human origins, the esoteric mysteries of life and much more. Those entrusted to work with them added all the wisdom and understandings of their particular tribe. Thus every one held a magnificent record of the times. Their purpose was to provide a treasury of information for humanity when you are ready to understand the concepts hidden within them. This will only be accessed when people can raise their frequency to tune into the vibration of the skulls and 'read' them.

What is the thirteenth skull?

A thirteenth crystal skull, the master, was fashioned from amethyst, and the information from the twelve was downloaded into it. Amethyst is connected with the brain. It has chemical inclusions which make it violet and help to hold information, which is why this crystal was chosen for the special record keeper.

I am told that because amethyst is attuned to the brain it helps to relieve headaches and migraines. To do so, lie down and place one on the third eye, which is in the centre of the forehead. You can tape it there if you wish to. Rest another an inch or 2.5 cm above the head and one on each side of the throat. If you have a sick headache, place an additional one on the solar plexus. An amethyst under your pillow at night assists sleep by soothing the rhythm of the brainwaves.

What happened to the crystal skulls at the fall of Atlantis?

Just prior to the final destruction of the islands, the priestesses of those temples where the skulls were kept defied danger and death to take their charges with them to their new locations. Each one was hidden, to be found when humanity was ready. The twelve were placed in a safe place; the thirteenth, the amethyst master skull, which was a much higher frequency, was dematerialised and withdrawn into the spiritual planes, where it has been placed in the charge of the Sphinx.

Have any been found?

Just one has been brought forward.

In 1927 Anna Mitchell-Hedges was helping her father, an archaeologist, explore one of the lost Mayan cities in the British Honduras, now called Belize. She saw a glint of light in a crevice and climbed down, emerging with the crystal skull, and she has been its guardian and keeper throughout her lifetime. She still has custody of it at her home in Canada. This was the one saved by Aphrodite, the High Priestess of Atlantis, who was later revered as a Greek goddess. It contains all the wisdom of her tribe. It is known as the Mayan skull and has been accredited with strange powers. People sometimes smell a sweet-sour odour, hear voices or singing, or see an aura round it. It is said to heal and make prophecies.

What about the other crystal skulls that have been found?

These are not Atlantean. They were fashioned in Egypt by the Wise Ones of the tribe that left Atlantis and do not contain the purity of information of the Atlantean skulls.

When will the other Atlantean crystal skulls be found?

When you are ready. If the information contained in them was accessed by humans in your current state of consciousness, you would blow up your planet.

Where are they now?

They are all safely hidden and will be found when their 'keepers' are ready to look after them.

Will they ever be found?

Yes. In the time of spirit.

2012

What is the importance of 2012?

The winter solstice of 2012 heralds the end of an old era and the beginning of something new. It marks the end of one 26,000-year astrological cycle and the beginning of a new one. It is also the start of a twenty-year transition. New higher energy has already started to come into Earth in preparation for the anticipated changes, and massive light will be pouring down to you in that year. Lady Gaia, the vast angel in charge of Earth, has decreed that Earth and all on her must rise in consciousness, so if you are ready, you will have an extraordinary opportunity for spiritual growth, a chance unique to these times. You have been prepared for this for hundreds of years.

Why is this shift taking place in 2012?

Every 26,000 years, or 25,920 years to be exact, there is a rare and extraordinary astrological alignment between Earth, the sun and the Milky Way when time stands still for a moment. This is known as a cosmic moment, a time of the unknown and miraculous, when things beyond human comprehension may happen. Concurrently the planets Neptune, Pluto and Uranus are configured to interact. The expected acceleration in spirituality may take place slowly to your human perception, but in cosmic terms it will be very fast.

Ancient Sanskirt writings describe this cosmic moment as the pause between the out-breath and in-breath of Brahma, or God. An astrologer told me that Neptune represents higher spirituality, Pluto transformation and Uranus change, and that as these energies work together it will cause a massive impact on the planet. This offers the potential for a huge shift in consciousness and we are called on to use these high energies wisely.

What will the angels be doing at the winter solstice of 2012?

The angels will be congregating to help you accept the new energy which will be available then. They ask you to prepare yourself. Set aside time for prayer and meditation or, if this is difficult for you, simply light a candle and ask the divine forces to help you. You may prefer to walk quietly in nature, but please recognise the importance of this day for your spiritual growth and that of everyone on your planet.

What is going to happen at the winter solstice of 2012?

The current projection is that some people will move into the fourth dimension, while a few, who are ready, will ascend. Others who could do so will stay to act as beacons of light to guide those on Earth who are waking up at this time. The angels do not anticipate a sudden or dramatic change. It is simply that the cosmic moment and the energies available will offer an extraordinary chance for enlightenment. It is expected that millions of souls will avail themselves of this unique spiritual opportunity.

What does moving into the fourth dimension mean?

When you raise your consciousness to a fourth-dimensional frequency, your heart chakra opens. With an open heart you cannot hurt another life form, for you recognise that in so doing you are harming yourself. Because you then have an expanded global and cosmic awareness, you seek peace. It is anticipated that peace movements will gain momentum after this time.

What does living at the fifth dimension mean?

It involves understanding that you are part of Oneness, and acting towards others as you would like them to treat you.

What is ascension?

When you ascend to a higher frequency you bring more of the light of your soul into your life. You may be carrying so much divine energy that you can no longer sustain a physical body, in which case you may choose to pass over.

The Mayans referred to 21 December 2012 as Creation Day. What is Creation Day and will something really happen?

The Wise Ones of the Mayan culture prophesied that the energy which comes in on Creation Day will ignite the kundalini force in many humans. This will once more activate their twelve chakras, which were fully working in the golden times of Atlantis but closed down as the frequency of that great civilisation fell. As the higher chakras of these individuals open, the genetic memories of their true divine selves will be stimulated and they will once more experience infinite possibilities. The light they can then access from Source will pour down through their higher chakras and flow into their Earth Star chakra, which is below their feet. This in turn connects them through the ley lines directly into the pyramids.

The pyramids are cosmic computers which also act as substations and energy generators, but they have lost their power. As the light of humanity once more connects with them and recharges them with energy from Source, there will be a rebirth of higher consciousness on Earth.

If enough people open to enlightenment and love, this will certainly happen. It will not be sudden, but the process will begin.

What is the Great Calendar of the Pleiades?

This is a cosmic calendar based on the movement of the Pleiades. The calendar ends on 21 December 2012. Currently, higher energies come to Earth from other galaxies. These are stepped down through the Pleiades, which acts as a transformer, so that humans and animals can cope with the force directed to them. Many star children, those whose souls come to your planet from other stars and galaxies, spend time on the Pleiades adjusting their vibrations and learning about Earth before they can be born to a human mother. After 2012 these high-frequency children will be able to incarnate directly, as their mothers will match their resonance.

Do souls come to Earth via planets other than the Pleiades?

Yes indeed. There are training establishments on the other planets, stars and galaxies. For example, many lightworkers have learnt about enlightenment in the universities of Orion before coming to Earth. Others train in technology and aspects of healing in Sirius. Some learn about heart centredness in Andromeda or Venus, while some are educated in Mars in the art of using their power as a warrior to protect the underprivileged, weak and defenceless. There are also those who have been schooled in several cosmic colleges before undertaking important roles on Earth right now.

If the astrological line-ups due in 2012 caused disaster before, why should it be different this time?

In the past, the consciousness of humanity was so low that when this alignment occurred it triggered wars and natural disasters. In those eras it did not affect the cosmos too much. However, things are now different.

The change that is currently taking place in your world is a microcosm of the macrocosm, for your entire universe is to raise its vibration. Earth is at its heart and as such has a pivotal role in its future progression. Lady Gaia has now decreed that your planet and all on her will move from a third-dimensional to a fifth-dimensional frequency. This means that a shift has to take place, the first time this has happened in aeons. Because the low frequency on Earth is currently holding the whole universe back, a great deal of help is being focused on to humanity. The cosmos depends on you!

What help is Earth being offered to help her prepare for 2012?

Because of the universal decree that Earth will start to ascend in 2012, beneficial astrological alignments were organised to prepare humanity for the occasion.

The harmonic convergence of 1987 brought in higher energies and raised the consciousness of people in general.

The harmonic concordance of 2004 bestowed more divine feminine energy to awaken compassion and open hearts.

A rare and auspicious double Venus transit is taking place. This planet transited the sun at the harmonic concordance on 8 June 2004. It will do so a second time on 6 June 2012. This special conjunction offers enormous opportunities for spiritual growth. It starts to balance the masculine and feminine energy within individuals and in the collective consciousness. It includes the potential to accelerate individual and planetary ascension. For this to take place you must be ready to raise your vibration and truly value all forms of life.

Special alignments will take place on 21 December 2012.

Angels are flocking to Earth to help humanity in an unprecedented way.

Unicorns are returning to help the people find their true divine selves.

Attention is being drawn to the wisdom of the dolphins and whales.

Higher-frequency children are being born and old souls are reincarnating.

By doing your part, you are not only helping others and the planet, but your own personal journey will be gloriously enriched too.

What will happen to those who are not ready to move into a higher consciousness?

If you are not prepared, you will miss the open gateway and at the end of your current incarnation you will continue your soul journey on another third-dimensional planet, which still embraces the pain and separation of lower understanding.

The Maori, African and Native American Indian shamans all prophesy a twenty-five-year period of purification followed by a shift in consciousness. Is this happening?

This purification is already taking place.

What is the twenty-five-year period of purification about?

In August 1987 there was an astrological configuration known as the Harmonic Convergence. At that time many lightworkers went to hilltops or sacred sites to pray and meditate for help for the Earth. The light of the prayers sent into the heavens was so enormous that St Germain, the Illumined Master, took the prayers to Source with a supplication for help for humanity. By divine grace he was enabled to return to people everywhere the Violet Flame to start transmuting the negativity energy around you. Although the Violet Flame was available to selected groups before this, its mass availability marked the start of the twenty-five-year period of purification.

Since then, Gaia herself has thrown off toxins, karma created by inhumanity. This She has done through earthquakes, volcanos, hurricanes, floods, tsunamis, fires, disease and disaster, in which many souls have left the planet, taking negative energy with them to be healed and transmuted in the spirit world.

The heartfelt prayers offered worldwide in response to the traumas everywhere have helped to purify every continent. And yet there is much more to do.

Has the Violet Flame merged with the Silver Flame, and why?

The angels have watched in wonder and delight as lightworkers have dedicated themselves to purifying their energies and healing others. As a result, in another act of divine beneficence, the Silver Ray of Grace and Harmony merged with the Violet Flame of Transmutation.

The Violet Flame transmutes negative energy.

The Silver Ray brings in something higher and more beautiful to replace the old.

What is the fifth-dimensional Gold and Silver Violet Flame?

The Gold Ray has now merged with the Silver Violet Flame. It is adding wisdom, angelic love and protection to the qualities of transmutation and harmony – a truly mighty combination that raises your consciousness to the fifth dimension.

How to use the Gold and Silver Violet Flame:

1. Wherever you are, you can call on the Gold and Silver Violet Flame. Think about a flame which includes every shade from lilac through purple to silver, sparkling with gold. Visualise it if you can.
2. Picture it surrounding people who are quarrelling.
3. Send it to people who are ill, unwell or out of balance. If you have anything wrong in your physical body, allow the Gold, Silver and Violet flame to bathe that part of you.
4. If you feel angry, afraid or negative in any way, imagine the flame around you. Feel it dissolving the old and replacing it with happiness. You can do the same for others.
5. Transmit it to places where there has been war or disaster.
6. Imagine it flowing along electricity pylons, phone lines and the Internet to purify the web.

Will I still be here after the winter solstice of 2012?

This depends on higher decisions taken by your soul. While many will choose to leave the third-dimensional reality before or soon after that date, the vast majority will stay.

Is it worth saving for a pension?

You are still responsible for your finances in your golden years. Either save for a pension, or open your abundance consciousness and manifest plenty for yourself. The world will continue, though there will be changes.

Energy

How does energy work?

The world is filled with energy, both visible and invisible. Humans currently respond only to what they can see and touch, in other words, to groups of particles that are dense enough to be solid. This means your reference points are objects, which are the low-frequency clusters of matter. However, invisible, lighter energy is also moving and changing, and it affects that which is visible.

One example is electricity (or gas, both invisible), which produces power, heat and light and considerably affects your life.

Your thoughts also have a charge that you cannot see, but which nevertheless influence dense matter.

EXAMPLE

A man had a stomach problem. His stomach was operated on, and for medical reasons the wound was not closed but a transparent plate was inserted. Doctors could see that when the man became angry or agitated, that area of his stomach became inflamed and engorged. When soft music was played to him or he was calm, his stomach visibly relaxed and the colour softened. They could literally watch how his thoughts were influencing his physical body.

How can a grain of sand moving in the Sahara affect a flower in the tropics?

Because everything is made up of energy, if one atom shifts, everything throughout the world is subtly affected.

EXAMPLE

You throw a pebble into a pond. The ripples touch the shore and a little soil is dislodged into the water. A seed was resting in the earth. Now it grows into a beautiful plant at the edge of the water. A child picks the flower and takes it to her mother, who is dying. It is placed on the mother's coffin where its simple beauty touches the heart of an old man. He decides to contact his son who he hasn't seen for years. And so the story continues . . . all because one day you threw a pebble into a pond.

Everything is a response to energy. What does this mean?

Your thoughts and beliefs send out impulses into the universe which affect everyone and everything around you. Some of your energies are magnetic, and they attract good towards you. Others are repellent, so if you radiate these, positive people, events, circumstances and the physical world will avoid you.

EXAMPLES

If you are needy you unconsciously send out vibrations attracting those who need to be needed, while repelling those who are independent. Therefore the kinds of friends you have are a response to the energy you send out. If you transform your neediness, becoming independent and self-reliant, your rescuing friends will automatically leave your life or behave differently towards you without you doing or saying anything.

If you fear you will never have enough money, this belief repels all forms of finance, which will stay at a distance. When you start to welcome prosperity into your life, new doors to abundance will automatically open as you attract a flow of wealth.

I have been burgled twice. My house is identical to my neighbours, so surely this is just bad luck?

There is no such thing as bad luck. The thoughts and feelings of everyone in the household radiate a collective energy, drawing in experiences both good and bad. If everyone in the house is peaceful, with a sense of self-worth and trust, their home has an aura of protection around it which keeps it safe from infiltration. If the people in the house are quarrelling and discordant, the aura of the home is broken. However, even if just one person in the house is afraid of attack or loss, or is angry or untrusting, a chink opens in the protective shield round the home, which becomes vulnerable. A potential burglar will unconsciously be drawn to that particular dwelling.

What can I do to keep my home safe?

Make your home happy and harmonious. Fill it with peace and love, then ask the angels to protect it. Please trust them to do so by letting go of all worry about it.

Steps to strengthen the light round your home:
1. Keep it clean, tidy and uncluttered. Negative vibrations form around mess and dirt.
2. Open your windows and cleanse your entire house inside and outside by playing a singing bowl, clapping, ohming or wafting joss sticks into every corner. Doing some or all of these things dispels any dark or stuck energy. Pay particular attention to the corners. Repeat this whenever disharmony arises, harsh words are spoken or you have been out with people of lower understanding or in a crowd.
3. Do the cooking, housework and other chores cheerfully. The more you laugh and are happy, the more quickly a strong energy forms round your home.
4. Play beautiful music, put up pretty pictures and place flowers in the house.
5. Do what you enjoy.
6. Every day take time to meditate, pray and bless all situations. These three actions create a powerfully protective aura.
7. Daily thank the angel of your home for looking after it.

Can I change anything in my life?

Yes. You are master of your destiny. Your thoughts and emotions send out the energetic vibrations which attract people, situations, events and material things to you. Transform your beliefs and your life must change.

What do I need to do to alter my situation?

If you seriously wish to transform something, you must be clear about it. First decide what you really want without letting anyone else influence you. Then focus on your vision, talk about it, imagine it and act as if it has already happened.

Ask your angels to show you what is unconsciously keeping you stuck in your situation. As you become aware of fears that are holding you back, pray for help to overcome these. Then sit quietly and meditate, letting the deeper blocks surface.

When you are prepared to take responsibility for dissolving these, you are ready for the new to appear in your life. Then it is time to live the change you want to be.

Remember, as soon as you are ready, your guides and angels will open the doors to the new.

Marguerite and Claire each wanted a relationship. They spent hours writing lists of the kind of partner they wanted. They talked endlessly about it and moaned about their old boyfriends. At last they were clear about what they were really looking for.

At that point Marguerite met a man and felt she was in love, but, before long, she was complaining about him to her friend. She focused on all the things she did not like about men and him in particular. The partnership soon ended and she decided that she never wanted to be hurt again. She closed her heart. She had not dealt with the second step that was needed to create change.

Claire watched this and realised that she still had lots of unconscious beliefs and fears about commitment. She decided to take responsibility for her own part in every relationship in her life. In her mind she went through her entire history with every single man from her father, uncle and brother to boys she played with as a child, lovers and her ex-husband. At each stage she wrote down her thoughts and feelings about each one, good and bad. Then she closed her eyes and visualised the unhappy situations being put right. In each case she encouraged and comforted her hurt inner child. After that she forgave the other people and herself and thanked them all for the happy and unhappy lessons they had brought to her. Finally she burnt the piece of paper.

Without her realising it, a huge energetic shift took place. Two days later she heard that her ex-husband had suddenly proposed to his long-term partner, having always declared that he would never marry again. Within a month she had met a very suitable partner, and they are still together.

What stops me from making the changes I really want in my life?

Being stuck always arises from unconscious fears and rigid attitudes. When you meditate, look within at your hidden blocks and beliefs. Make determined efforts to think and act in positive, open, life-affirming ways and your life will change.

What if I change and it hurts someone else?

You are responsible for your own life, and others are responsible for theirs. Of course you should never deliberately or maliciously hurt someone. However, when you remain true to yourself, the universe will adjust all situations for the highest good of everyone concerned.

I was stationary when another car hit me. Surely I am completely innocent?

This is about energy, not about guilt or innocence. At some level you were a magnet for the accident. Remember that anger, whether conscious or denied, attracts such events.

Ask yourself these questions. Do you allow other people to abuse you emotionally or physically? Do you feel used, unappreciated, misunderstood or not good enough? If the answer is affirmative, you will be holding a ball of anger inside you. It is time to claim your power.

My friend is the angry one. I am friendly and good-natured, but I get attacked. Why?

Your friend's anger is conscious and the consequences are obvious. However, as a child you learnt to bury your anger and be nice to everyone in order to get the love, attention and popularity you craved. Eventually it became second nature to be pleasant to everyone, but there was a cost. In order to feel loved, you stopped being true to yourself. You gave away your power to do what you wanted to. Then you had to deny the anger you felt. The buried rage lies within your energy fields and attracts these problems.

What can I do about my suppressed anger?

Underneath anger is fear, which is a denial of your God self. It separates you from your true magnificence. Open your heart to Source and your lower feelings must dissolve.

Suppressing your anger became a survival mechanism, because as a small, vulnerable infant you believed you had to be nice in order to be loved. Just remember that your inner child needs to be reassured that it is safe to express your feelings. Words like, 'But I genuinely am a nice person,' or, 'But I like being kind to people,' may trip from your lips and help you to resist appreciating the truth.

Start by watching your thoughts. These rise like bubbles from your consciousness and hold clues to what really is going on within you. Instead of saying to yourself, 'That was an unworthy thought,' or, 'I don't really feel like that,' acknowledge each one and accept that it came from somewhere inside you. Then remind your inner child that it is OK to feel cross or upset and help him or her to find a safe way to express it.

My friend says I am an accident waiting to happen. What does this mean?

Perhaps your friend can sense your frustration or anger, which is like an unexploded bomb waiting to go off and cause problems in your life. Alternatively, your deepest fears may attract an 'accident'. There is a way to avoid this unpleasantness. Learn to acknowledge your true feelings and find the courage to express them appropriately. This will defuse the hidden tension.

I want to go out in a miniskirt and low-cut top like my friend, but my brother says it is asking for trouble. What should I do?

What do you want to attract? Your clothes and the way in which you wear them are overt signals to other people, while your beliefs and attitudes also send out unconscious energy. These messages magnetise friends, acquaintances and situations to you. Any trouble that you draw to yourself becomes your karma.

My friend calls her daughter a little devil. She means it jokingly, but I worry that her choice of words will affect the child. Is this possible?

All words have a resonance in the individual as well as the collective consciousness, and will draw this energy to the child, impacting upon it.

Is this also true when you thank someone for being an angel?

Oh yes. Through the vibration of the word, the person you call an angel is being blessed by angelic energy.

Karma

What exactly is karma?

Karma is a way of ensuring that you learn to take responsibility for your actions by returning the consequences of your decisions to you. It is the mechanism by which you learn and evolve, and literally means 'wheel' or 'circle'. As it ensures the spiritual working out of all things over lifetimes, it is a fallacy to think that anyone 'gets away with' anything.

How do you stop yourself from getting bad karma?

Give and receive in balance. If you give something away, allow yourself to receive in equal measure, and if you are given something, gratefully repay it in some way. This includes taking from your state or government, so if you accept a benefit, make sure you give something back to the community in return.

How does God punish people who have done cruel things?

God is love. Love does not punish or condemn. It shows the soul a higher way of being and softens the heart with love and understanding. However, after each lifetime, during their assessment, the soul of the person who has perpetrated wrong becomes fully aware of the consequences of their actions. The Higher Self wants to experience for itself what they have done to another and also to repay. Karma is a soul choice in order to experience and balance.

Who decides on the karma?

After you have died, you go through a life review with the support of your angel and guides. You see and understand the true consequences of your thoughts, words and deeds. You and your spiritual advisers then decide what you need to experience in order to learn the lessons of that lifetime and to right any wrongs.

Who are the Lords of Karma and what do they do?

The Lords of Karma are a group of highly evolved angels who are in charge of the balance of right and wrong, good and bad. They take decisions about individual, national, collective and world debt. Because these burdens have in some cases become so huge, you can, in meditation, approach the Lords of Karma to request divine dispensation for yourself.

You may petition them for release of some or all of your karma, which, if granted, will ease your most difficult challenges. You may also ask for divine exemption for your friends, family, ancestors, a country or the world. Each time such grace is granted, it lifts everyone's load.

What is instant karma?

It is the immediate return of the consequence of your thoughts, words or deeds, so that your karmic account is kept balanced for you. For example, if you give someone short change in the morning, you will very soon find money taken away from you. A less evolved soul seemingly gets away with things in the short term, so instant karma gives you feedback from the universe about your spiritual level.

Who qualifies for instant karma?

Until recently, only those who were sufficiently evolved were entitled to instant karma. However, this grace is being extended so that more souls are accessing this possibility.

How is a backlog of karma reduced?

The spiritual agreement made with the archangel who oversees your earthly progress often entails paying regular instalments towards your accumulated karma. In karmic terms this happens as challenges, burdens or a compulsion to serve a person or society.

Who decides on your karma?

The universe works on energy. When your spirit passes, you will review your life with your guides and angels to see the consequences of your actions, good and loving as well as those based on fear or anger. Together you will decide what you still need to learn and how you will repay those you have hurt or harmed in any way. Before your next incarnation this is genetically programmed into you as limitations or gifts, and your guides and angels ensure you meet the perfect people and situations at the right time to fulfil the blueprint of your life. Your attitude to your conditions, however, profoundly affects your repayment plan.

If you have a huge backlog of karmic debt, you may choose a very difficult incarnation in order to deal with much of it in one lifetime. Only a determined soul will do this. Many prefer to experience gradually over several lives.

How much free choice do we really have?

Your oversoul freely chooses your genetic inheritance, your circumstances and the people and situations of your life. Where a condition is karmic, in other words decided by your soul before birth, you must deal with it. Your guides and angels undertake to synchronise meetings and ensure you are in the right place at the correct time. Your belief systems are karmic, a result of past life and family conditioning. How you respond to the conditions decreed by your soul are up to your personality, which makes decisions and chooses your attitude. Your thoughts, words and actions profoundly affect your situations, and if your reactions are consistently enlightened your life changes.

If you plan a train journey, you know the stations it will stop at beforehand. They are set in stone. However, you can freely decide to get off at a particular location and spend time exploring. You can choose whether or not to talk to your fellow passengers or whether to look out at the view, to read a book or to sleep. Depending on your temperament, you will find things to grumble about or will take the inevitable challenges lightly.

EXAMPLE

Doug and Margaret's beloved only son was killed and they were understandably heartbroken. Their marriage broke up under the strain. Doug turned to the bottle and drowned his sorrows. Margaret decided to use her life for the higher good. She went to Africa to work in an orphanage and found new happiness and satisfaction. Both were faced with the same karmic circumstance chosen by their souls. Each personality reacted differently.

Is there new karma being earned now?

Yes, but not as much as many people imagine. Many of the dreadful happenings are the completion of old karma.

Is there a spiritual working-out for all things?

Indeed there is. No one ultimately gets away with anything, so there is never any need for humans to take revenge into their own hands. The long reach of karma ensures that all things are worked out in a divinely perfect way, though this may take lifetimes, depending on the dictates of the souls involved.

What about the justice system?

Humans are co-creators, co-rulers on Earth. Justice with integrity helps to balance karma, but only where the criminal is enabled to see the error of his ways. Rehabilitation dissolves karma. For the growth of humanity it is important that justice is seen to be done. (See *Repayment of Karma*, p.57.)

Has humanity sunk as low as it did before the fall of Atlantis?

Because current technological knowledge is not as advanced as it was in Atlantis, the opportunity for descension is more limited. However, the parallel trend towards the ungodly is already observed. The spiritual world is saddened to see humanity once more falling into the temptation of genetic manipulation, cloning and silicone chipping, experimentation with nuclear power and medication to control, enrich or serve the ego.

Even in the darkest times of Atlantis the leaders actually rejected the use of fossil fuels as being too damaging to the planet. You are currently abusing Mother Earth beyond anything the

Atlanteans perpetrated. They went past the point of no return. The angels remind you that you can still change your lives and return to the glory of a higher way of being.

Action to help the planet

Actively respect all life forms. Try not to purchase or support that which is produced by diminishing another human being, animal or plant.

~ Prayer of higher intention ~

Angels of light, fill my heart with love and respect for all life forms. Help me to recognise the divine in all things so that by thought, word and action I align with the highest will. Strengthen my intention to live my life according to the purest vision. At the same time open me to compassion for those who transgress the Spiritual Laws. Amen.

I told a lie to protect my mother's feelings. Does this earn karma?

When you try to protect another soul from hurt, you are preventing them from learning their lessons and this earns karma. You might like to consider that you were actually trying to shield yourself from feeling your mother's pain.

A dog ran out in front of my car and I killed it. Do I owe karma?

If you were driving sensibly and cautiously you do not owe karma, but if you were travelling recklessly, then you do. Sometimes subsequent feelings of guilt become a burden, even though the action itself does not qualify for penalty. Remember that the universe gives you whatever you believe you deserve.

Why did that dog choose my car to run into?

There could be many reasons. Here are a few questions which may enable you to discover why you attracted this situation. Were you able to remain centred in the midst of horror? Were you filled with compassion for the animal or were you thinking of yourself? Did it remind you to drive more consciously? Did you try to find the dog's owner and console him? Were you able to hold the dog in the light and pray for it? Was it a wake-up call, telling you your life was on the wrong lines? At the time of the accident were you angry or even feeling murderous?

How do I know if I still have karma to pay?

If you still owe karma, your life will present it to you in the form of challenges, restriction or the desire to help others.

John did not particularly like children, but his job as a driver entailed doing school runs. He tried to get out of it but always seemed to find himself driving kids. What he really wanted to do was become a chauffeur. Then he attended a past life regression course where he became aware that he had been cruel to youngsters in another life. He realised that he was paying back karma and went through a releasing exercise in which he forgave himself and received the forgiveness of the spirits of those he had harmed. For the first time in his life he felt contented. Within a month, the job of his dreams came up and he knew that his karmic debt to youth was cleared.

Tragic things keep happening to my son. All of his friends seem to have died and his girlfriend committed suicide.

Your son has a belief in tragedy. This attracts people into his life who have soul contracts to die in sad circumstances. None of it is by chance. It would be really helpful for your son to change his belief system.

Exercise to change your beliefs

When you do not like what is happening in your life, your unconscious beliefs need to change in order to attract something happier.

1. When you focus on what has occurred, watch what thoughts come up and write them down. Do not dismiss any of them.
2. There will be patterns within the mass of thoughts. Extract the main beliefs.
3. Then write down the opposite, the positive that you wish to attract.
4. Picture the good things happening.
5. Make affirmations of what you want to create.
6. Forgive yourself for drawing in the old.

∼ Visualisation ∼

Here is a visualisation which may help you pinpoint the underlying cause of your problems and heal them.

∼ *Find time and space where you can be quiet and undisturbed.*
∼ *You might like to light a candle and call in your angel to help you. You do not have to believe in angels to receive their assistance.*
∼ *Mentally thank your unconscious processes for trying to protect you and remind them that you are now ready to bring the causes to conscious awareness so that you can heal them.*
∼ *Focus on what has happened and be aware of where you hold the tension in your body.*
∼ *Breathe into that part of you and ask that any images or memories surface.*
∼ *If a memory or picture presents itself to you, talk to it. Find out what it is trying to tell you. Reassure it and help it to feel satisfied.*

~ *Visualise all the negativity being transmuted in a gold, silver and violet flame.*

Do companies earn karma, for example fast-food chains which sell junk food, cigarette companies or drugs companies?

Yes. Where a company sells its products in the full knowledge that they are harmful, the owners, directors or workers may all earn karma. The amount depends on the attitude, intentions and degree of understanding of the individual.

Do you still earn karma if you were carrying out the orders of someone senior?

Every individual is responsible for his or her actions and the consequences thereof. However, if a soldier believes he is fighting for a just cause and follows orders which result in death or injury, the karma is less severe than that for a soldier who battles without principle.

FINANCIAL KARMA

Does bankruptcy incur a karmic debt?

If you owe money, you are inevitably tied to the creditor over lifetimes until it is repaid.

Do rapacious financial institutions bear karma for the problems they cause?

Indeed. Those in charge of the decisions bear karma and, in some cases, so do those who administer the rules of the financial institutions.

If I owe money when I die, do I owe my creditors karma in my next, life?

This depends on the feelings and attitudes of all parties, but in general terms you will owe those creditors until it is repaid unless they are willing to release you. When the circumstances are right, your Higher Selves will orchestrate a life together in which you have the opportunity to repay.

My husband paid off my credit-card debts, which I care-lessly ran up. Do I owe him karma?

If you feel indebted to him, then you owe him karma. Guilt attracts anger, and the unpleasant feelings are consequences of your actions! When the time is right, in this life or another, your soul will urge you to repay him in some way.

However, if your husband freely and open-heartedly paid off your credit cards, leaving you feeling loved and valued, the karmic balance is reduced. Nevertheless, your Higher Self will provide you with another opportunity to learn about handling money in this incarnation or another.

My father paid my university fees. Do I owe him karma?

This depends on a number of factors. Several people asking this question would each receive different answers. It depends on the attitudes of the giver and receiver. If money comes with an agenda, karma is set up. If it is given freely, without attachment, there is perfect balance.

So, if your father paid the fees lovingly and generously expecting no repayment, emotional or financial, and you received in the same vein, there is no karmic debt.

If your father scrimped and saved because he loves you and he wants you to do well, the money comes with the hook that you must succeed. This creates a karmic cord.

In the case of the father who toils to pay because his heart bursts with pride and love for you, and he only wants your highest good, no karma is created for he is equally contented whether you go to university or not, whether you do well or not.

Where the student and his father agree that the child will repay the university fees, then the loan is his karma until it is repaid.

When I was deeply in debt, my financial adviser told me that I might just as well spend, spend, spend and then go bankrupt. This seemed to me immoral and I did not do it. If I had done, would I have earned even more karma? Does he get karma for suggesting this to me?

Yes, if you profligately spend when you are already in debt, this earns financial karma. And your financial adviser also earns karma for suggesting such an immoral course of action to you. When a person deliberately tries to influence another to do something that is not in accordance with the highest principles, his soul has more to learn.

I owed money to the Inland Revenue when I went bank-rupt. Does this mean I owe them karma?

Remember that karma is a way for you to experience what you have done to others. You owe society a debt because you have not paid your share of the community fund.

I went bankrupt because I owed money on my credit cards. Surely it didn't harm anyone because banks have loads of money. I don't get karma, do I?

Yes, you do. Your Higher Self will bring into your life more learning about managing money until you can do so responsibly.

But what about the karma of banks and other financial institutions who charge high rates of interest on money that they don't even have? Do they have no responsibility for the suffering they cause?

Yes, they do. Each individual who acts as an agent for a spiritually corrupt organisation takes on a proportion of the karma. The more responsible your position, the more debt you incur.

What about banks who tempt people to borrow money they can't repay?

Each individual is responsible for what they borrow. At the same time, where moneylenders are consciously and cynically targeting the weak and vulnerable, they do earn karma. In the case of an impersonal institution, those who take the decisions as well as those who implement them take on some of the spiritual debt.

I work for a debt-collecting agency and am expected to use dubious methods. I hate my job but cannot find anything else. What can I do?

Every single individual creates their own reality. Your current situation is the result of your beliefs, attitudes, thoughts, words, actions and choices. If you wish to change your life, you must transform your inner world. You can start immediately by making constant affirmations about your self-worth, value and ability to find the perfect spiritually enhancing job. Then decide what you really want to do and focus on your vision. This is your way of impressing on the universe that you are ready to move into something new, honourable and fulfilling.

⌒ Affirmations to change your job ⌒

Say these aloud at least ten times a day and silently repeat them as often as you can. Add your own affirmations.

⌒ I deserve a worthwhile job.
⌒ I deserve to be well paid.
⌒ I feel good about my work.
⌒ I really like my co-workers.

> ~ I enjoy what I do.
> ~ I work in an honest way.

Exercise to gain clarity
Remember, you are not seeking a lifetime job. Your quest is for the next step.

1. Consider these questions and write everything down, however trivial. Be sensible and reasonable.

   What makes you feel happy and fulfilled?
   What sort of work gives you a buzz?
   Do you want to work indoors or out, or a combination?
   Do you like being alone or with others?
   Do you like serving others?
   Do you need to be creative?
   Do you prefer to do something physical?
   Are you artistic?
   Do you like teaching?
   How much do you want to earn?
   Do you want to work for yourself?
   If you knew you would be successful, what job would you do?
   If you were already wealthy what would bring you satisfaction?

2. Sit quietly and picture, sense and feel yourself doing a variety of jobs until one feels right.

Exercise to find your perfect work
1. When you have decided what you would like to do and how much you would like to earn, write it down.
2. Draw a picture of yourself in the job and also your bank balance with the money in it.
3. Light a candle and thank the angels and the universe for bringing this work to you.

4. Take steps to prepare yourself for this job and watch out for it.

GROUP AND COLLECTIVE KARMA

Why would a God of Love choose a whole community or society to suffer in order to repay previous pain or debt?

God does not make these decisions. God is Love and magnanimously offered humans free will to make their own choices. Humanity has continually chosen to perpetrate suffering on its brothers and sisters. Throughout history whole groups, societies or families have taken soul-level decisions to return together to experience in their turn what they did to others. Then they are subjected to the abuse, violence, subjugation or pain that they in previous lifetimes meted out. In this way they can understand what such suffering feels like and learn the lesson never to treat anyone in that way again. When they take a decision to end their behaviour and to forgive themselves as well as those who made them suffer, the wheel of karma will stop turning.

Many groups reincarnate again and again into the same entrenched conditions, repeating cycles of inhumanity. If this applies to your society, stop now and bless those on the other side. They are your brothers and sisters.

Why would a God of Love allow the entire black society of South Africa to suffer under apartheid in order for the spirit or souls to become better, richer or to experience enlightenment?

This was something done by humans. You used your free will to subjugate and disempower others and it had nothing to do with God, who offered you free will and witnessed your choices. The whites who set up apartheid were younger souls who were still earning much karma. The blacks who allowed themselves to suffer under the impositions of apartheid were mature souls who were repaying karma, and were at the same time demonstrating to those who were less evolved, qualities of forbearance, patience and fortitude.

Fear and ego, which feel separate from God, promote feelings of separation, superiority, difference and cruelty. Love always promotes Oneness, co-operation, caring, harmony, valuing others and equality.

What is collective karma?

This is the karma earned by the entire world which has not yet been repaid. For centuries these debts have been lying unheeded in the cosmic bank account. However, now, as your planet and all on her are moving into a higher dimension, the collective liability must be balanced. Consequently individuals, groups and even countries have undertaken to pay off some of the burden.

Do countries have karma?

Oh yes. Where a country has ill-treated its immigrants or visitors or has invaded, cheated or betrayed another nation, it owes them recompense.

EXAMPLE
The massive flood of immigrants into many European countries from countries they have colonised, plundered, invaded or cheated is one karmic consequence of their past actions.

Do cities have karma?

Where bad or unwise decisions are taken by city leaders, the consequences become its karma.

What is ancestral karma?

An incoming soul undertakes the collective karma of seven generations of his ancestors. This is genetically programmed into the individual, attracting his life conditions and influencing his health.

After an Atlantis seminar in which I took the participants through an ancestral karma-release programme, Rachel emailed me to say that she had lost seven kilos in weight in the week after the course. She knew it was because she had released the karma of one of her ancestors she was playing through her physical body.

Do religions have karma?

Missionary religions who endeavour to convert peoples of other customs and impose their beliefs on them ultimately have to repay for the damage they have done.

REPAYMENT OF KARMA

Does forgiveness help a criminal?

Very much. When you hold on to anger, judgement or fear towards another soul, a psychic link is formed between you. The two of you are karmically attached until it is dissolved. That cord inevitably draws you together again, so that you reincarnate at the same time. Your anger, judgement or fear, however deeply unconscious, will cause you to punish that soul in some way, until you in turn bear karma with its inevitable consequences. And so the wheel keeps revolving.

When the victim forgoes punishment and pardons the perpetrator, the debt is cancelled. Both souls are released. The one who committed the bad action must also ultimately forgive himself or herself.

When you absolve another from guilt, it assists the whole of humanity, for your release of the bond raises the consciousness of all. Others follow suit.

Are all the terrible things that happen a result of karma?

Some, but not all, of the more dreadful events taking place on Earth in current times are the working out of deep karma. Prayer and supplications for grace greatly assist your world.

I did bad things as a teenager. How can I repay the karma?

Grace dissolves karma and this involves unconditional love. If you cannot repay the people you initially harmed, help others with an open heart and your debt will be released. When the guilt and drive to do this fade, it is over.

Some people get away with things all the time. Why?

Everything works out spiritually over lifetimes, so ultimately no one gets away with anything. Younger souls tend to accrue karma because they are unaware of the consequences of their actions. However, as they reincarnate and gain more wisdom, they have a desire to repay what they owe. Then they undertake lives where they serve society or help other people.

My friend is such a good, kind person, but terrible things keep happening to him. This seems so unfair. Why is this? And how can he change it?

In earlier lifetimes your friend did some bad things, as most souls do in their early incarnations. Now that his understanding has matured, he has a longing to balance the wrong he perpetrated. Part of this involves experiencing what he did to others, and he agreed to this at a higher level before incarnation.

As a result of his past lives your friend also has an unconscious belief in terrible things happening. The universe arranges itself so that his convictions are satisfied. Unpleasant circumstances are inevitably drawn to his energy, and people step forward to serve him by doing nasty things to him. In this way his karma is activated, and his attitude towards these challenges dictates whether his debts are increased or decreased.

He is already repaying his dues through goodness and kind acts. Now he needs to watch his thoughts and recognise his underlying beliefs. Then, with affirmations, healing, courage, prayer, meditation, positive visualisations, by seeking the good in all situations and self-forgiveness, he can alter his destiny so that he only attracts good things.

I am caring for my senile husband, who no longer recognises me. Is this karma, and why does God let this happen?

In the eyes of God, your husband is mentally, emotionally, physically and spiritually whole and perfect. The life situation or karma is created by you and your husband.

What you can do is pull back all the negative emotions you have sent to your husband and to the universe. Then picture your husband in light and surrender him to the love and care of the angels. Here is an exercise which will help all carers, and is appropriate however much they love their dependent.

Visualisation for all carers
1. Sit quietly, breathing in and out until your whole body feels relaxed and your mind calm.
2. Picture the person you are caring for in front of you.
3. See or sense the effect of all the frustrated thoughts you have sent to him or her or to God. What is this energy like? Is it thick, thin, grey or black, odorous or putrid? What is it doing? Is it clinging to you or to the other person? Has it formed a cord between you, or a stabbing dagger, or is it strangling you or him with a rope?
4. Ask the angels to wash all this sticky energy away, leaving you both free.

5. Picture your dependent as he or she used to be, full of life force and energy. If you cannot do this, envision his perfect divine self.
6. Surround him in a golden ball of light and imagine yourself handing it to the angels.
7. Take a few moments to thank God for taking your loved one into His care. Ask for the strength, patience, love and whatever else you need to handle the situation.
8. Feel your angel's wings enfolding you and know that help is coming to you.

You may need to do this exercise several times.

I feel condemned to a life of drudgery looking after my elderly parents. What can I do?

You build your life with your emotions and, most importantly, your beliefs. Your beliefs are that you deserve to live in drudgery and servitude, and this has become your karma. Your deeply held presumptions are lack of self-worth, lack of deservingness, guilt, expectation that nothing good happens and that life is a hardship. Under spiritual law, those that truly love you at a soul level enter your life to mirror back to you your underlying convictions. In this case your parents have undertaken this task, but you are now all trapped in a situation that is not serving the growth of any of you.

The Law of Resistance says that what you resist persists. Most people fight against unwelcome situations by focusing on their grievances. Whatever you give attention to is created in your life. So, tell the universe what you want and soak yourself in the good feeling as if you already have it.

Exercise to change your situation
1. Watch your thoughts until you are clear what your beliefs are. Then write affirmations, which are positive statements in the

present tense about who you truly are or what you really want. Remember that your divine essence is worthwhile, beautiful and deserves a happy, love-filled life.

2. Repeat each affirmation ten times, twice a day, or more if you can.

3. Decide what you do want. You may want a carer to come in twice a week to give you some free time. You may want to live on your own and pop in once a week to see your parents. You may wish to get married and live in Australia.

4. Know that the universe will give you your heart's desire as long as you are clear that you want it and believe you deserve it.

5. Remember that if something is not for your highest good, it is not appropriate for those affected either.

6. When you have clarity about what you really want, picture it, feel it, talk about it, experience it as if it already is. At the same time, picture your dependents being looked after in a wonderful way and being totally happy about it.

My son is disabled. Why him? Why me? It's so unfair.

At a soul level, both you and your son chose your situations for this lifetime. Therefore be assured that spiritually it is totally fair. There are many reasons for such choices, most of which force you both to learn lessons.

REASONS WHY A SOUL WOULD CHOOSE A DISABLED BODY

If the soul is inexperienced on Earth, it is a way of ensuring he will be totally looked after throughout his life.

If the being has had a number of lifetimes and earned a deal of karma, it may be a way of restricting them from creating more.

They may have offered themselves in service to give the family and carers lessons and tests in love, acceptance, patience, compassion, empathy or faith.

In another life they may have constantly affirmed they wanted to be looked after or safe.

Most highly evolved souls who choose restrictive bodies do so to test themselves for qualities such as surrender, patience, self-acceptance, strength, courage, faith or understanding.

REASONS WHY A PARENT WOULD, AT A SOUL LEVEL, AGREE TO BIRTH AND BRING UP A DIABLED CHILD

The parent may owe karma to the incoming soul, and the loving care bestowed on them cancels the debt.

At a soul level the parent may so love the child that he or she offers a lifetime of service to them.

The parent is undertaking lessons. These may be about guilt or restriction, or about selfless love and acceptance.

If the child has to be looked after in a home, the parent is learning lessons of loving detachment.

The parent and child together are teaching each other about compassion and caring.

EXAMPLES

A man who, in an earlier life, carelessly impregnated many women and took no responsibility for his children chose a life where he was too disabled to express himself sexually.

A man who ordered people's hands to be chopped off for stealing in an Eastern life chose to experience a Western life without a hand.

A cruel prosecutor and his equally vicious son chose to incarnate in their next life as mother and daughter, believing that female bodies would soften their outlook to some extent. However, realising that their consciousness had not changed and that they would both have continued to be unkind and to misuse their power, their souls chose for the daughter to be disabled. As a result, the mother learned about love, caring and compassion while the daughter learned dependence and surrender to love.

Why does karma only last as long as you wish it to?

The currency of karma is love. As soon as you are truly remorseful, are ready to forgive yourself and others and can open your heart to unconditional love, your debts are cancelled.

What do you mean, karma only lasts as long as you wish it to? I want my disabled body to be whole. That isn't possible, is it?

Currently there is a belief in the collective unconscious that it is impossible to regrow limbs and heal a number of congenital disabilities. Spiritually, of course, as you align yourself to your divine blueprint you must automatically become whole. But at present, unless you can attune yourself to your divine perfection and have the faith to overcome the limiting mass consciousness, you must pass over when you are ready to hand over your karma. Then you can return in a different body.

Does a sentence in prison mitigate karma?

Spending time in gaol does not in itself dissolve karma. The attitude of the prisoner is what frees the debt. Remorse, kindness and spiritual practice are some of the ways in which the reckoning can be reduced or cancelled.

In some cases prison offers an opportunity for the offender to change his life direction and thus reassess his due. In others, time behind bars prevents the prisoner from accruing more karma. Sadly, for many their time in custody merely affirms their victim-consciousness, hardens their hearts and causes them to be influenced by others who are dark. Often their misdeeds continue when their sentence is over, so they are setting up an unhappy future incarnation.

Patrick was given a year in prison for a small traffic offence in which a woman was slightly hurt. On the face of it, this seemed a monstrously unfair sentence. However, his mother said that it was the best thing that happened to him. It shocked him so much that he changed from being wild to calm, sensible and responsible. He used his difficult year as an opportunity to change his direction, and it probably saved his life.

What is the spiritual perspective on prison?

Punishment is not a substitute for love. However, a few souls need to be incarcerated for their own safety or that of others.

Life Purpose

Does every soul have a purpose?

Yes, every soul has a purpose, something it wishes to learn, accomplish or teach. An undertaking is often quite general. Perhaps four people incarnate with a mission to understand animals and spend their lives working with them in some way. One may do research with different creatures. Another may work in a kennels or a zoo. Another may write a book about them. The fourth may have their own pets. How each fulfils their purpose is up to them.

What was Mother Theresa's life mission?

To show to the world that everyone is important in the eyes of God. She also demonstrated, by living example, qualities of service, joy, humility and faith.

What was Walt Disney's life purpose?

Walt Disney was a highly evolved soul who incarnated to tell people about the elementals, such as fairies, elves, pixies and gnomes, and also about the essence of animals. He chose to fulfil his mission by making films to draw to public attention that which he had agreed to teach. When he passed he ascended, his work well completed.

What was John F. Kennedy's mission?

He was a bringer of peace.

Did Marilyn Monroe have a soul purpose?

Her incarnation was to reveal to herself and others that beauty is only skin-deep and does not ultimately bring happiness.

Did Gandhi fulfil his destiny?

He was a highly evolved spirit who fulfilled his mission in a wonderful way. He demonstrated to the whole world that harmlessness is enormously powerful, and still stands as a reminder and flame of truth to many.

Why do so many Great Souls have difficult lives?

Like all in a human state, they have dross to burn to purify their souls. They must also demonstrate to others how to overcome challenges with courage and integrity. By going through adversity themselves, they act as living examples and become beacons of light.

What about Profumo?

He was teaching himself about the use and misuse of power. Having learnt about its temptations and misuse, he demonstrated with humility and devotion the correct use of power through service. His true spiritual growth occurred when he dedicated his energy to help the disadvantaged.

What were the missions of Hitler and Mussolini?

Their missions were about using the power of love. Both failed when they closed their hearts and fell for the love of power, which they used without compassion for control and self-aggrandisement. In future lives, possibly not on Earth but on another third-dimensional plane, they will try again to learn about love. They will experience lives where they are rendered impotent to harm anyone and have mothers whose hearts are open.

Does anyone incarnate with a destructive or warlike mission?

This would not serve anyone's higher soul purpose. However there are souls, like Hitler and Mussolini, who have had many dark incarnations, where the likelihood is that the same pattern will manifest. Nevertheless, the divine spark within them still yearns to find the light.

How can I find my life purpose?

Ask yourself one question: What makes your heart sing? The answer will give you clues to your mission.

I feel I am on the wrong path. How can I find my mission?

Your guardian angel holds the blueprint for your life mission. Give yourself time and space, then relax and listen to its promptings. If you feel a desire to change your life, follow this soul urge. Your angel will lead you in the right direction and open doors of opportunity for you. Remember to ask for help, and watch for signs to guide you.

Will numerology or astrology indicate my life purpose?

In the hands of a capable and sensitive practitioner, either of these sciences will help you to pinpoint your mission. Remember, a life purpose is rarely to perform one specific task. It is usually much broader than that.

Could my life purpose be just to experience depression and sadness?

How would such a path serve your spiritual growth? It is very unlikely. Only a very rare and powerful soul would undertake such a mission in order to transmute through his own energy field part of the collective cloud of depression and sadness.

My life is so burdened. I feel I have undertaken too much for one lifetime. Is this possible?

No. When your soul chooses your life with the guidance of your masters and angels, it only allows you to undertake what you are capable of. It is the decisions you have made while on Earth and your attitudes to conditions that have made your life so very difficult. When someone wilfully takes the wrong path, life can become too onerous, so meditate for the right direction and ask the angels to help you reduce the load.

I feel I have been marking time all my life, and now have a sense of excitement that my mission is about to be presented. Is this possible?

Many souls, especially those who are more evolved, spend much of their lives waiting for or looking for their destiny, which is only presented to them in later years. However, every step of the path offers you lessons which will prepare you for the work ahead. So walk every step wisely.

My life is all over the place. There are so many things I want to do and accomplish that I feel as if I am juggling everything and not moving forward. What do you suggest to help me?

Yes, you are doing far too many things at once. First, take a decision about what you really want to achieve, pulling three or four threads out of the jumble. Write down those specific goals and read them to yourself every day. Allow the others to fall away for the time being.

I can always see two sides to everything, so I'm pulled this way and that. It is exhausting, so how can I direct my energies towards a single goal?

It is excellent to have an overall view. However, you must decide on your goal and see it with a single eye.

At present you are metaphorically driving a carriage with two horses, each pulling in opposite directions. Your thoughts are giving each horse different instructions, so all your energy is tied up in controlling the animals. Decide which path you want to follow. Here is a very powerful exercise to help you harness your energy and move quickly towards your goal:

> ~ **Visualisation to reach your goal** ~
>
> ~ Stop the carriage and get off.
> ~ Talk to the horses. Explain what you are trying to achieve and get them on your side.
> ~ Then say, 'This is my goal. Will you work with me?'
> ~ See them nodding agreement.
> ~ Get back into the coach and drive it straight along the road.
> ~ From time to time over the next few weeks, check in to see that the horses are galloping in the same direction.

Nature

Why do I feel more relaxed and peaceful when I walk by water?

Water is a cosmic cleanser, which is why you feel peaceful when you walk near it. It draws in and absorbs your negative energy, leaving you feeling better.

If you place a glass of water by your bed at night, any lower energy hanging round you will be absorbed into it. Remember, do not drink it in the morning. And don't water your plants with it, for though some greenery will transmute the negativity, many leaves are too delicate to take your toxins through their systems.

Why do I feel better when I am out in nature?

Trees, plants, grass, water, the elements, as well as Mother Earth, draw in your negativity and transmute it. Fire, which includes the sun, burns up the dross. If you go out in the wind, the air blows away the cobwebs of your mind. When you walk in nature, the earth draws off your anxieties and worries. Nature also radiates positive energy which you can breathe in so that you feel better.

Why does it help to hug a tree?

The essence of most trees is love, so they enfold you in it and help to soothe you. They are also keepers of wisdom.

What is the purpose of trees?

They are part of the ecology, balancing and purifying the air, offering shelter for birds and small animals, shade for other creatures, wood for building and fires as well as fruit and nuts to eat. Each one graces the planet with its beauty and offers something slightly different.

They are also keepers of ancient wisdom. Certain things are encoded at a physical level for scientists to decipher, but the entire history of a place is psychically held by many wise old trees, the record keepers. When your frequency rises you can 'read' this information. Trees act like a whispering worldwide web, passing on information through the nature kingdom. In the summer they spread it through the leaves and in the winter through the roots.

The elementals of the trees are in touch with each other all over the world. They see the past and future and know the weather forecast. Remember to ask a wise old tree for advice.

A wise octogenarian friend of mine told me how she used to go to her favourite venerable old cedar tree for guidance. One day she had a dreadful dilemma to resolve and did not know what to do. She told the tree her problem, and asked, 'Whatever am I to do?' Into her head promptly came a three-word reply! It was the last thing she expected, but she said, 'If that's your advice I'll do it.' And fifty years on she laughed as she told me, 'It worked a treat.' But she would not reveal what she asked!

*

On another occasion the same wise friend was sitting under a tree with a companion. At the same moment they both received into their minds, 'You'll just get away with it.' The two ladies looked at each other, startled. Then they realised it was the tree talking about a garden party they were putting on the following weekend. They took those words as guidance and got everything cleared up early, just before the rain came.

*

A row of fifty-foot leylandii trees bordered my house and eventually I had them taken down. Another neighbour asked me to remove some untidy hawthorn trees which straggled from our adjoining hedge. When my lovely spiritual gardener went to do this, the trees said to him, 'No, now that the leylandii have gone, we are Diana's protection!' Needless to say, the hawthorn remained, and I thank them.

Exercise to connect with a tree

1. Sit underneath or hug a tree. If you cannot do this physically, think of one you know and imagine you are sitting under it.
2. Mentally honour it and thank it for allowing you into its aura. Remember that old trees are venerable beings.
3. Make your mind as quiet and still as possible, perhaps by focusing on your breathing.
4. Open your heart and 'feel' anything that the tree wishes to impart. You may have a feeling of peace or love. Or you may sense its dignity or strength. You may even be open to impressions or pictures of the local history. Alternatively you may receive a downloading of ancient wisdom.
5. Thank the tree for anything you have experienced.

When I was a child I had a book full of pictures of flower fairies? Do they really exist?

Oh yes. Fairies look after flowers. They help them to grow and develop their beautiful colours. Just as you have angels to watch over you, flowers have elementals to tend them. However, there are now fewer of these beautiful spirits as so many natural meadows and wild habitats are disappearing and being replaced with chemical-filled gardens and concrete.

How can I see a fairy?

You have to be psychic to see the elementals. However, if you go to a lovely place in nature where it is still and quiet, the veils between the worlds are thinner, and you may just glimpse or sense the fairies that gather in such a place. Often you will just be aware of a light dancing amongst the flowers.

Can I do anything to encourage fairies?

If you have a garden, make a fairy corner. Let it be pretty and think of the fairies when you work on it. Keep the area chemical-free. Then just know that they are there.

Fairies can be very naughty, just like small children. They can untie shoelaces and make you jump by rustling a leaf behind you. They will mischievously hide the gardening implements you are using, so when something goes missing remember to ask them to return it. You may have to wait a day or two! They also love to make you laugh.

Why does God allow one species to decimate another, for example the grey squirrels ousting the red ones?

Left to itself, nature brings everything into equilibrium and harmony. God created the original divine blueprint and humans used their free will to tamper with it. When you started to interfere with the natural world, the divine balance was lost.

Is it spiritually allowable to alter the course of a river?

The innate wisdom of a river allows it to flow in a perfect way, finding the path of least resistance. When the route is altered or interrupted, consequences reverberate throughout the planet, and eventually the water power will reassert itself.

Will Earth survive with what we are doing to nature?

The question is not whether Earth will survive, but whether it will continue in a form that can support life as you have known it. The answer lies in your individual and collective decisions. Treat every aspect of nature with respect and support only food, clothes and businesses that have an ecological ethos.

Religion and Spirituality

What is the New Age?

It is literally a new era. For the past 2000 years the world has been under the influence of Pisces, a period during which humanity gave up their power and allowed priests and others to be a channel for the divine communications. Now Earth has moved into the jurisdiction of Aquarius, which will influence you for the next 2000 years. The New Age of Aquarius is a time when individuals are expected to access ancient wisdom and make their own connection with God.

Has organised Christian religion had its time?

The dogma of Christianity has served its purpose, but the Christ energy will remain for eternity.

Who was Jesus? Was he the son of God?

Jesus was the most spiritually evolved being ever to incarnate on Earth. A son/daughter of God is a Being of Light carrying the energy of Source, once diluted. He was one of twelve sons/daughters of God, and the only one to serve in this universe.

Why was He chosen to carry the Christ energy?

The Christ energy is a high-frequency light of unconditional love. Jesus was chosen and trained to bring this light into his energy field, because he was the only human capable of doing so at that time. Now, as the people's vibration rises, more are able to carry at least some of the Christ light.

How diluted are people in general?

Most people are Source energy two or three times diluted.

What is ascension?

Ascension literally means investing more of the light of your soul into your personality on Earth. The effect is that you rise to a higher dimension. When you carry more than a certain amount of light you can no longer maintain a physical body, and at this point most people will pass over naturally, leaving their physical body on Earth in the usual way. However, there have been a few highly evolved beings throughout history who have dematerialised their physical bodies on ascension.

Is it true that the planet Earth is ascending?

Yes. By divine decree of Lady Gaia, who is the Illumined Angel who looks after Earth, the planet and all on her are ascending through two dimensions from a third-dimensional planet to a fifth-dimensional one. Your soul is being offered an unprecedented opportunity for spiritual growth over the next few years.

What if someone is not ready to ascend with the planet?

Those who are not ready will simply reincarnate to continue their experience on another third-dimensional planet.

What is the difference between religion and spirituality?

Religion is spirit clothed by man. Where there are dogma and rules, pure spirit becomes restricted. Spirituality allows people to be themselves, free to use their intuition, to commune with nature and the spirit world.

Where does superstition come from?

When people lost their connection with the divine, they no longer used intuition or tuned into spiritual guidance. Then they allowed themselves to be influenced by happenings.

EXAMPLE

If something good occurred on a day when you turned in a circle three times, three turns signified luck. If the same thing happened on a second or third occasion, the sign was confirmed and became entrenched as a superstition. This is why these beliefs vary in different places.

Which is the best religion?

At the top of the mountain all religions are exactly the same, but as they come down the slope the paths get further and further apart.

The essence of each religion is love, light and spiritual truth. No one is better than another. All are pathways to God. However, as humans have distorted the basic, pure teachings, the sects have differentiated and become separate journeys. So people now incarnate into specific parts of the world in order to experience the religion through which their soul wishes to learn.

Why was so much cruelty perpetrated in the name of Christianity?

The Church fathers valued the religious dogma of Christianity, not the essence. When the logic of the left brain is valued more than the wisdom and love of the right, it inevitably leads to disconnection from feelings and spirit. Because the hearts of those attracted into them were closed, missionary religions perpetrated cruelty in order to control and manipulate others. This has nothing to do with spirituality or even religion, and individuals as well as the Church bear appropriate karma.

Does the Catholic Church bear karma for knowingly sheltering priests who abused children?

The institution and all concerned carry a terrible burden of karma. It is a truly dreadful thing to harm innocent children.

Do the bishops who knowingly sheltered priests who abused children bear karma?

Oh yes. Where anyone has knowingly colluded in children being harmed, their spiritual progress in future incarnations will be severely curtailed.

Has the Church done more good than harm?

Yes, the Church has done more good than harm. It has offered hope, comfort and solace to millions of individuals.

What happens when religions are male-dominated?

Those who no longer listen to the feminine wisdom and become disconnected from their spiritual connections form religions with a focus on limitation and exclusivity rather than a higher perspective. They then persecute, exclude or condemn women and those that do not follow their limited path. This has nothing to do with spirituality.

Why is Islam in ascendancy now?

Missionary religions move like waves across the planet. Christianity had an opportunity to influence widely for many centuries. Now a new wave, carrying different lessons, has started to rise.

What are the lessons of each religion or denomination?

Every religion has a yin and yang aspect, shown in the table below. Each teaches about light, love and peace on one hand and on the other offers tests to its devotees. Before incarnation the oversoul chooses the religion which offers the challenges and experiences needed, positive and negative. Souls often decide to try a variety of pathways in successive lifetimes, especially if they have been particularly dogmatic. Such individuals may well transfer their rigid attitudes to their new creed.

Protestantism	Unconditional love, forgiveness.	Dependence on intermediaries, intolerance.
Catholicism	Transcendence.	Guilt, shame.
Judaism	The chosen ones.	Worthlessness, rejection.
Islam	Faith, tolerance, peace.	Manipulation, blind faith, anger.
Buddhism	Peace, harmlessness, enlightenment.	Anger, suppression.
Hinduism	Faith, balance.	Confusion.
Paganism	Oneness, reverence.	Too terrestrial, superstitious.
New Age Spirituality	Ascension.	Illusion, ungrounded.

Is there such a thing as original sin?

It has always been known by spiritual people that souls incarnate with karma. During evolved times these limitations, which a soul chooses to place on itself for learning and to balance past misdeeds, were recognised without judgement. Wise people offered love and higher teachings to assist the understanding of the sufferer and this acted as grace.

When the masculine energy took over the Church, which then denied the wisdom of the feminine, karma was translated as original sin. Lack of spiritual understanding meant that simply being in a physical body was judged, and even innocent babies were considered to be bad. The angels never criticise. They look with love and compassion on every human being and try to guide and help them into higher ways.

Who was Mary Magdalene?

Mary was a high-born, very evolved and holy woman who was the spiritual partner of Jesus during their incarnation together. She was one of his disciples and never his sexual partner or wife. As the Church became more male-dominated, it tried to demoralise women in order to take their power away. Mary Magdalene was both powerful and pure, so the Church vilified her with false accusations. In accusing women of being 'Eve', sexual seducers who led men off their path, the Church fathers devalued both the female sex and the holiness of sexuality.

Did Jesus and Mary Magdalene marry?

No, however when Jesus reverted to the energy of Joshua Ben Joseph, after the crucifixion, he and Mary married.

Did they have children?

No, not while he was Jesus. Afterwards he and Mary had Sarah.

Was Jesus celibate?

Yes. His energy was so pure and high that He was beyond the need for sexual expression. His preparation before incarnation, vision and focus throughout his ministry and attainment as Jesus, was to bring in the highest energy known on Earth, the Christ consciousness.

My guide Kumeka and the angels told me that Jesus and Mary did not marry or have children yet I am very aware that highly respected esoteric schools, who have access to deep occult truths, teach that Jesus and Mary Magdalene married and had progeny, who later founded the continental royal houses. I was puzzled by this seeming anomaly and was discussing it with Rosemary Stephenson, who is an angel teacher and carries the divine feminine energy. I said that there must be a higher perspective that I had not grasped yet in which the angels, Kumeka and the esoteric schools were all correct. Suddenly, pure white rings of light started to flow from her dog. The lights flickered on and off. Then we could feel the proximity of loving, powerful presences and our bodies were running with energy. St Germain entered on my right. Jesus stood on my left. Mary Magdalene, Mother Mary, Mother Theresa, St Clare, St Catherine of Sienna, Joan of Arc and St Theresa of Avilla came in behind me. It was awesome. Mary Magdalene spoke to me. She said that all these seemingly contradictory statements were correct. My question had been whether Mary Magdalene and Jesus were married and had children, to which the answer is No. Jesus attained that name for three years while he carried the Christ energy. Later he reverted to Joshua Ben Joseph, married Mary and Sarah was born. For me, everything fell into place and it was a wonderful example of the importance of asking the right question.

Did Jesus die on the cross?

No. Thanks to his advanced ability to control his mind and physical body, he was able to enter a state of suspended animation on the cross. He ascended into a higher frequency. Those who took him from the cross and tended him were highly evolved Essene healers with special powers, who were able to help him back into his physical body and heal him. So he lived and continued his incarnation.

Soul and Spirit

What is a monad?

The monad is defined as the original spark from Source, known as the I AM. This is a mighty light, almost beyond the current comprehension of humans.

What is an oversoul?

It is a descended portion of your monad or I AM presence. The oversoul is the combination of all your soul parts, each of which goes out into the universes to experience. It is this higher aspect, with its wide perspective and accumulated wisdom, which takes decisions for your soul before incarnation.

What is a soul?

The soul, or Higher Self, is the total of all you have learnt on all levels to that point. It is the aspect of you that guides your personality on Earth.

Can there be more than one aspect of your oversoul on Earth?

This used to be rare, but as the planet is rising in frequency more souls and their various aspects want to incarnate to experience the current spiritual opportunity. It is now possible for people to meet other aspects of their soul, which may have undertaken very different lives. This is not necessarily an easy meeting. For example, one may be living in a strict religious sect, learning tolerance and openness within restriction, while another might be floundering in a hedonistic part of the world, trying to create balance; and yet another may be a politician, endeavouring to practise honesty and integrity in a world of temptation, and they may have little in common on the surface.

Can two people belong to the same soul?

Souls can divide into up to twelve aspects, so two or more people on Earth may belong to the same one. Of course other parts of it may be out of incarnation or experiencing something quite different in another part of the universe.

Is it possible for only part of a soul to incarnate?

The entire oversoul is a great entity, so it is very rare for the whole energy to enter one body. This may happen at times of change or turbulence, when a great soul or Mahatma is born in order to raise the frequency of the world.

Other aspects of your soul may, of course, currently be on another planet or in a different universe.

If only a tiny fraction of a soul enters to learn a single lesson, it may not have sufficient resources to live a fully independent life, so it may create a physically or mentally disadvantaged body and will need to be looked after. Of course there are other reasons for a soul to choose a dependent incarnation.

Did Jesus bring in his whole soul energy?

Yes.

What is a spirit?

Your spirit is part of your soul and holds your consciousness. Your physical body is a sheath to house your spirit, which can leave when you sleep and sometimes when you meditate.

What is your ego?

Your ego is the aspect of your personality that keeps you separate from others and God. It is learning certain lessons.

What happens to all the spirits when people die?

The universes are vaster than you can conceive, and there are many planes of being simultaneously existing on different frequency bands. All can be accommodated!

Where do the ghosts live?

They live amongst you in the astral planes, which is a frequency that only psychics can see and access.

Why is the planet so crowded?

Because you are approaching 2012, which marks the end of a 26,000-year astrological cycle on Earth and heralds a cosmic moment offering unprecedented opportunities for spiritual growth, souls from all over the universes are petitioning to come to Earth now. Some want to complete their karma while they have the chance. Others wish to ride the wave of opportunity.

Where have all the people now on the planet come from?

There is not a finite number of souls for Earth, which is just a small planet in one of thousands of galaxies in one of twelve universes. There are trillions of souls throughout the universes, all experiencing on other star systems. Because Earth is such an important place of spiritual growth at this time, many of these beings are visiting your planet now to take a physical incarnation.

What happens to your spirit when you die?

Initially your spirit will experience whatever you expect, whether it is fire and brimstone or heaven. After your expectations are fulfilled there is a period of readjustment, especially for those who have been indoctrinated with specific or limiting beliefs. You may then receive healing from angels and those in spirit who are trained in such arts.

You will meet with your guides and angels, possibly even the Lords of Karma, to assess your life. During this discussion, you will take a decision together on whether you need to reincarnate quickly or wait for hundreds of years, or even whether you have earned liberation from reincarnation so your soul can soar into higher dimensions. If you have unresolved karma, you are bound to this planet until your debt is repaid. After this you may decide to continue your soul education on Earth or on another planet.

At some time your spirit will be reunited with your beloved soul family in the inner planes. Whether you succeeded in your mission on Earth or not, you take back to your oversoul your learning, experiences and understanding from your life so that it can absorb it and grow.

Don't souls go to heaven when they die?

Yes, if that is where they believe they will go. Heaven is a plane in the seventh dimension, so those who are able to raise their frequency to this level after death will, for a time reside in the beauty and light of this place with the angels.

Why don't I die when I fly out of my body during sleep?

While you are alive your spirit is tethered to your body by a silver cord. When you die, the silver cord is cut and you are set free from your physical body.

What do people do between lives?

There are millions of choices in the inner planes. Your spirit may wish to serve in some capacity, for example as a healer, a teacher, helping babies who have passed over, developing new ideas to help humanity, working with animals. The opportunities for service are endless.

You may desire to help a child or grandchild or group of people who are still in incarnation.

You may wish to develop your creativity as an artist, musician or architect.

You may wish to be an ambassador in the inner planes.

It may be time for you to train for a new role, in which case you may spend a period of time in one of the universities of light on another star system.

ASTRAL TRAVEL

What is astral travel?

When your spirit leaves its physical sheath and travels into the emotional planes you are astrally travelling. This can happen if you project your spirit while you are awake, in which case, ask your guides to protect your body. It also naturally occurs while you are asleep, in which case, your guides automatically protect your physical form.

Where does your spirit go at night?

It is free to travel where it will. Your consciousness is housed in your spirit, so if your focus has been on anger or worry, you will go into the astral planes, which are the planes of emotion. This can be very exhausting, so you may wake up tired. It is important to calm yourself before you go to sleep, perhaps by reading or meditating, so that you can go to the higher realms. In that case you may visit the realms of the angels, Illumined Masters, dolphins or your spirit guide for help or education. You may enter healing or teaching temples or journey to your home planet. Your sleep time may even be spent assisting others to pass properly, giving healing, solace or teaching.

Can I affect where I go in my sleep?

While you are awake and conscious, you can plan your night-time journey. It is helpful to decide each morning where you wish to go that night and clearly state what you wish to accomplish in your sleep. Then you can affirm it during the day, which impresses the consciousness of your spirit. Last thing before you go to sleep, focus on your planned destination and you will travel there. However, you must keep in mind your desired goal. There are limitless places to go, but choose somewhere for your spiritual or emotional advancement.

Do I always go where I ask to at night?

No, your intention may not be clear enough or your vibration may not be able to reach your desired destination. Also, your guides and angels may want you to go somewhere else, in which case you will hopefully have surrendered to their higher wisdom. You can ask to return from your night's journey with an explicit dream, to give you feedback.

Can I meet my loved ones in my sleep?

Yes, this happens. When spirits are drawn together by mutual love, they meet on the inner planes while they are asleep. The happiness of this often sustains them during their waking hours, even though they may be physically apart. So think about your loved ones before you go to sleep.

Can I meet my future husband in my travels at night?

This does occasionally happen when there is a fated relationship involved and the two have not yet met. They connect in the inner planes in the months and years beforehand, and when they finally meet physically, there is a sense of déjà vu or soul recognition.

Alan was a policeman, solid and grounded, not given to flights of fancy. He had a very vivid dream in which he met a beautiful woman and knew she was to be his wife. A year later, when he saw her at a party, he recognised her at once. They have now been happily married for nearly twenty years and still glow with happiness when they talk about each other.

Can I visit my dead mother while I am asleep? She passed very recently after a short illness and I miss her dreadfully.

You can ask to visit her if it is for the highest good. However, remember you mother may be in hospital on the other side receiving healing, as she has recently passed after an illness, and may not be ready to receive visitors. Or she may have moved on to a plane where she can no longer connect with those on Earth. She may even already be part of another plan. It is quite likely that your spirit will visit your parent and, though you will probably not remember the details when you waken, you will be sustained by the feeling of solace and love engendered by your meeting. It will help her too.

My little girl is dead to the world at night, while my boy sleeps lightly and wakes easily. Why is this?

Your little girl's spirit travels far during her sleep time. She returns to her planet of origin, which is not in this universe, for soul refreshment and learning. Such travel can be very tiring.

Your son originates from a closer planet in this universe and has to journey less far in his sleep state.

When he was a baby, one of my sons screamed for a long time when he woke up both in the morning and from his day sleep, though he is growing out of this. Can you comment?

It is very difficult for your high-frequency child to adjust to life in a body. He has not been to Earth many times and is not used to the material planes, so he screams to express his discomfort. He may not wish to go through his chosen life experiences. This can also happen if a baby or small child is tense and their free spirit finds it difficult to constrict itself into the tight sheath. Of course, it is important to check there is no physical cause.

I always feel grumpy in the mornings. Why is this?

Unconscious matters that you have not dealt with are brought to the surface during sleep. In the morning, while you are in touch with these pressures, you feel grumpy until you have repressed them again and can forget them! However, it is an indication that you need to explore your past and clear a backlog of stuck emotions. That will free you to wake up sunny and happy!

My friend practises astral travel in meditation. Is this safe?

When you fall asleep naturally, your guides protect your physical body so that no other entities can slip into your sheath. However, if you practise astral travel without setting in place protection, you might have a problem. Mediums who leave their bodies sit in a circle so that the other members can watch out for them.

You should never touch someone while they are out of their body, and especially do not move them, for they could go into shock and be quite ill. Although their silver cord should draw them back to the right place, occasionally a spirit has difficulty finding their body again if it is not where they left it. And if someone who is astral travelling has a problem coming back into their body, hold them in the Christ light, which is a very high-frequency energy brought to humanity by Jesus 2000 years ago, for this will assist them in returning.

Is it possible to travel out of your body to another place without consciously intending to do so?

If you are strongly emotionally linked to that place or person, you can project yourself there out of your body without knowing you are doing so. The other person may sense or see you.

Sheela met someone on a healing course, with whom she felt a great affinity. When she got home she would wake up at 6 a.m. each day and see him standing in the corner of the room. This continued for two weeks until she spoke to him on the phone. She discovered he had been on an early shift and would think about her as he drove to work.

What is the purpose of astral travel?

Some people use it to locate missing objects or people. Mostly it is used to connect with loved ones or places.

What qualities do I need to be able to practise astral travel?

You need to be able to focus and concentrate your mind so that you direct your spirit where you want to go.

All my children loved to travel. When Lauren left university she flew off to the East with her rucksack and her sense of adventure. At first she sent postcards and I received the odd phone call. One day I realised I had not heard from her for some time. My intuition told me she was safe, but I decided that three months was too long without contact. I mentioned my concern to a friend who immediately said, 'Well, find her on the astral.'

'Of course,' I thought.

That evening I sat down to meditate, directing my spirit to seek my daughter. Within moments I found myself in a beautiful sunny bay fringed with white sand and palm trees. Seconds later Lauren appeared in blue shorts, slim, with long brown legs. She was laughing and looked very happy. I said to her, 'It's time to phone home.' She nodded. I came out of meditation feeling completely relaxed, knowing she was fine.

The next day I received a call from her. 'Hello, Mum. It's me. I'm coming home. Can you meet me at the airport?' It transpired that, within moments of our astral meeting, she had suddenly decided it was time to return and had immediately gone to book her flight!

Can your spirit be attacked on the astral planes by someone who is angry with you?

Yes. The astral is the plane of emotions. It is a murky place to enter and you should always wear a cloak of protection. If your spirit is attacked by someone who is jealous of you, you may wake feeling drained and exhausted. You may even have physical scratches on your body or sharp pains where you have been psychically stabbed.

This is why it is so important to clear your emotions and direct yourself into the spiritual realms.

GROUNDING

What does being ungrounded mean?

Imagine your body is a jug and your spirit is the water which fills it. Your spirit is designed to fill your physical presence. If it does not come right down to your feet you are ungrounded.

What are the symptoms of being ungrounded?

Common symptoms are a cracking headache, nausea or pain in the stomach, faintness, tension at the back of the neck or painful eyes. If your body is tense somewhere, that is where your spirit cannot fully enter. You may also feel you are floating, not quite with it or anxious.

Of course all these symptoms may indicate something completely different, so it may be appropriate to have such physical manifestations medically checked.

After I meditate I often feel as if I am floating and slightly out of focus. Why is this and what can I do?

If you feel floating, you are ungrounded. To get yourself back into your body, stamp your feet, stretch, turn your neck from side to side or get up and move about. If you can, walk in bare feet on the grass so that Mother Nature can help to bring you in. Take Bach Rescue Remedy, eat something sugary or have a cup of tea.

Exercise to help someone who is ungrounded
1. Ask the ungrounded person to sit sideways on a hard chair. This is so that you can access their back.
2. Rub your hands together and hold them up for angelic blessing.
3. Place your hands on their shoulders. You may feel warmth or tingling, but if you don't, do not worry.
4. Imagine roots going down from your feet and your friend's feet into the earth to anchor you.
5. Remain like this for a few minutes.
6. Feel the aura above your friend's crown and push it gently down towards their head. This can help to push them back into their body. However, if this feels uncomfortable to them or you intuitively feel it is not right, stop immediately. Instead massage the back of their neck or their solar plexus.
7. Kneel down in front of them and place your hands on their feet.
8. When you have finished, bring your arms down between you to symbolically sever your energies from each other.
9. Visualise a deep blue cloak of protection round the other person and yourself.

My partner is very cerebral. Is this connected to his cold feet?

It may well be. Those who think or read a lot have much of their energy round their heads and none at their feet. Where there is energy there is heat, and where there is none you are cold.

You could help them by using the grounding exercise above, or you may be able to practise step 6 only, gently pushing their energy field down into their body.

I sometimes jerk when I am meditating. Why is this?

Those are moments when you are drifting into a sleep state and your spirit starts to rise out of your body. As you unconsciously realise what is happening, you jerk back in again.

I fall asleep when I meditate. What can I do to stop this?

Concentrate one hundred per cent on your breath or the voice of the person who is leading you. Check you are grounded. Be disciplined and consistent about your spiritual practices to raise your frequency. Also remember that on occasion you may have been taken to a spiritual place by your guides and angels.

A friend told me that when she has fallen asleep and astral travelled during meditation, it takes time to wake up. However, if she has been taken to a spiritual place she is instantly back, alert and aware at the end of the session. So she can tell which she has been doing by the way she returns.

I am normally healthy but occasionally wake with twenty-four-hour flu. I can't raise my head off the pillow and feel terrible all day. Then it is gone next day. I don't have a temperature. What is this?

The symptoms you describe are those of someone whose spirit has come back into their physical body crooked. For some people this happens very easily, so they can often be slightly or even badly off centre.

When your spirit departs for your night-time adventures, it visits a number of places. Usually it will return gently and you will wake feeling refreshed from your spiritual sojourn. However, if you are tense, it may not be so easy to re-enter properly. Or if you are disturbed during your journey, your spirit may precipitate too quickly, out of alignment, back into its sheath.

How do I deal with my spirit being out of alignment?

Twenty-four-hour flu symptoms, without a temperature, indicate that you are quite badly off centre. Anything that can relax you will help – a massage, a warm bath, Rescue Remedy or, in extremis, an aspirin. If these do not work, go back to bed and sleep. If you can really let go and relax, your spirit will exit and come back in straight.

On occasion the off-centre symptoms you describe last for forty-eight hours. Why is this?

The most common reason for this is that you were so tense that your spirit still could not come back in straight. Another reason may be that you did not sleep deeply enough the first night, so your spirit did not leave your body properly, which it needs to do to come in again in perfect alignment. Thirdly, part of your soul may have split off and needed more time, and maybe even help, to retrieve itself.

I work with physically disabled people and they often describe the symptoms of being ungrounded. Why is this and how can I help them?

Because many disabled people have tension in part of their body, their spirits sometimes have difficulty in entering fully. The exercise for grounding helps. So does healing. Anything that will enable them to relax will assist the process. Try relaxation journeys, massage or breathing techniques.

I often feel ungrounded but my friend never does. Why is this?

Some people's spirits slip out of their bodies very easily. Others are so solidly earthed that they simply do not have this experience.

My daughter is tense, anxious and a daydreamer. I feel she is often far away. Is she ungrounded?

She could well be. Perhaps you can help her to relax and re-assure her that she is safe. Encouraging her to walk, spend time in nature and eat sensibly will help her. Physical exercise also assists.

I have panic attacks, and someone said I was ungrounded. Could this be true and what would help?

Panic attacks are one consequence of being ungrounded. For some people, because they are not fully in their body everything seems slightly unreal, unfocused and unmanageable. Then they breathe too shallowly and this pulls them out of their body more. A regular regime of relaxation practice and breathing exercises should help you. Then you will have tools to use if you have another recurrence. You may also need to explore any specific triggers which cause you to react in this way.

A good hypnotherapist could help you to learn to breathe properly, explore your underlying fears and reprogramme your unconscious beliefs.

Space

Why did the Challenger space shuttle blow up in 1986?

In human terms this was a terrible tragedy, but from a cosmic perspective the disaster was inevitable. The space shuttle exploded because the intention of those who worked on the project was to conquer space. It came from arrogance and ego, with a lack of respect for the wonders of creation. Even the name, Challenger, defines the intention.

Is space exploration always wrong?

Where space is explored in order to expand the boundaries of knowledge and to discover the wonders of the universe, it is spiritually acceptable. Each project must be entered into with respect and a sense of reverence; then the successes and new understandings will be momentous and enriching to human life.

Is there life on other planets?

There are indeed planets supporting third-dimensional life forms in other universes. These have not developed into the same shapes as you, but they experience a similar consciousness.

Higher-dimensional beings, who do not need to be supported by food, water and oxygen as you do, dwell throughout the cosmos. These beings currently vibrate at a frequency beyond your range of vision and hearing.

Are there UFOs?

Yes, there are UFOs. On other planets and stars, as well as in universes beyond yours, there are intelligences and life forms, many of which are more technologically advanced than you are.

Are the clouds which I sometimes see in the shape of a spaceship actually spaceships, or are they clouds which happen to take that shape?

A spaceship has a very high frequency, so that condensation forms round it when it rests, just as it forms round an angel. If you see a cloud in the shape of a spaceship, a craft is or has recently been there.

The most spectacular UFO clouds I have ever seen were in the early morning when I was walking the Camino in Spain with a friend. A huge cloud in the form of a perfect flying saucer appeared. The top of it opened up and several smaller saucers rose from it one by one and flew off, rapidly evaporating. Then another big saucer cloud came up from behind. Once more the top opened and several craft emerged from it. This recurred without ceasing for twenty minutes, while we watched in awe.

93

What is a mothership?

It is a huge spacecraft from which smaller ones are launched on their missions.

While I was in New Zealand, crossing Te Anau lake to see the glow-worm caves, I glanced up and glimpsed a mothership. I saw it only for a moment, but it was like a huge liner with row upon row of lights as if from windows, and the whole craft was glowing. A never-to-be-forgotten moment!

Who is Commander Ashtar?

He is a highly evolved being, head of the Intergalactic Command. He is in charge of millions of spacecraft who patrol your universe as part of the Brotherhood/Sisterhood of Light. They keep a benign and watchful eye on Earth and its inhabitants to protect you.

Are there spaceships belonging to unfriendly aliens?

Yes. Do not focus on them or give them any energy. Only that which you nourish with your thoughts can touch you, so concentrate only on the good and light.

Spiritual Matters

AURAS AND CHAKRAS

What is your etheric body?

It is the spiritual counterpart of your physical body and exactly reflects it. It can be felt radiating about one inch from the person. If someone loses part of their body, for example an arm, he or she can still experience sensation or pain where the limb was. This is because the consciousness remains in the etheric spirit.

What is an aura?

An aura is a coloured electromagnetic field which surrounds every living thing and is made up of the energy of their beliefs, thoughts and emotions. A rock, crystal, plant or tree radiates a simple light. A human being has an emotional aura as well as a mental and a spiritual one. These are seen as bands of coloured light by clairvoyant adepts, while sensitive people can feel the different layers with their hands.

Can one person's aura affect another person?

Absolutely. If your aura is radiant and full of beautiful colours it can light up those of others. If you are warm, compassionate and loving, your aura will enfold and comfort people near you and this will happen without your conscious knowing. If you are a healer, your aura will reach out to touch and help those who need healing even if they are strangers. An optimistic aura will ignite hope in the hearts of those in despair.

Can one person's aura change the atmosphere in a room?

No one is an island. Your auras all permeate each other's. One person of peace and wisdom entering a room can affect everyone. The opposite can also be true if you allow it. However, higher frequencies transmute lower ones.

Which is more powerful, a dark aura or a light one?

Light consumes darkness. Healing dissolves pain. Love soothes hurt. Light is infinitely more powerful. One golden aura can light up a million souls.

What is the purpose of an aura?

First, it spreads information about you to others, who unconsciously read your energy fields. Second, when you draw it in, it acts as a protection or buffer between you and other people and situations.

How can I read auras?

Everyone consciously or unconsciously reads auras. Ask yourself the question, 'If I could see that aura, what would it tell me?' Then let answers surface.

Exercise to see auras

If you wish to practise seeing auras, start with healthy trees or mountains. They have very strong radiations, especially on a sunny day. Just let your eyes relax and look obliquely at them and you may see a band of light round them, sometimes coloured, often full of sparkles. After that, practise on people. Only ever do this with the highest intention, and bless the tree, mountain or person afterwards.

Does an aura change colour?

Yes. Your thoughts and emotions profoundly affect the colours in your aura.

Susan Phoenix Says:

'I took my aura camera to one of Diana's seminars in Dublin to photograph the participants' auras before and after the workshop. By the end of the session every photograph invariably showed a greatly expanded auric field of pure gold, illustrating, I feel, that divine angelic energy had entered each individual's aura. This beautiful energy was reflected in the smiling, happy faces who sat before my camera.'

(Dr Susan Phoenix is the author of *Out of the Shadows – A Journey from Grief*, published by Hodder Mobius, and, with Jack Holland, *Phoenix – Policing the Shadows*, by Hodder and Stoughton.)

What is a chakra?

Chakra means 'wheel' or 'circle' in Sanskrit, and is an energy vortex. This means it is a spiritual point on your body which takes in and gives out energy. Currently there are seven main ones, though spiritual people are beginning to access once more the twelve chakras which were part of your original divine blueprint. There are also many subsidiary chakras, including those in the palms of the hands, through which healing light is transmitted, and those under the feet, which help to ground you to Earth.

When I first started to work as a hypnotherapist, I was helping a client to open her heart centre. Suddenly a pure pink, vibrant and vivid light burst from the centre of her chest. Feelers of light moved round the room delicately touching and sensing objects. I was transfixed, watching for several minutes, and felt blessed to be shown a heart chakra working.

What happens if some chakras are stuck, so that your energy is not flowing?

This is how you will feel if your energy is stuck:

Base chakra: You will feel very anxious and constantly in survival mode.

Sacral chakra: You will be out of balance sexually or emotionally

Solar plexus chakra: You will feel full of fear and anxiety.

Heart chakra: You will be afraid to love or trust.

Throat chakra: You will have an inability to communicate how you really feel or what you truly believe.

Third eye chakra: Your intuition will be limited. If it is locked open, you are too sensitive to psychic influences and atmospherics.

Crown chakra: When your crown chakra does not open, you cannot connect with your Higher Self.

What happens when your chakras are open and flowing?

Base chakra: You feel safe physically and materially.

Sacral chakra: You feel emotionally warm and loving, sexually mature, happy and able to give and receive nurturing.

Solar plexus: You feel peaceful, wise and powerful.

Heart chakra: You are able to love unconditionally.

Throat chakra: You can say what you truly feel. Therefore you act with integrity.

Third eye chakra: You are very intuitive, clairvoyant and can heal others.

Crown chakra: You connect to your soul or Higher Self.

What can I do if I think one or more of my chakras is stuck?

Your chakras clog up when your thoughts and beliefs hold them in tension, so affirm positive statements into them and hum, sing or chant into each one in turn. You can also energise a stuck chakra by massaging it at the front and the back. It is even more effective to exercise the whole area, for example you can release your throat chakra by moving your head in circles. Yoga is particularly useful as it was designed to free the chakras and bring them into alignment so that yogis could enter deep meditation.

ENLIGHTENMENT AND ASCENSION

What is the difference between enlightenment and ascension?

Englightenment is a state of being in which the consciousness expands to include all that is. An Englightened One can transcend lower limitations, control body functions and take power over his or her environment and circumstances.

Ascension is a state of doing, of drawing down more of the light of the soul and monad into the physical body. This raises the consciousness, expands spiritual awareness and can enable physical changes to take place.

Both happen in stages. You can sometimes receive illumination about a subject and take a big step forward in understanding and growth. That is an expansion of enlightenment.

Do enlightenment and ascension take place simultaneously?

They often do, but enlightenment often precedes ascension and prepares the person to receive more of the soul light.

How can I attain enlightenment and ascension?

Spiritual disciplines can accelerate this process. It may be a path of prayer, sacred mantra chanting, yoga, meditation or one of many devotional practices, but they must be performed regularly, with focus and concentration.

Spiritual visualisations and journeys, heart opening, forgiveness decrees, karma-release exercises, working with angels and Masters, calling on such energies as the Gold and Silver Violet Flame and the Mahatma energy all assist with spiritual attainment. Discipline, devotion, humility, service with love and heartfelt joy are keys. Seeing the divine essence of everyone and everything, and treating all with due reverence is important. Watching your thoughts and acting consciously for the highest good also opens doors to higher aspiration.

MASTERS AND GURUS

What is a guru?

A guru is a spiritual master who takes on students to teach and initiate them into a spiritual understanding.

Do I need a guru?

In the Piscean age it was considered acceptable and even desirable to have a guru to lead you. For many it was a safe and comfortable way to move into higher spiritual understanding. However, planet Earth is now under the influence of Aquarius. The lesson of the Aquarian age is to take mastery of self and create your own channel to the divine. Therefore people no longer *need* a guru, but many still choose to follow one, especially in the East.

Are all gurus good?

Many are and some are not. As with everything, you are called on to use discernment and discrimination.

When I meditate, a smell of lilies often wafts over me. What is this?

Lilies are one of the highest vibration flowers, so if a higher Master or angel is with you, you may smell their lily perfume. Masters such as Quan Yin, Mother Mary, and Mary Magdalene often announce their presence with the perfume of this flower, as does Mother Amma, who is still alive.

I stayed at Mother Amma's ashram in Kerala, India for a few weeks, and when I returned home I often smelt lilies as her spirit visited me during my quiet times.

What do masters mean when they say life is a dream?

They understand that while you are in a body it is easy to feel that the material life – work, money, success, possessions – is most important. However, in the great scheme of things this is an illusion, for only spiritual attainment means anything when your spirit leaves its physical sheath.

They also understand that you dream your life into being with your thoughts, thus you constantly create what you picture, whether it is intentional or not.

GENERAL MATTERS

How are new ideas and concepts given to people?

When it is time for expansion on Earth, the seeds for new inventions, technology or scientific advancement are dropped into appropriate receptive minds. Many such seeds fall on barren ground, but where people allow them to grow, similar ideas are generated in different places, often far apart. If these ideas are widely scattered so that thousands of people pick them up at the same time, a wave of change is triggered.

Sometimes information is selectively planted in a few receptive minds. Then similar books may be written or new inventions produced simultaneously by two people in different parts of the world. When this occurs, no one has stolen anybody's ideas, for such concepts come from spirit and individuals have simply responded with synchronicity to seed thoughts planted by the angels.

EXAMPLES

When more blue healing energy was called for on Earth, the same thought about blue jeans was planted across continents and the masses started to wear them. Magenta became fashionable when it was time for the influence of the divine feminine to enter the planet.

How is it that people are in the right place at the right time?

If any individual needs to be at a certain place at a precise time to take part in a project the angels and guides start whispering into their mind to prepare them. In due course they will think it is their own idea and will start to make arrangements. The angels then open doors to facilitate their move in perfect timing to the appropriate location.

If a larger project is being planned, a general call is put out to souls across the planet and some respond. This may happen up to five years beforehand to allow for preparation.

In response, and quite unconsciously, the volunteers intensify their studies, change course in mid-stream, decide to visit a particular place or person, or move house. And then they find themselves exactly placed to take part in the plan.

Behind the scenes the angels and guides work continuously and tirelessly to help you fulfil your destiny. They orchestrate all chance meetings, coincidences and synchronicities.

How can I help to bring about fairness, equality, justice and integrity in the world?

When you decide on a vision or a cause, tell the Principalities about it. They are the higher angels in charge of big worldly projects. As you impart your hope to these great illumined beings, focus on it as if it has already taken place. The angelic realms, who do not have free will to act but must wait for humans to ask, can use your supplication, intent and visualisations to bring in a better way of being.

EXAMPLE

If a country was withholding signature to a peace agreement, to fair trade or ecological improvements, your vision of the signed document, together with your prayer to the Principalities, enables them to nudge those who are in power. Of course, it needs many people working with prayers and visions to affect a change, but you may be the one to make the difference.

Never underestimate the power of one person, or a group of people, working with the angels for change.

Why is there such a focus on angels now?

Just over 20,000 years BC there was a period of 1500 years, during Golden Atlantis, when the spiritual energy on the planet was very high. During this time everyone could see and communicate with his or her angel. It was a time of peace, love and co-operation. However, people eventually succumbed to ego and the frequency on the planet declined. The higher angels and those wondrous spiritual beings of the angelic realms, the unicorns, withdrew.

For centuries the energy on the planet devolved, culminating in the terrible darkness of the Middle Ages. Eventually Source decreed that angels come to Earth to try to lift the situation. At the same time certain highly evolved souls, like Leonardo da Vinci, incarnated to bring in spiritual wisdom. Great painters, sculptors, writers and creative people offered to be born to add their beautiful light to the effort to raise the vibration of the planet. They painted or carved the angels that they saw or felt. This was the rebirth of the planet, the Renaissance. The energy peaked for a time, then alas, it declined.

Around 2012 you are offered a great opportunity for spiritual growth. This is why the angels are being sent to prepare you to receive the higher energies available.

A few years ago no one talked about angels. They asked me to write *A Little Light on Angels*, and when I did so the media tried to ridicule the concept. Now lots of people are wearing brooches or have angel stickers on their cars. They are openly discussed, and more people are connecting with them or looking for white feathers and other signs. They really are making their presence felt now.

What effect do stars and planets have on people's lives?

Every star or planet has a magnetic effect on Earth and on people. Depending on your place and time of birth, different ones will influence you to varying degrees throughout your life.

The effect of the cosmos on you is rather like that of the tides. When you understand its movements, you can take an opportunity when it is in full flood. On other occasions when the heavens dictate differently, you may decide to hold back until the current is right for you. In that case you can constructively spend your waiting time preparing your boat, rather than battling against an adverse flow. However, it is your choice whether you align with your astrological alignments or use your determination, skill and strength to set your course regardless of the conditions you will meet.

It is well understood, for example, that the moon influences the flow of water. Humans coined words like lunatic because it was observed how the different phases of the moon profoundly changed the emotional and mental state of certain people.

Mercury is connected with communication, so if it is in retrograde, you may find them being disrupted. If Saturn touches your chart, this stern taskmaster makes sure your situation is in order before it allows you to move on.

*

Carole was having a very difficult time. She lost her job and got a temporary one where she did not earn enough to meet her outgoings. Her car had to be repaired. Her credit cards were at their limit. She had to borrow from friends and family, so she sold almost everything she had. She had to cancel her mobile phone, her email provider and every single thing she could think of, but still she could not make ends meet.

In despair she consulted an astrologer, who explained that Saturn was over her chart and everything was being stripped away from her to teach her about the essentials of life. She was told that this situation would last another six months and then there would be an incoming tide of good things. Armed with this knowledge, she was able to remain resolute in the face of overwhelming challenges. She handled each financial crisis, went through bankruptcy, sold all she possibly could and even learnt to economise for the first time in her life. She focused on her health, cleaned and painted her flat and generally used the time to prepare herself for the tide to turn.

True to prediction, after six months she was given a rise and her temporary job was made permanent. She could make ends meet and see light at the end of the tunnel. She remarked that without the understanding astrology offered her, she would have given up.

Unicorns

What are unicorns?

Unicorns are seventh-dimensional ascended horses who belong to the angelic kingdom. Because of their purity they appear as shining white creatures with light pouring from their third eyes, and this looks like a single horn.

Why are people talking about and seeing unicorns now?

Unicorns were constantly available and visible to the people of Golden Atlantis around 20,000 BC. However, when the frequency spiralled down, the unicorns withdrew from the planet. Now at last you are raising your individual frequencies and that of Earth, so that these magnificent creatures can once more walk amongst you. Those who have eyes to see will see them.

Where can you see them?

Unicorns, like all spiritual beings, can be seen where the veils between the worlds are thinnest, that is in nature and in beauty spots or natural high energy points. But if your frequency is light enough, they will come to you wherever you are.

Why are they called unicorns?

The word 'uni-corn' literally means 'one horn'. You call hard skin, such as hoofs and horns, corns. Clarivoyants see these beautiful beings as horses with a single horn spiralling from the third eye. In fact this protuberance is pure energy pouring from the forehead, in the same way that an angel emits light in the shape of wings and a halo is a visible radiation from a spiritual person's crown.

Are angels to humans as unicorns are to horses?

Simplistically yes, though a human does not become an angel, whereas a horse may ascend to become a unicorn. Generally animals evolve to become humans, but in the case of a few highly spiritual animals, some of them may ascend into the angelic kingdom.

Sai Baba, the Indian avatar, told his devotees that his pet elephant would be a human in her next life.

105

Why are unicorns coming to Earth now?

Unicorns are on Earth now to help with the great spiritual transition taking place on your planet. They have come under grace in response to the prayers of humanity for assistance. While the angels were sent under directive from Source, the unicorns have been attracted by the light of those who are pure and radiant. Their aim is to remind you all again of your innocence, in other words the original essence that you had when you became a divine spark. They are also bringing you hope, wisdom and enlightenment.

What do the unicorns do in the spiritual realms?

The unicorns are keepers of ancient wisdom, magic and mystery. They hold pure visions for humanity and for beings in other planes of existence, though their concentration is now focused on Earth, to help you ascend.

Why do unicorns have a horn of light?

Their third eyes are so developed that the light emitted is as sharp and clear as a laser beam. It directs wisdom and enlightenment into people. If it is channelled into your third eye or heart chakra, you will receive a charge of spiritual information and knowledge or be energised with qualities of beauty, clarity, purity, nobility, grace, healing, joy or peace.

Who do the unicorns approach?

If you are a person of good intention and courage, unicorns will drop thoughts into your mind that will assist the world. They will also encourage and steady you to bring your mission to fruition. They work with anyone who has a vision to help others or is manifesting a plan for the higher good. They also connect with the pure in heart and those who have an earnest desire to walk the spiritual path.

How can the unicorns help me?

Where you have a vision beyond yourself, the unicorns will strengthen you and enable you to maintain your dignity, self-worth and honour as your project moves forward. They whisper inspiration, connect you to the spiritual realms and bring healing to your soul. A unicorn will also help you to manifest your personal aspirations.

Can unicorns heal?

Yes, unicorns heal at a most profound level by touching and repairing the soul. They reconnect you to your spirit to rekindle love and inspire hope. They offer grace, which transmutes the spiritual, mental and emotional blocks and heals the physical body.

Does everyone have a unicorn?

In ancient times of wisdom, your unicorn stayed with you throughout your life. In current times this does not happen. Few experience the presence of their unicorn from birth. However, as you develop wisdom, strength and higher ideals, your unicorn will approach. Its energy is so special and so light that it comes towards you briefly and then retreats, several times, like waves, until you are strong enough to contain it. You may be able to think of people who radiate confidence, nobility, self-worth and dignity. They are connected to unicorn energy.

Why do children seem drawn to unicorns?

Unicorns and children have a natural affinity because their essence is pure. Youngsters who have newly left the spiritual dimensions are innocent, still in touch with wonder and magic. Unicorns remind them of this and they can play lightly together.

It was the bright light of the new highly evolved children who are incarnating now on Earth that first attracted the unicorns back towards your planet.

I often see angel clouds, but I have never seen a unicorn cloud? Why not?

When an angel pauses to watch over someone or something, vapour forms where it has been. Then, if the conditions are right, this will turn into a white cloud in the shape of that angel. Unicorns tend to spend less time watching from above. They come down to Earth and observe from a different angle. However, on occasion they do view from on high, so on a clear day you may see a unicorn cloud.

When my friend was saved from drowning, he was sure a horse was holding him up in the water but he could not see anything. Could that have been a unicorn?

Oh yes. It was not your friend's time to pass over and his guardian angel and a unicorn were holding him up and giving him strength and encouragement to hold on until help arrived.

I often dream of white horses. Could they be unicorns?

Sometimes they are. They connect with you during your dreams to take you into the higher spiritual realms. A unicorn dream is very special, for it means they are close to you and encouraging you to bring your visions to fruition.

As a child my daughter loved to make daisy chains. She also talked of unicorns. Are the two connected?

Daisies represent purity and innocence, and a daisy chain embodies those qualities. So it may well be that your daughter's love of these qualities drew the unicorns to her. Whenever you see a daisy, hold it in your mind's eye as a symbol of purity and remember the unicorns.

Once a horse has become a unicorn, does it incarnate again?

Up to the present time this has never happened. However, because of the unkind and disrespectful way some horses have been treated over the centuries, a few unicorns may incarnate in the near future. In this case they will appear as radiant white physical horses with a beautiful light. Because of the dignity and authority they carry, people will respond to them differently. You will start to remember that horses are great spiritual beings who are gracing Earth with their presence. They will then be treated with honour, dignity, respect, kindness and love.

Do unicorns leave a symbol?

Like angels, unicorns will leave a little white feather to tell you that they have been near you. Unicorns love white flowers, from a simple daisy to an exotic lily, so you may find yourself aware of a cluster of such flowers or notice a single bloom in an unexpected place as a reminder that they are near. They resonate with the vibration of the colour white.

Also, in unconscious recognition of their presence, people are creating unicorn paintings, statues, songs and decorations, all of which act as symbols to remind you of their energy.

Can unicorns dissolve karma?

Their unconditional love and light offers grace, which indeed dissolves karma.

Can you send a unicorn to touch someone?

Yes, your thoughts create a bridge of energy which a unicorn or an angel can use to connect with people to help them. They will illuminate minds and hearts where this is possible. You can ask a unicorn to illuminate and inspire teachers, leaders and those who have an influential role in the world.

EXAMPLE

Newspaper editors are very influential and this responsibility is not always carried with integrity or for the light. Whether for local, national or international journals, magazines or papers of any kind, you are invited to participate in the prayer and visualisation below. You can adapt this to people in any walk of life.

~ **Prayer to the Unicorns** ~

I now ask the unicorns to approach the editor of . . . . . . to touch their mind with wisdom, light and integrity and their heart with love, peace and kindness.

~ **Visualisation to send help to the unicorns** ~

~ Picture a bridge of white light going from you to the person in question, who you may or may not know.

~ See a shining unicorn travelling along this path to the other individual. It is directing the light from its horn into their mind and then their heart.

~ Hold a vision of the recipient sitting in a radiant aura and see this light surrounding all their work.

What element do unicorns belong to?

Unicorns are essentially of the air, but they also love water. You will find them where waterfalls cascade like a bridal veil, or where waves crash on to the rocks. They also enjoy the earth, particularly the green cloak of nature which brings balance and new growth.

~ **Visualisation to work with your unicorn** ~

~ Take a few moments to breathe deeply and relax.

~ Picture yourself out in nature, in a place of beauty, where the veils between the worlds are thin.

~ Be aware of a cluster of pure white flowers. Gently touch their petals and you may even be able to smell their perfume.

~ Nearby is a waterfall or stream, cascading and frothing in the clear air.

~ A shimmering white light is approaching and a magnificent unicorn steps out of the light towards you, radiating such love that you feel encompassed by it.

~ Relax more deeply as the beautiful creature comes close and tilts its head towards you. Light pours from its horn into you. Open up to it.

~ Tell the unicorn of any wish, dream or vision you have and ask for its help. Wait for any impressions or response you may receive.

~ Think of someone and picture a white light going from you to that person. Ask the unicorn to touch that person to inspire or help them in an appropriate way. Sense what takes place.

~ Thank the unicorn and watch it moving away and out of sight.

~ Open your eyes and return to the material world.

SOCIAL
QUESTIONS

Alcohol, Drugs and Addictions

What are addictions?

Addictions are a last, desperate attempt by your ego to stop you from dealing with those energy blocks that prevent you from accessing your true divinity.

What are the spiritual effects of alcohol?

Alcohol lowers your frequency, making spiritual connection more difficult. In excess it creates holes in your aura, so that negative thoughts, emotions and entities can enter and affect you. Soft drugs have a similar effect.

Tom and Angela were both clairvoyant and so was their daughter, Rose, who was almost sixteen and very psychically sensitive. Rose visited a pub one evening, where many entities lurk. One attached to her. When she arrived home she was screaming and crying for, being clairvoyant, she could actually see the ghost holding on to her. It was the spirit of an alcoholic who had died but remained stuck on the Earth plane, attached to gratifying his addiction through living drinkers. He was continuously repeating into her ear, 'Have another drink. Have another drink.' She was terrified and could not get rid of him. Luckily her parents knew what to do and released her.

They were so glad that she could see and hear the spirit. Another teenager without Rose's gifts would have felt quite unwell and would constantly have wanted another drink to satisfy the man on her back, without having any idea what drove her.

Exercise to help teenagers
1. Light a candle.
2. Ask the Principalities, those of the angelic hierarchy in charge of big business, towns and countries, to bring a higher consciousness to the owners and managers of pubs and clubs where teenagers are binge-drinking and taking drugs.
3. Picture the youngsters receiving light, which fills them with self-respect, happiness and a sense of worth, so that their lives find direction and purpose.
4. Hold the vision of a new generation opening to their true spiritual potential.

~ **Prayer for teenagers in pubs** ~

Angels of light and love, thank you for surrounding all pubs and clubs where youngsters gather. Touch the hearts and minds of the owners and managers with a sense of responsibility. Enfold and protect each young person who enters. Help them to find direction and purpose in their lives. So be it.

What are the spiritual effects of drugs?

Soft drugs have similar effects to alcohol, in that they close down your spiritual connections. Hard drugs do permanent damage. LSD affects the brainwaves, causing them to move out of synchronicity. The inevitable loss of spirituality results in a lifetime of restriction. Every choice you make has consequences.

Why would someone choose a lifetime of spiritual restriction?

Some people who have the potential to be highly spiritual have taken decisions, often when young, which alter the course of their destiny. Sometimes it means that, by default, they then choose to learn through frustration and disappointment. Both these emotions are master teachers. Those who sought, consciously or unconsciously, a quick and easy way to enlightenment through the use of hallucinogens may need to lay the foundations of light for their next incarnation.

It is the personality that makes choices to do drugs, often out of desperation and despair when they cannot sense the light ahead. Others see this as an easy option or a social pleasure, without understanding the true implications of their actions.

My friend used to take LSD. She has read that you block your spiritual progress for that lifetime if you have taken it. Now she is depressed and suicidal, and I am afraid for her. What can I do?

This is a question with two parts, and the first is about you.

Your task is to take responsibility for your own life and spiritual growth, so do examine what underlies your fear for your friend. Are you afraid of not being good enough to help your friend? Are you afraid of loss and separation? Are you scared of being lonely without her or that you will become depressed if she dies? Do you feel it will reflect on you if she is depressed?

When you resolve these questions within yourself, your light will be strong enough to help her without your personal issues interfering. Then you will be able to demonstrate true empathy and compassion, which is a highly evolved state. The greatest gift you can give another is to be happy yourself.

Your friend became depressed when she learnt that her previous decisions have consequences that she does not like. This tendency to respond to life's disappointments in this way was possibly one of the original reasons she took LSD. There are many paths to choose in life which can lay positive foundations for her next incarnation. Opening her heart to children, animals or people, the path of service, learning, teaching or working with nature are a few suggestions.

What are the spiritual effects of tobacco?

Tobacco clouds your aura, so forms a smokescreen which prevents you from seeing both your darkness and your true magnificence. On a physical level, smoking tobacco suppresses feelings of lack of self-worth and self-esteem.

Why are so many people becoming addicted to alcohol and other substances?

All addictions are ways of coping with your most difficult emotions. At this current time on Earth, in preparation for big changes in consciousness worldwide, everything hidden is surfacing to be explored. Secrets, unconscious drives and denied emotions are all being revealed, and this applies to individuals and families as well as society as a whole. This is rarely easy for humans, as it is painful to deal with long-suppressed feelings and concealed truths. In addition, many are feeling lost and confused in your current permissive, materialistic and chaotic societies, so that readily available drink and drugs offer a palliative to ease their tribulation.

More high-frequency energy is now flowing into Earth than ever before, and this will help to move many sufferers through the fire of addiction into the pure light of their souls.

Are more sensitive souls incarnating now, and are they more likely to become addicted?

Yes. There are many more highly evolved spirits incarnating now, with missions to bring in the light for the changes ahead. However, such sensitive beings are vulnerable to chemical substances, and some, caught in the trap of addiction, have lost sight of their pre-life aspirations. Hardy souls rarely become addicted.

Why are some people violent when they are drunk or on drugs, even though they are gentle when sober or clean?

Those who are violent when drunk or on drugs are expressing the anger that rages inside them and which they can control when sober or clean. Alcohol and certain substances cause the critical censor between the conscious and the unconscious mind to step aside. This means it can no longer do its office of keeping the lower urges at bay. Those individuals are then driven by their inner demons.

I have a tendency to be addictive. I am a workaholic and exercise excessively. Does this affect me spiritually?

All addictions, whether to food, substances, work, shopping, sex, starvation, exercise or television, are escape mechanisms enabling you to avoid uncomfortable feelings. Those emotions you are suppressing form energy blocks in your aura, so that your true spirituality cannot flow. As you recognise what you are doing to yourself, you can take a conscious choice to face the unpleasant feelings.

The angels suggest that next time you have a craving or addictive feeling you make a little space for yourself. Breathe deeply, focusing only on your breath. If possible go outside into nature, for earth, trees, flowers and wildlife will help you by absorbing some of the dark vibrations.

Exercise to face feelings
1. Sit or walk.
2. Ask your guardian angel to help you.
3. Notice where the feeling is held in your body.
4. Breathe deeply into that part of the body.
5. Observe the memories that come up.

119

6. Remind yourself that these are past and have no power over you.
7. Congratulate yourself for surviving, even if it is only for a short period, without resorting to your addictive behaviour.
8. Thank the angels for helping you.

Children

CONCEPTION TO BIRTH

Does every baby have a guardian angel?

Yes. Every baby that is born through a physical mother has its own guardian angel.

When does the soul connect to the foetus of the baby?

This happens at different times depending on the origin of the soul. Those from Orion and Sirius attach to the mother moments before conception. Others come in much later. Some arrive almost too late, in which case the baby may be very slow to take its first breath.

Was Jesus a divine conception?

Yes. The vibration of God was implanted into Mary. There was no physical connection, a cosmic truth only comprehensible to the minds of mystics.

What is the higher purpose of sex?

The divine concept of sex was the loving union of a couple in a moment of ecstasy. The orgasmic moment projected the physical release of the sperm to join the egg. It also provided the energy to draw the appropriate soul from the spiritual realms. In this way the material and spiritual world work in perfect harmony.

What is the higher perception of IVF, known as test-tube babies?

The angels love all babies, whatever their origin. They are souls who desire so much to experience life on Earth that they are prepared to grasp any opportunity which is presented and are willing to be conceived in challenging circumstances. They are birthed through a human mother, so each has a guardian angel.

What if the egg is donated from another woman, but the father's sperm is used?

This is a soul choice by all the beings involved and offers lessons to each of them.

What is the best way to prepare for conception?

When the parents have higher spiritual understanding, they meditate before their child is conceived to discover what kind of soul they can best serve and to connect with one such who is awaiting incarnation. Holding this intent, they make love in order to draw in this baby to start its physicality. Parenthood is considered to be a very important act of service as well as a spiritual responsibility, and such babies are welcomed wholeheartedly. These children enter from the pure spiritual realms.

Is abortion spiritually wrong?

There is no judgement in the spirit world. Incoming souls choose their destiny. Many couples engage in intercourse unconsciously driven by their low self-esteem, lust, neediness or loneliness. These prospective parents consider their own selfish needs and give little or no thought to the requirements of the soul that is entering through their physical union. The conception of such an unwanted baby brings lessons to both the parents and their families.

Where this happens, the soul has agreed to come into incarnation through these particular individuals and in many cases it already knows that the consequence will be a termination of its journey to Earth. This is what it has agreed at a higher level.

In India a doctor has been imprisoned for aborting a foetus because it was female. What is the angelic perspective?

The soul of the aborted child knew that the outcome of the mother's pregnancy would be a termination. In this case, the Higher Self of the baby was offering to redress its own karma. Please take a moment to send prayers for her spirit as you read this. Even if it is several years later, those prayers will assist her.

The doctor who performed the abortion on the grounds that it was a female child was not on his planned spiritual path. Therefore the soul (not the human persona) of the doctor offered to be a 'sacrifice' to draw the attention of the world to the inferior status of girls in India.

This was a plan set up in the spiritual world to help bring about change and higher understanding. The question is not whether it is spiritually allowable to abort a foetus on grounds of its gender, but how the societies throughout your world can value girls and boys equally.

The laws and customs of certain societies make it difficult and expensive to give birth to a daughter. What can be done?

Change the laws and customs. Do this by envisioning the ineffable thought held in the mind of God. Male and female are equal parts of a whole. They always have been and always will be. Perfect truth vibrates in the hearts and minds of all, so at some level every human knows this. It was originally the doubts of women about their worth that allowed this imbalance to be perpetrated over the centuries. Now courageous women are incarnating to reclaim the power of females. Movements will erupt in unlikely places as the scales of the genders balance once more. In the meantime, make sure that you value boys and girls, men and women equally and, in doing so, teach others to do the same.

What happens to the spirit of an aborted baby?

It has a number of choices. One is to remain in the astral world attached to its family, in which case it grows up in spirit and experiences through their growth. In this case, if the aborted spirit holds feelings of sadness, rejection or abandonment, its negative emotions may cause a cloud to hang over its relations. On the other hand, where the departed soul is wise and loving, it can truly assist its loved ones from the spirit world.

The second choice is to wait until one of the parents or both are ready to birth him or her. In this case the termination merely postpones its entry into physicality.

Thirdly, the aborted soul may return into the spirit world and continue with its assignations and work on the other side.

Fourthly, it may reconsider its options with the help of its guides, angels and spiritual advisers and choose another set of birth parents.

The souls of all such babies benefit greatly from your loving prayers. Mother Mary and her team of spirit helpers take care of them.

~ Prayer for the soul of an unborn baby ~

Beloved Mother Mary, I ask you to look after the soul of this unborn baby. May the angels enfold him or her with love and light and help him or her to make wise choices about their future spiritual journey.

Why do miscarriages occur?

When a baby miscarries it can be a tragedy for the parents. But remember that the journey the soul set out on into incarnation is a formidable undertaking. A spirit may simply need to touch the Earth plane, so it withdraws after a few weeks of pregnancy. Or it may have elected to give one or both of the parents a wake-up call or lesson by being conceived and then departing. Occasionally the being may simply have decided that the proposed lifetime is too difficult, so it leaves prematurely.

In some instances the mother's body is not ready for this particular experience, so she should check her health. It may simply be that her longing and stress render her body too acidic to carry the baby to term, or that the mother, father or both are not in the right mental, emotional, physical or spiritual space. Their past-life beliefs may even interfere with the full-term entry of a new baby. In that case it is important for them both to examine and explore what really is taking place at an inner level.

As I was writing this I was talking to an acquaintance of mine about her little girls. She remarked that she had had five miscarriages before her two children, and then added, 'When I look back, I don't think I was ready for them at that time.' I admired her insight.

Why are some babies born damaged?

The soul of the baby coming in commands its circumstances and conditions, so there are no accidents and no chance. The people who are present or even not present at the birth are taking instructions at a higher level from the Higher Self of the baby.

At an Earth level the seeming mishaps, mistakes and problems which occasionally happen during or after birth teach, test or give experience to all the participants. Nevertheless, each individual must take personal responsibility for his omissions and commissions. Carelessness or malpractice incur karma.

What choices does the soul make pre-birth?

Before conception, the soul of the child communicates with his angels, guides and spiritual helpers. Together they decide the desired gender as well as the conditions that the soul needs for its growth or teachings. The prospective parents of the child are minutely examined because they both supply the child's genetic inheritance. Siblings, grandparents, aunts and uncles and extended family are also agreed at this point. Some specific needs, such as a desire to be in the same age group as a specially selected sibling or marriage partner, may also affect this choice.

Because the astrological impact at the moment of birth is vitally important, the time and place of birth are carefully calculated and considered. What is the atmosphere there? What are the emotions and feelings in this place? They all affect the baby. The more evolved the soul, the fewer options are available to it. Sometimes such a being has to wait hundreds of years for an entry opportunity with the right conditions and desired emotional links.

Why are some babies born premature?

This is a choice made by the Higher Self of the child, knowing the probable conditions into which it will be born. These soul choices provide the challenges and difficulties it wishes to undertake. For those who are very focused on life, it is a test of willpower. They put their energy into fighting for survival. Others weaker or less determined are not clear about the strength of their desire to undertake an incarnation, and they will allow themselves to pass over. For some, it was never part of the plan to experience more than a few hours, days or weeks on Earth.

Is it right to keep very premature babies alive?

This is a question that has only arisen since human advances in medical technology. Now many very premature babies are kept artificially alive to satisfy the ego of doctors or the neediness of parents without consideration for the highest good of the newcomer.

While many of these children are offering themselves as sacrifices to teach lessons and provoke spiritual questioning, please offer prayers for their highest good without attachment to whether they stay or return to spirit.

Why do multiple births happen?

In earlier times there were always a few sets of twins born each year. The survival of triplets was rare, while the birth of quads occurred very rarely. Those souls chose to incarnate together either for mutual support or to resolve a particular karmic issue.

Of course babies still choose to make the journey into life together for these considerations, but now there are more reasons for doing so. Because the chances of surviving a multiple birth without damage are much greater and so many souls wish to experience current world conditions, two or more may agree to share the vehicle when the chance is presented. The use of IVF treatment offers a physical opportunity that was simply not available before.

Why would one twin die while the other lived?

Each soul has a different karma.

It feels appropriate to repeat the story I tell in *Light Up Your Life*, where a lady was expecting twins. The night before their birth she dreamt that a boat came to shore. On it were a handsome prince and a beautiful princess. As they landed, the prince stepped ashore and helped the princess on to dry land. Then he got back into the boat and sailed away. She knew that the boy would die and the girl would live. And next day, when they were born, that is exactly what happened. She realised that her son had accompanied his sister on the journey to Earth and that was the experience they both needed. Of course this did not stop her from mourning her baby, but she did understand the spiritual reason for his death.

126

If everything is a soul choice, why are conjoined twins born?

This is the result of a wish expressed deeply and fervently in a previous incarnation by two beings never to be parted again. The strength of their soul desire translates into a physical bonding.

Is it spiritually correct to separate conjoined twins?

This varies. For some such souls, only death should separate them. For others, the desire to be together diminishes when they find themselves restricted by a physical link. In the latter case it is spiritually correct to use modern medical practices to enable them to lead individual lives.

The parents and doctors should always connect with the Higher Selves of the conjoined twins in meditation to sense whether it is permissible to perform such surgery on them. It must be done from compassion, never from the ego of the parents or medical teams.

Can we influence the kind of child we have?

Yes, the parents and extended family can meditate for the kind of soul to whom they can best offer support. Then they can pray for a child with these particular qualities or characteristics.

When they were ready to start a family, a couple I know meditated together and asked for a spiritual soul to be born to them. Their daughter is beautiful, high-energy, full of light, intelligent, individual, fun, stretches all the boundaries and is a complete handful. When they were ready for a second child, they asked for a calm and spiritual soul! Soon after his birth I held him and could see the Tibetan monks around him. He is indeed a totally different character, calm and considered. Both are absolutely fabulous, though I could be biased, as they are my grandchildren!

How can I spiritually support the conception and birth of my child?

If you are the mother-to-be, before conception offer yourself as a vehicle to the incoming child. When both parents prepare themselves physically, emotionally, mentally and spiritually to bring in the baby, they are helping greatly to relieve his karma.

All dedicated prayers, meditations, hymns, chants and mantras soothe and support the soul before conception and during pregnancy as well as after birth.

When I asked if I could to tell the story about about my grandchildren, their father, Greg, reminded me of the mantra we chanted for Finn. I had arrived at their house to look after two-year-old Isabel while Lauren, my daughter, went into hospital for the birth. The baby was overdue. Lauren's first labour had lasted for thirty-six hours and she was already very tired, so we decided to chant the Sanskrit mantra, Om Namo Bhagavate Vasudevaya, a favourite of theirs. We dedicated it to the child arriving soon and to a short safe labour. As we chanted, the vibration in the room was extraordinary. Three hours later Lauren went into labour and three hours after that Finn arrived safe and sound.

Greg said to me later, 'The energy that poured through on that night as we chanted, just hours before Finn was born, was amazing and clearly linked, as if he was responding to the mantra.'

Teenagers

Why are we being presented with a teenage mob culture now?

Teenagers need to belong, so they form groups. They have always done so, for it is part of their growth. However, their behaviour is now out of balance because family structure is breaking down and they feel confused about their place in the community. Because the elders no longer offer wisdom, discipline or direction, the youngsters do not know where to channel their energy, so they wander round in gangs in an aimless way.

When current teenagers were children, many of their parents overprotected them, afraid to let them play outside or explore their neighbourhoods. Instead of listening to them and loving them, they gave them material possessions and let them watch inappropriate television or videos, often violent. Children who are overprotected remain immature and dependent, so they become disillusioned, undisciplined adolescents, with little confidence or self-worth and no outlet for their vital force. Life appears pointless and fruitless, and many are deeply depressed, feeling disconnected from their Source. Their behaviour reflects the malaise of the adults around them.

The pendulum will start to swing towards equilibrium as society itself becomes more balanced and responsible.

How can we help the teenagers?

Teenagers need compassion, love, discipline, direction, encouragement and hope. Every time you condemn their unruly behaviour or are frightened of it, you are sending a dark energy into their consciousness and pushing them deeper into their illusion of separation. You must see the divine in the youngsters. The Higher Truth is that they are all perfect and have always been so. Picture them in their perfection and ask the angels to use you as a bridge of light into their minds and hearts. Bless them individually and collectively with such qualities as compassion, love, discipline, direction, encouragement and hope. Each time you do this from your heart, you will create an opportunity for the angels to help them.

Why are teenage gangs so destructive?

Those who feel uncared for close their hearts and cannot feel. As a result they can be destructive, violent, cruel and even self-harming.

129

No one hears their pain and they cannot hear anyone else's. They are deeply afraid and hurting.

These teenagers build their own family in gangs and take substances to dull their feelings. They express their disillusion and anguish by becoming angry, aggressive and, when they have no safe form of expression, violent or dangerous.

A child who feels loved, respected and understood can empathise with and feel for others, which automatically means he could never hurt or harm anyone or anything.

Reminder

When you open your heart, you are surrounded in an aura of love which can enfold and heal the anguish of those who come into contact with you. As you remind them that it is safe to love and be loved, they can begin to remember who they truly are.

Why are teenagers drinking and doing drugs?

On a physical level, too many parent and adult role models have abrogated responsibility for the wise and sensibly disciplined rearing of adolescents. Television soaps set around pubs are the current projection of family life. Alcohol and drugs have been made socially acceptable and readily available with no vision to take their place.

On a spiritual level, some teenagers have lost trust, hope, sense of purpose and spiritual connection, and a few are committing slow suicide through drink and drugs.

Why are girls starting to become violent?

The old order where men dominated the world is coming to an end. During the thousands of years when the masculine controlled the feminine, women had no option but to accept bullying, beating, poverty, the constant bearing of children, unfaithfulness and all forms of abuse that the significant men who owned them

– fathers, uncles, brothers, sons and husband – cared to mete out.

All old unresolved feelings are coming to the surface now to be released or dealt with.

Many girls are taking on the unexpressed rage of their mothers, grandmothers, great-grandmothers and other female ancestors. They do not know how to heal these feelings or to channel them appropriately, so it is manifesting as violence.

However, when women recognise that at some level they collectively colluded in their disempowerment, they take responsibility for their past, present and future. They become Masters. They claim their power. Then each can make new choices of ways to behave and be. When this happens all anger evaporates and each individual has healed her family tree.

The rewards are inner peace, a sense of self-worth and happiness for herself as well as her descendants.

What can we do to offer children and teenagers an alternative?

Many of those who are currently children or teenagers are high-frequency spirits who are full of energy and need to channel their vital force into sports, creative endeavours, spiritual understanding or other appropriate outlets.

Girls as well as boys need fathers to swim, play tennis or do some other sport with them, not take them to watch someone else doing it. Their artistic, musical and creative efforts should be respected and encouraged.

Action to help children and teenagers
Lobby for more sports facilities. Encourage local acting groups to put on plays with roles for young people. Set up painting groups or any sort of creative class. Let youngsters care for animals and those less fortunate than they are.

131

~ Visualisation to help young people ~

— Light a candle and focus on the flame.
— Breathe deeply.
— Close your eyes.
— Ask for the hearts and minds of children and teenagers everywhere to be opened to a higher purpose.
— Picture angels going into schools, colleges and wherever youngsters gather, lighting them up with hope.

What is the spiritual understanding of current education?

Children learn best in quiet, relaxed, harmonious places with teachers who encourage, inspire and offer sensible discipline. Currently education is out of balance. Schools are too stressed, for they honour left-brain knowledge and learning while devaluing the right brain.

Left-brain learning is logical, linear, rational, scientific, mathematical, computer-orientated. It forces youngsters to take in other people's ideas and regurgitate them, producing clones. Because of the emphasis on rules and orders, sensitive children feel stifled and often become depressed, rebellious or cruel.

The right brain is responsible for originality, creativity, imagination, rhythm, song, artistic ability, spiritual connection and an open heart. In societies with a focus on the development of the right brain, caring, empathy, trust, nurturing and inclusivity is encouraged and valued. This leads to relaxation, peace and contentment but sometimes lack of decision-making powers or financial acumen.

From a spiritual perspective, education systems need to adjust to include right-brain development. The rewards will be immense – interested, balanced youngsters with a sense of safety and belonging who express their creativity and originality and at the same time feel good about caring for others, especially the disadvantaged.

Do reading and writing block our spiritual potential?

In excess, yes. When all the focus is on reading and writing, the left brain develops to the exclusion of the right. It is through the opening of the right brain that you make your spiritual connections.

Left-brain dominance involves too much acceptance of others' ideas, while spiritual progress depends on creativity and originality.

How can we help children and teenagers to express their life force?

Love, listen to and spend time with your children. Youngsters need openness, encouragement and freedom. They need challenge and adventure, within a structure of discipline. Provide more sports facilities, especially school playgrounds. Create adventure opportunities and outlaw the blame and claim culture. Let children and teenagers be creative, paint murals on the walls, plant beautiful gardens in wasteland, travel in other countries and meet the people, do service work and understand teamwork. Encourage more wise, strong males to engage with the younger generations.

Would initiations for boys help?

Yes. In initiatory societies, boys feel comfortable in their manhood and this in turn means that they can honour women, children and those who need help. (*See also SOCIETY – Is there an advantage to initiatory societies on p.211.*)

What about initiations for girls?

Females have always had internal initiations – menstruation, childbirth and menopause. These need to be honoured and celebrated again. A girl who celebrates her womanhood and is proud of it becomes a happy mother and values men for their role.

INDIGO, CRYSTAL AND RAINBOW CHILDREN

Who are the Indigo, Crystal and Rainbow children?

These are enlightened souls who have been born at this special time of the evolution of your planet. They have not incarnated on Earth before. They have arrived now to teach their families and all who come into contact with them about a higher way of being. Indigo children are so named because of the predominance of the colour indigo in their auras. They tend to be psychic and have healing powers. Crystal children have crystal-clear auras, so they have clarity to see into other realms, including the angelic realms. Rainbow children have rainbow auras, bringing in the full spectrum of colour and making them more balanced.

Do these special children bring in karma?

No. They enter without karma, but there are challenges marked in their astrological charts which are inevitably lessons for their families and those with whom they come into contact.

Where do the high-frequency children come from?

All Indigo, Crystal and Rainbow children originate from Orion, which is the planet of enlightenment. They have never incarnated on Earth before, so this material plane is very difficult for them to understand. Nor have they been to other training schools in the universe. Their only home has been Orion. Because their Spirits are so pure, teachers from other planets have come to them to initiate them into cosmic understandings.

What is special about them?

Not only are they very high-frequency children, but they are very psychic and often enlightened. Many have gifts of healing and telepathy as well as clairvoyance. Some have advanced powers which need to be carefully nurtured and trained.

Are particular parents found for these children?

Yes. Great care is taken before they incarnate to find families who can look after them and help them to cope with life on Earth. However, because of their sensitivity, this is not always enough to enable them to make the adjustment.

Who are the autistic children and how can we help them?

Some Indigo, Crystal or Rainbow children withdraw into autism because their vibration is so high and pure that they cannot cope with the energy around them. They have shut down their gifts and talents, so in order to help them reconnect with them, raise your frequency. Of course not all autistic children are Indigo, Crystal or Rainbow souls. There are some very evolved beings reincarnating who also cannot manage the low frequency on Earth. Again, it assists them if you can raise your consciousness.

Other autistic children have reincarnated with heavy karma. By taking on this condition, their souls have limited their options, and this prevents them from earning more karma through misdeeds.

Whatever the soul reason for autism, you can help these children by enfolding them in love and by asking the angels of healing to work with them.

Death and Dying

COMAS

Is coma similar to death?

No. While a person is in a coma, their spirit is attached to their physical form by a silver thread.

Some people in comas are terrified of dying. They want to come back to their families, and from the inner planes are pleading and begging for help. Such frightened beings need reassurance and prayers to assist them for the highest good of their souls. This will help them to return to their physical body or pass safely and happily into the light, whichever is right for them.

Others do wonderful work while in a coma. Their spirits, free of their body, may channel healing or visit people to act as intermediaries or comforters. They can often accomplish things that the angels cannot because their vibration feels more familiar to those they help. Those who are doing these tasks are quite content, for they know that their outer physical shell will remain until their work is done. Prayers for their highest good will assist them and those with whom they are communicating.

Is it spiritually correct to turn off life support when a person is in a persistent coma?

With the advances in medicine without equivalent spiritual under-standing, many disturbing questions are being presented to humanity. In spiritually enlightened times, healers examined the patient's energy fields containing their soul record to see if it was their time to pass over. This would be done with the intention of serving the patient's highest good, so if the patient had reached their allotted time, the families and healers would uncord themselves and set the patient's spirit free. The physical body would automatically follow.

In current times, family or friends can so easily hold on to their loved one by the sheer force of their desire. This may oppose the higher will of the sick person and, therefore, may trap them in a state of limbo.

You must learn to meditate to connect with the patient's Higher Self and receive an impression of what the soul wants. Assuming that he or she is ready to pass and that the intention of all concerned is pure and open-hearted, then it can be spiritually correct to turn off life support. However, it is never a lightly made decision.

What if a person does not need a life-support machine, but continues to breathe and remain in a vegetative state?

This is slightly different from the question above. If the person is breathing unaided, there are many lessons for the family to learn. Patience is one; detachment another. Compassion, understanding, empathy, love, courage and discrimination are all developed by such situations.

It may be that the patient has a contract to pass at a particular time and is waiting for this. An example would be when there is a specific astrological alignment imminent, which will assist him into his ongoing journey after death.

Frequently the spirit of the person in a vegetative state is afraid to let go. Maybe they want to watch over the children or grandchildren. Perhaps they are terrified of dying. Please take spiritual action and offer prayers for their highest good. Because they may need reassurance or permission to leave, release your loved one physically, emotionally, mentally and spiritually.

Bear in mind that sometimes the spirit of the apparently absent person is doing incredible spiritual work out of body, perhaps healing others or spreading peace.

Many years ago I was asked to see a lady who remained in a persistent vegetative state. She had two small children and a husband, but simply was not in her physical body. The family wanted her to return. I only saw her once and thought it very sad and quite hopeless. After I had seen her, my guidance came through very clearly. I was told that she did not wish to return to her old life but was terrified of letting go and passing over. I was asked to work with her in my quiet times, connecting to her spirit and reassuring her that it was all right for her to die. I was to tell her spirit that the children would be looked after and her grandmother was waiting for her on the other side. I did this every day for three weeks. Then she let go. Though it was heartbreaking for the family, ultimately it allowed them to move on with their lives.

THE PROCESS OF DYING

What is the best way to help someone on their deathbed?

This partly depends on their beliefs. If they are totally spiritu-ally unaware and absolutely do not wish to acknowledge anything beyond the physical world, hold your counsel. Just let your consciousness permeate theirs and assist them. Mentally give them permission to leave, send them love and silently offer prayers for their safe passing. They will telepathically receive your messages and be helped. Please use your intuition, for many a dying atheist suddenly becomes aware of deceased rela-tives waiting for him and of the angels beside him, and is unex-pectedly open to hearing about God and the spiritual dimensions.

Where the dying person is spiritually aware, offer them love and permission to go. Either do this silently or aloud, depending on what feels right. Sometimes a loved one tries to hold on for you because they think that you need them. If you sense this is the case, gently remind them that you too will be looked after by the angels, and that it is all right to let go and experience the wonderful freedom and joy that awaits them. It is often very comforting for such a person to surrender on the energy of your prayer. Whatever the circumstances, it is very important to be ready and willing to release the person.

Was an angel there when my husband died?

Oh yes! No one dies alone. Not only is your guardian angel with you when you die, but a higher angel comes to help with the passing too. Your husband was taken into the light.

Sensible nurses, grounded people full of common sense, have often commented to me that they see angels waiting for patients to pass over. Then they know they are about to die.

Why do some people die in such horrible ways?

The method of death is a soul choice. Often it reflects the way they lived their life. The person who lives on the edge may choose to pass over in a spectacular way, while the quiet person may die gently during sleep, though this is not necessarily so. Even when a death appears to us to be violent, the person may not feel pain. For example, many who die in fires leave their bodies before the burning starts. Remember their angels are there to help them. However, if someone's soul dictates that he must undergo a difficult experience as he dies, his angels cannot exorcise his karma for him.

What happens to the souls of people who have committed terrible acts, such as Adolf Hitler?

Usually, after death they will spend much time in a healing sanctuary until they are ready for their life review. If their souls have undergone many lifetimes of darkness with a heart closed and immured to the pain caused by their decisions and actions, they will undergo extensive rehabilitation. If, however, during their assessment they felt compassion for their victims, they will be given the opportunity to learn about love in the inner planes before returning to Earth.

Where prayers are received which ask for the suffering and eternal damnation of these human monsters, the consequences for their souls are dire. However, where there are requests for mercy, like sparks of gold, from their loved ones and lightworkers, the angels can take these and weave them into a flame to place in their hearts. Thanks to those prayers, in their next incarnations they are born into a position where they can do no harm. They will enter into a loving family and at last have the opportunity to learn about love.

My husband was driving soberly and safely when he was hit head-on by a drunk driver. My husband was killed while the drunk walked out unscathed. Where is the justice in this?

On an emotional level this is very sad and traumatic for you and your family. Be assured that if it had not been your husband's time to die, his guardian angel would have prevented it.

On a spiritual level, your husband's soul or Higher Self made the decision to return to the light in this way. People sometimes offer their method of passing as a way to draw attention to bad things that are happening on Earth, such as driving under the influence of alcohol or drugs. The waves of anger, shock and horror exert pressure, for this is needed to change attitudes and laws. From the heavenly realms it was also hoped that the drunk driver and all who knew him would be so appalled by this devastating occurrence that it would change their lives.

Seemingly unjust happenings are often the resolution of karma.

Your entire family was offered a wake-up call by the terrible bereavement, for death often accelerates people into a deeper spiritual search for truth.

BABIES AND CHILDREN

My child fell to his death from an upstairs window and I keep thinking of what he must have gone through as he fell.

As your child fell, there was only a moment of fear before he was held by angels and taken to the light. He felt nothing but joy. Also it was his time to die.

Where was his angel when my child was drowned?

Your child's angel was holding him lovingly and helping him to make the adjustment to leaving his body. If it had not been your child's time to die, his angel would have 'miraculously' saved him.

Why do babies die?

When a baby is born it has a spiritual get-out clause that allows it to abort its mission to Earth in the first six to twelve months. For sensitive souls your planet may seem a very difficult place to live, so, despite the love and care of parents, an infant may feel that its chosen task is too difficult. Choices freely made while in spirit feel very different when confined in a physical body.

Some children come in specifically to offer their parents and extended family lessons, one of which may be detachment, the lesson of letting go of a loved one who has taken a decision to pass over.

Sometimes a soul may have left a previous incarnation prematurely or with just a small amount of karma to complete, so it only needs a few days, weeks or months in a physical body to complete it. That is a pre-life decision.

If an infant decides to depart, his angels will help him return to the light.

Why are some babies stillborn?

The stillbirth of a child is inevitably a terrible shock and tragedy. The angels enfold the parents as well as the spirit of the dead baby in love while trying to help them see the higher picture. Remember that if the soul of the child has a one hundred per cent commitment to live, its angel will ensure that the perfect conditions are provided for its safe entry. There are no accidents.

It helps the soul if you name it, acknowledging it, and send prayers for it. Do light a candle for your child and bless it.

Why do cot deaths happen?

In the first six to twelve months of life, the soul has a karma-free opt-out clause, which allows it to withdraw back to spirit if it decides that life is too onerous. Exercising this right is the spiritual reason for a cot death. Of course, a physical cause will often present itself to enable the baby to achieve its objective.

The spiritual hierarchy considers life to be a huge opportunity and privilege, but it is never intended to be a right. These babies exercise their opt-out clause and their angels assist them. Many wait for the full six months before taking a decision.

Why do children die?

The Higher Self of the child chooses his or her life mission. A five- or ten-year contract may be all that is needed to complete the desired work. Perhaps the youngster only had a few lessons to learn, or is needed as part of another plan on Earth or elsewhere. Occasionally the child is preparing the way into the family for other children who are not yet born.

Perhaps the parents needed the lesson. More often, because the death of a child is so painful, it triggers the family on a spiritual seek-and-search.

While it is very rare for a child to die accidentally before his time, this does not absolve you from the responsibility of looking after your children diligently.

My teenage son died in a car accident. Is he all right?

As your son died he felt no fear or pain, for he saw a beautiful white light coming towards him. He is perfectly happy and whole now in the spirit world.

THE TIME TO DIE

How do you know it is the right time to die?

Apart from in the rarest and most exceptional of cases, if someone has died, it was their time. However, prayer and supplication from their loved ones can occasionally make a difference. The willpower of the person to stay alive can force a change in pre-chosen decisions, as can the will to commit suicide.

I know someone with four teenage children, one of whom had asthma all his life and was very poorly. One day she went into his room with her daughter and was shocked to find he had passed over in the night. Her daughter looked at her and reminded her quietly, 'Mission accomplished, Mum.'

In what circumstances would someone die before their time, and what happens to their life blueprint?

Murder, suicide or wilful accident may occasionally shorten someone's life, in which case they would need to reincarnate to complete their time. This may be for days, weeks or a few years. The universal computer run by the Lords of Karma would make adjustments and allow for new possibilities.

My husband survived a terrible ordeal at sea while the others all drowned. Why did he live?

His sheer will to live took him through the experience, and this decision earned him the right to continue his life. Also it was not his time to die.

My brother went to visit all the extended family for the first time before he died very suddenly at the age of forty-one. We felt he was saying goodbye. Did he know he was dying?

Not consciously, but at a soul level he knew and wanted to say goodbye. It was also his way of bringing the family together.

Do some souls unconsciously give their families a hint that they are about to pass over?

Yes, they do, and it can be done in many ways. Children especially try to warn their parents in order to mitigate their shock.

It also often helps the loved ones to understand that the death happened in divine right timing.

Crista's beautiful, vivacious daughter died in an accident at the age of twenty. A week before she passed, she showed her mother her palm and remarked that she had a very short life line. Her mother, who understood such matters, was shaken but said that she was sure it didn't mean anything. However, it was the girl's soul's way of indicating to her family that it was her time to go and preparing them in some small way for the bereavement to come.

*

Pauline and her family took their five-year-old daughter to the seaside for a holiday. On the first afternoon, the child said to her mother, 'Mummy, I want to go home.' Her mother replied, 'Don't be silly, darling. We've just arrived and we're going to have a lovely holiday.' The child looked at her and said slowly, 'Mummy, you don't understand. You can't stop me. I'm going home.' She died that afternoon and her mother realised that her little girl had been trying to tell her it was her time to return to the light.

*

Amelia was the child her parents had been told they would never conceive. She was beautiful, light filled and the joy of their lives. She loved to play in the garden, watch the wildlife and be out in nature. One day when she was six, she came home from school and said it was a waste of her time to keep learning things. She did not want to do her homework for it was more important to be outside. Next morning she died of a brain haemorrhage.

Is it possible to renegotiate your soul contract to die at a particular time?

This occasionally happens, but it is relatively rare. Sometimes a soul will return from the brink of death to help a loved one, and in such a case they have renegotiated their contract for the sake of another.

My father was on the brink of death. The hospital said it was a matter of hours and there was nothing they could do. Everyone said goodbye, but my mother was old and could not conceive of living without him after sixty years together. Then suddenly the specialist said he was to be given food, which would probably kill him, but was the only chance. Within two hours my father was talking and on his way to recovery. I remain convinced that he renegotiated his contract and agreed to stay for another two years to help my mother. Although he eventually passed before her, that extra time enabled her to get used to the idea of living alone, and I feel it was a gift from his soul.

How much leeway does a soul have about the moment of death?

This varies depending on a number of factors.

If the next stage of his journey is waiting to unfold, he must leave on time in order to participate. His soul may have agreed to help a loved one or a number of people more effectively from the other side. In such a case his Higher Self will ensure he passes at the appropriate moment to do this.

If the dying person strongly wants his loved ones to be at his bedside before he passes, he may be able to postpone the moment of death for several hours. If his Higher Self wishes his spirit to depart before they arrive, it will do so. Both these scenarios are agreed by the souls of those involved and co-ordinated by the guides and angels of all concerned. It is never chance.

Occasionally it is vital that someone passes at the astrologically correct time, under a particular stellar influence. If they need to catch that tide to take them on a specific spiritual journey, there is no leeway about the moment of passing.

Occasionally, when a famous person dies, a huge current of energy is built up by the prayers of the masses. Sometimes those who are waiting for death decide to leave at about the same time to take advantage of this tidal wave of love and blessings to help them on their journey.

Why do some people wait for the arrival of their loved ones?

This is an unconscious decision taken by the Higher Selves of those involved. It is always arranged by the angels and guides and is not by chance. Here are a few reasons for taking such soul decisions:

By waiting to be surrounded by loved ones, the dying person leaves with a feeling of contentment, love and completion.

In some cases the loved ones give the dying person the energy needed to pass. This happens when the family and friends are spiritually ready for the departure.

The family or friends feel that the dying person loved them enough to wait for them to arrive and this helps them to adjust.

It brings people together.

Meeting at a deathbed offers an opportunity to resolve old issues.

Those who are grieving can support each other.

Collective prayer is very powerful and can help the departing spirit.

Why does someone make a decision to die alone or before specific people arrive?

Your Higher Self may know that the emotions of the loved ones will hold your spirit back, making it difficult for you to leave if they are with you.

You may be so closely bonded that it does not matter energetically whether you are physically together or not, so you leave in divine right timing for you.

When someone is not there to support a loved one as he dies, the feelings may set the bereaved person on a search for spiritual meanings.

The dying person may have a belief in independence, loneliness or that no one is there for them. This may or may not be true. It is just a belief but all humans carry their beliefs with them throughout their lives and play them out to the end.

Why do some people die when their loved ones leave the room?

It takes energy to pass over. Very often, loved ones are holding on to the dying person without even realising it. As they leave the room, the spirit seizes the moment when the cords have been relaxed to exit the body.

Can I consciously affect my way of dying?

Every thought, belief and action of your life, conscious or unconscious, affects your life and, of course, your death. Decide how you wish to die. If you are very clear about it, tell the angels and they will help to bring it about. However, as with all things, add the proviso, 'For the highest good of all,' or 'Let God's will be done.' The reason is that your ego may have one idea, but your Higher Self, who sees the overall picture, may have a different opinion about your method of passing.

I don't want to be a burden on my family by living until I am senile or physically incapable. What can I do?

This is a threefold question.

First, if you believe you are a nuisance or a burden, you may become one, while if you value yourself, you will be honoured in old age. If you need to change your belief system, constantly affirm your worth. Then start now to act as a wise and valuable member of your family and the community.

Second, senility comes about when people do not wish to take responsibility for themselves. Recognise that you have consciously or unconsciously created your life. Take mastery by visualising yourself being happy, healthy and mentally clear right into your old age.

Third, be responsible for your health by eating good food that

147

nourishes the body and brain. Drink pure water. Laugh a lot. Take yourself lightly. Keep your thoughts and emotions wholesome, happy and capable.

You can be a wise, happy, healthy and beloved old person.

MURDER, EUTHANASIA, SUICIDE

Why do murders take place?

At a higher level, many murders are contracts between the two souls, even if they seem to be strangers. Victim and perpetrator are corded together by karma which is activated across lifetimes.

However, new karma is still being created. If a person's life is taken, they will reincarnate to complete the lost years in a different body, and they and their murderer will be bound by fate until reparation has been made. No one gets away with anything, for there is always a spiritual working-out.

Prayers for the victim are, of course, really helpful, as are those for the murderer, for ultimately all must return to love and equilibrium, for you are all part of the Oneness.

Is there ever a Higher Purpose for a murder?

Occasionally there is. Firstly, when humanity refuses to listen to spiritual guidance and continues to promote ignorance or ill-conceived laws, the Higher Selves of a group of people may plan a murderous plan so shocking that change is forced through. In these cases the souls of the victims and perpetrators have agreed to the circumstances. They have sacrificed themselves for the eventual good of all.

Secondly, the Higher Self of a person chooses that he die by murder to focus attention on the good he has done or something he believes in. This happens where death in ripe old age would not have the same impact on humanity.

EXAMPLES

The Hungerford massacre resulted in a change in the gun laws in England in a way that individual murders had failed to do.

The shootings of school children in America has provoked debate about the gun laws but more will die in this way before the people see the light.

Sometimes groups of people agree to pass over together at an accident black spot or in a train disaster to accelerate change.

The murder of Gandhi sent a shockwave throughout India and the whole world, resulting in peace for a time.

Reminder

Life is considered to be tremendously precious. Any murderer, whether it is a spiritual contract or not, bears karma.

Why were two innocent little girls murdered in Soham? Was the name of the town significant?

At a higher level, everything is perfect. *So-ham* means 'the breath of God' in Sanskrit, and the divine light shone very brightly in the two little girls. They epitomised purity and innocence, so when their souls volunteered to pass over in this shocking way, it was in order to touch the hearts of the world. They succeeded. Their deaths drew attention to the insidious darkness that was creeping into schools and places where vulnerable children gathered. It started a process of change. People also began to think or say *so-ham*, 'breath of God', unconsciously focusing on the divine. The angels took the children directly into the light and their souls are shining beacons in the spiritual planes.

Do the angels judge murder and manslaughter differently?

Angels never judge. They only witness, for the actions of humans are often incomprehensible to loving beings.

Because they see the whole picture, they recognise the conflicting energies that provoke one person to kill someone else.

They observe that wilful intention to harm only happens when the heart is tightly closed and that such a murderer may have to undergo lifetimes of painful experiences before their heart opens. The angels are also aware of the remorse or lack of it in the perpetrator. Remorse indicates that their heart is opening; lack of it that their heart is still closed. These factors are all taken into account by the Lords of Karma when decisions are taken about the next learning the soul needs to undertake.

What happens to the murderer after his death?

Initially they will experience what they expect to experience. After that, when they are ready, they will be shown the consequences of their actions on the lives of their victim's loved ones. This review is an awesome and terrible thing for the soul to undergo. With their angels and guides they will decide what they need to experience in order to repay. Then they will either reincarnate when a suitable family is found or enter a rehabilitation or training establishment to be prepared for their next life.

EXAMPLES

One murderer may be horrified when they see the consequences of what they perpetrated on Earth. They may reincarnate with the person they hurt and be driven to serve that person throughout their next life.

Another may feel no compassion, in which case, in their next incarnations, they may experience love being taken from them. What they did to another is done to them, so that they can feel the loss for themselves.

Should I send love to murderers?

It is always appropriate to send love. You may not like someone's actions, but if you close your heart to them, you have allowed their energy to affect you. When your heart opens fully you will experience the joy of Oneness.

Action to send assistance to murderers

Quit all judgement. You do not know the story behind anyone's life, their karma or the higher plan.

Light a candle and ask the angels to help you see the divine in everyone.

When you hear of murder, picture a candle being lit in the inner planes and the light going to the victim.

Visualise a pink light going into the accused person's heart and a gold light to their mind. Then cut any cords you may have formed to that person with your judgements or preconceptions.

But it's not fair to the victim to send love to the murderer, is it?

Sending love to the murderer may help them to open their heart, and this will eventually assist the person they have harmed. Please send the victim your love, light, healing and prayers too. Ultimately you are all One.

Are there spiritual consequences if you kill someone accidentally?

This depends on the intention of the person.

If you are driving home, soberly and carefully, a child runs out in front of you and you cannot avoid hitting them, then there is no karma involved. However, the effect this has on you is a spiritual consequence.

If you are driving home drunk, too fast, carelessly or without due care and someone runs in front of you and is killed, then you must repay karma, sometimes over lifetimes. This is so even when it was that person's time to die.

Is there ever a case for euthanasia?

Spiritually, the opportunity for life is prized beyond almost everything. However, there are cases where someone's physical life becomes unendurable. In this scenario, if the person is ready and it is their genuine free will to die, euthanasia can be acceptable. But this is a dangerous path to walk because such a decision must be taken with an open heart and the highest integrity. If there is any suggestion whatever of pressure on the patient, the karmic consequences can be dire.

Are people who commit suicide cowards?

The angels make no judgement. They observe that for many it is an act of great courage to take their own lives. No one knows what another is suffering, mentally, emotionally, physically or spiritually.

Why do some people commit suicide?

A few know it is their time and respond to the call to go home. Others feel that they need to abort their mission on Earth for they sense they are on the wrong path or can do more helpful work on the other side. Most simply cannot cope with what is happening in their lives. You all discuss the challenges and lessons you wish to undertake before you incarnate. For many, life feels too onerous and they cannot cope any more. They need a rest before returning to try again, for the tests they rejected may be more difficult next time.

Does a suicide pass over properly?

This depends on the state of mind of the person at the point of death. Often the mind is disturbed or so distressed that they cannot see the light. An angel of death is not sent to guide a suicide over, so they may have difficulty finding their way. It is vitally important to say prayers for the safe passing of all those who choose to die by their own hand.

What happens to people who commit suicide?

There is no judgement. Someone who commits suicide is as loved and welcomed on the other side as anyone else. They will be lovingly assisted to look at the life choices they made and how they handled them. If they exited before they completed their lessons, after healing, and when they are ready, their spirits will return to Earth to finish their original mission which will then be more challenging and difficult than before.

As I am writing this it is pouring with rain outside. The weather seems fitting, for this morning I went to the funeral of a friend who committed suicide. I will call her Anjy, though this is not her real name. Anjy had cut herself off from all her connections in the months before her death, yet the chapel was full. Others who could not attend were meeting during the evening to light candles and say prayers for her. I wonder if she realised how many people did care for her? And if she had, would it have made any difference? I suspect not.

On the day she died a close friend had intended to call on her, but at the last minute could not go. Would her visit have stopped Anjy from taking her life?

We believed that she had taken a clear decision, so that her guardian angel had stepped aside in deference to her free will. For if it was not her time to die or her positive choice to end her life, her angel would have orchestrated an interference in her plan.

∼ Prayer for those who have taken their own lives ∼

Dear Angels, please light the way for those who have taken their own lives. Enfold them in your wings and surround them with love. Lift the anguish from them and let them find strength, courage, love and true peace.
Amen.

PASSING OVER

I'm not sure if my mother, who passed over last year, is all right. What can I do to help?

If you have an uneasy feeling about your mother, any loved one or even a stranger who has passed, ask Mother Mary to find them on the inner planes and help them. Mother Mary has a wonderful angelic energy, full of love and compassion, and she will undertake to do this.

～ **Prayer to help someone to pass** ～

Beloved Mother Mary, Queen of Angels, please find . . . . . .
on the inner planes. Enfold him/her with peace, love and
healing and guide him/her to the light.

The visualisation below will add power and energy to your prayer.

～ **Visualisation to send further assistance** ～

～ Light a candle.
～ Picture the person for whom you are inviting assistance. You may not know the deceased personally but may have heard about them or read about them in the media, and your intuition and compassion are prompting you to help. In that case just sense them.
～ See Mother Mary meeting them and enfolding them in a beautiful blue colour. Then watch them walk away together into the light.

If your angel is there to help you, why do some people's spirits remain as ghosts?

There are a number of reasons why some people do not pass properly into the light. If a person is very afraid of death, their fear may keep them stuck on Earth. Similarly, if someone is very attached to loved ones, their home or even drugs or alcohol, the Earthly attachment may be stronger than the quiet call of the angels. Unfinished business can also hold a spirit back in the material plane. Some individuals who die very suddenly are in shock and do not realise they are dead, so they wander round looking for their loved ones. This may be for years, but time feels much shorter to them.

These spirits simply do not see the light and so cannot go to it without help. A few of them may remain for hundreds of years, but all will eventually return to the light when assistance comes to them. Your prayers help enormously.

What does a rescue medium do?

These are people who see spirit. They have a light which attracts to them those who have not passed properly, and they can help release the stuck soul to the light. There are also others, who may not be consciously psychic, who perform this rescue service in their sleep time. They may wake feeling very tired, especially if they have been assisting with the aftermath of a disaster.

Is it always right to help a stuck soul to pass over?

As with all things spiritual, it depends on the individual situation and the desire of the spirit. So tune into the person and get a sense of what is right.

Many years ago, when I started running small workshops, I used to hire a local church hall. To my consternation and that of the attendees, whenever we went into silent meditation, piles of books would seemingly be

155

pushed from the table and land with a resounding crash on the floor. We sort of got used to this, but then, during the quiet times, footsteps would run across the stage. They sounded like those of an angry child, and some people were afraid.

Kumeka, my spirit guide, told us that the ghost was the spirit of a girl of fourteen who had been involved in an accident outside the church hall about forty years before. She had been carried inside, where she had died. He said that the girl did not know she was dead and was not ready to pass over, so we could not interfere with her free will to stay. He added that she wanted to be acknowledged and was angry because she thought we were ignoring her. This may sound stupid – certainly it felt silly sometimes, especially when new people came to the workshops – but from then on we started our sessions by acknowledging the girl. We never heard another squeak from her! I am sure that in the perfect timing, the right person will help her to return to the light.

*

I had another experience with a ghost that was quite different. She was an old lady who had lived in my house during her life. She loved her home and did not want to leave. She would often sit quietly in a corner or watch out of the window of my study for me to return if I had been out. But she was quite sad and was leaving a heavy energy in the part of the house she stayed in.

I would have let her be, but three things happened within a few days of each other. The previous owner of the house before me phoned to tell me about the ghost of an old lady her son had often seen. The following evening, I was introduced to a medium who told me that there was a lady haunting my house who was lowering the energy of certain rooms with her sadness. She described those parts of the house with uncanny accuracy. A friend who slept in the guest bedroom, which used to be the master bedroom before the house was extended, was freaked by the old lady peering at her in the night.

I decided that in the physical world it is now my home and she was interfering, so a group of us gathered one evening to cleanse the house and to persuade her to go to the light. She rushed from room to room to avoid us, but eventually saw her grandmother and her angel waiting, and left in a great rush of energy.

Interestingly she returned almost immediately to say, 'Why did you make me pass when I didn't want to?' We explained it was now my house and she accepted that and thanked us, saying it was the right thing and she was happy.

What should you do if a stuck soul visits you, seeking help to pass over?

Call in the angels to help them and direct them to turn and see the light. As soon as they see it they will leave and you will have done a real service.

Certain people who carry a special energy can see disembodied spirits, and of course lost souls are attracted to them. There are so many stuck souls seeking help that some mediums feel overwhelmed by the demands on them. It is also your right to state you will only be available at specified times or even that you no longer wish to do that work.

I still remember a lady who came to see me in the days when I was a hypnotherapist. She was terrified because people who had died kept visiting her, wanting to talk to her. She wanted me to hypnotise her to stop this! Of course I could not do so. The problem was that she was a Roman Catholic and her priest had told her that it was a sin to talk to or help the spirits. She believed him and did not wish to hear anything different, so her mind and her soul were in conflict and I do not know if she ever resolved this.

I sometimes smell disinfectant in the house. It is only there for a moment and I have tried to find where it comes from without success. My aunt, who was a nurse, died last year. Could it possibly be connected with her?

Yes, when your aunt in spirit comes to see you, she carries the smell of disinfectant to let you know that she is calling.

Incidentally, she is now working on the inner planes as a nurse, which was a job she loved on Earth.

My neighbour committed suicide. Why should I go to her funeral?

Your neighbour's spirit may need your prayers and love more than anyone. Please attend her funeral with an open heart and compassion for her. And remember she may have heard the clarion call to go home and responded in the only way she knew how.

FUNERALS

Can your funeral help others?

In recent years there have been two very public funerals that helped many people. The first was Princess Diana's. Her death was a catalyst for millions of people to release their own blocked emotions, and in numerous cases lifetimes of grief were discharged and purified. The prayers, flowers and focus on her death created an enormous funnel of energy, which enabled millions of stuck souls to pass into the light with her. She headed a vast procession of souls into the higher dimensions and there were flocks of angels waiting to help them.

The second was the Pope's. Again, the prayers, hymns, chanting and emotional release created a great wave of energy which took souls into the higher realms. Many people who were sick or old took advantage of this current to let go of their physical bodies. Of course, there are always angels present at a funeral and people are comforted by their presence.

Is there any point in sending flowers to funerals?

Flowers contain a pure spiritual essence. The angels are able to extract this and amplify it on the inner planes, then they use it to help the spirit of the person who has passed. Flowers also raise the energy at funerals, which helps the bereaved as well as the deceased.

Is it helpful to the deceased to attend the funeral?

The collective energy can help the spirit of the deceased to pass properly into the light. If the person has already fully passed over, the prayers and love will energise their soul. But go only if you have love in your heart. If you attend a funeral bearing hate or anger, it will not help the deceased; nor does excessive grief assist the passing process, as this prevents the soul from moving on.

Is it better to be cremated or buried?

Whatever you believe is best is correct for you. Different societies and cultures have created their own burial rites, based on their beliefs, customs and the climate in which they live.

What are the advantages and disadvantages of burial?

If the body is healthy and pure, the flesh nourishes the earth and provides nutrients for future growth. Also, some people find it comforting to visit a grave and know their loved one is lying in hallowed ground.

The disadvantages are that if the body is riddled with disease, the earth eventually takes in the sickness and has to cleanse it. When someone is buried, it is easier to remain connected to the material plane, for earth is a feminine, nurturing, holding energy. And very occasionally, if the spirit of the deceased is earthbound, he may be attached to the physical remains and stay around the graveyard.

What are the advantages and disadvantages of cremation?

Fire is a powerful, masculine, purifying force, so that much of the astral or mental energy surrounding the body of the deceased is transmuted during the cremation ceremony. The spirit of the deceased, therefore, is cleansed and this makes the onward journey easier. At the same time the fire purifies the physical body, the outer shell of the spirit, so it is more difficult, but not impossible, to stay attached to the material plane.

The disadvantages are that a cremation often seems very final for the family and friends, who may wish to have a burial plot where they can visit their loved one. A resting place for the urn of ashes can help with this.

Is an elaborate funeral more helpful to the deceased than a simple one?

The angels see the quality of love that goes into the arrangement of a funeral. It is the love and prayers that help the departed, not the sophistication of the event.

Is a wooden casket better than a wicker one?

No.

Family

PARENTHOOD

What is the true role of parents?

The true role of parents is to provide a perfect balance of masculine and feminine loving energy in which to bring up their children. The elders' spiritual responsibility is to encourage and develop the child's innate talents and to create safe and appropriate boundaries for each one. This includes listening to and hearing the youngster's needs and responding accordingly.

Why are there so many single mothers now?

On a physical level, this is the consequence of the breakdown in society. For the first time in hundreds of years, women have claimed the right to express and explore their sexuality. However, as yet many do not have the maturity or understanding to do so as wisely as parenthood requires – it is one of the most important spiritual responsibilities to undertake.

Many girls and women are having babies to satisfy their personal needs, not that of the child, and western society has permissively supported this. In addition, so many souls are clamouring to be on Earth during this time of great spiritual opportunity that they are agreeing to enter through any vehicle, however seemingly immature or unsuitable.

Is it the spiritual right of every woman to have a child?

No. Women incarnate to experience many things, not necessarily motherhood.

Why are so many fathers abrogating responsibility for their children?

This, too, is a consequence of the breakdown of society. Many youths are taking on parenthood when they are too immature and without any clarity about their role. It is difficult for those who lacked good fathering role models and are no longer supported by an extended family structure to be an effective parent.

In addition, those women who have had no appropriate maternal role model have unrealistic expectations, with the result that they push their partners away.

Spiritually, when a father abrogates responsibility for his children, he bears karma towards them, possibly for lifetimes, until the lessons are learnt and forgiveness as well as self-forgiveness is found.

The same, of course, applies to mothers.

Can the karma created by absent or irresponsible parenting be dissolved?

Inappropriate family patterns and behaviours often stretch back over several incarnations and through generations. At last, many parents and grandparents are waking up to their true spiritual natures and responsibilities. They are beginning to understand what they have unwittingly done to their children and are seeking forgiveness and new ways of relating. Families are being healed. When the remorse is genuine and the lessons learned, the Lords of Karma are offering grace to free the past. If you believe you are ready for this, ask for a karmic release, but this must be requested from your heart.

EXAMPLES OF HARMFUL PATTERNS

Parents who are physically or emotionally absent for their children.

Imposing your will and desires on your children, such as expecting your son to follow you into the business.

Overdisciplining or underdisciplining are equally detrimental patterns.

Making your child into a confidante when he or she is too young.

Buying your child's affection rather than acting with integrity.

Speaking badly of their other parent in front of them.

Not communicating with the child's other parent or expecting your child to act as an intermediary.

Shouting at your child or ignoring them.

Lying to your child.

Treating them or one of their siblings as a favourite.

Not loving them. Letting them feel they are a nuisance. Not valuing them. Disempowering them. Refusing to recognise their gifts and talents.

Wishing they were a different gender.

Control by force.

~ Prayer to the Lords of Karma ~

I recognise that I have perpetrated this family pattern on my children — (name the pattern or patterns). I now wish to set myself and my children free from this behaviour. I vow to discontinue these attitudes and actions. I ask for grace that the underlying beliefs be erased from my consciousness and that the karma be dissolved. So be it. It is done.

~ Visualisation to release a family pattern ~

~ Picture your child in front of you. He or she may be alive or dead, an adult or a baby.
~ Say, 'I am truly sorry that I have done this (name the behaviour) to you. I ask you to forgive me.'
~ Wait for a moment to sense if this is coming.
~ Then say, 'I forgive myself.'

If you sense your offspring is not ready to forgive you, ask your angel to tell his angel you wish to apologise. Then repeat the exercise the following day or week, until the energy changes.

You can, of course, talk directly to your child of your new understandings and remorse, but it may be helpful to do the visualisation first.

What is the spiritual role of grandparents?

They are part of the support structure for the young ones. Very often there is a strong soul bond between grandparents and their grandchildren, which can be more readily expressed without the responsibilities of being parents.

ADOPTION

Why would a soul choose a parent who gives him away for adoption?

There are many reasons for this – adoption is never by chance; it is always divinely chosen and perfect. Before the baby is conceived it discusses its future possibilities and lessons with its angels and guides. In the case of adoption, the choice of birth parents as well as adoptive ones is made at this time.

Often adoption is a karmic consequence from other lives. Occasionally the adopted children wish to experience a lifetime without blood ties. How will they feel? How will they adjust to this? Will they harbour a sense of rejection? Can they feel belonging in such circumstances? Others really desired to be brought up by the adoptive parents and had to choose a different vehicle for entry in order to reach their true family. Some have karma with the birth parents, which is satisfied by the opportunity for life both mother and father have provided. In other instances the incoming soul, out of love, offers a lesson to the birth parents before moving to its destined relations.

Why do so many adoptive children have a soul-longing to meet their birth parents?

Where the adopted child has a really strong soul connection with the birth mother or father, he or she will long to meet them again.

In some cases the mother or father has never truly let go of the baby and is constantly calling it back. This will profoundly affect the child as it grows up, especially if it is sensitive.

My sister had a baby adopted twenty years ago. She never stops thinking about him and wants to trace him. What would be the most spiritual thing for her to do?

There are, of course, actions she can take in the physical world to set this in motion, but on a spiritual level the most important first step is to release the boy emotionally. For many years she has been sending distraught feelings to her son, throwing a huge energetic cord round him which causes him great turmoil. The psychic uncording will set both of them free to do what is for the highest good. Unconditional love does not form an attachment and can never be lost.

Uncording her son will enable both souls to make higher choices without the negative emotions, such as neediness, longing, control, desperation or guilt, clouding the issue. These feelings have a repellent quality that will keep the boy away from his birth mother. Love, joy, independence, caring or peace have an attractive quality that will draw his spirit towards her.

A week after she has done the exercise below, the mother can meditate and ask the angels to help her find the spirit of her son in the inner planes. When she has a sense of his presence, she can tell him of her love and desire to meet him. This is very important, but she must make it clear that she wishes to do only what is for his highest good. Then she may listen to his answers.

If your sister finds the above exercise difficult, she can sit quietly and ask her angel to take a message to her son's angel. This message should be couched in terms of love, saying that she would like to meet him but respects his choices and will do what is right for him. If the meeting is for the highest good, her son's angel will wait for an appropriate moment before dropping the thoughts into his mind. If he wishes to meet her, the angels will bring them together when she starts to trace him.

Exercise to uncord from your adopted child
1. Sit quietly and relax as deeply as you can by focusing on your out-breath.
2. Invoke Archangel Michael to help you. You may sense his presence as he stands at your side.
3. Picture the baby you left or the child or adult you feel they are now. If you cannot conjure a picture, think about them.

4. Explain to them that you would love to meet them. However, you wish to do whatever is for his highest good. Because you love them, you offer to set them free emotionally. If they choose to come to you, you will be delighted, but if they prefer not to, you will accept their decision.

5. See them in front of you and sense the emotional cords you have sent out to each other.

6. You may like to touch those cords to get an idea of how thick they are and what texture they have.

7. Ask Archangel Michael to cut the cords and send light right into the roots to dissolve them at a core level.

8. Be aware of Archangel Michael's sword cutting through the cords of emotional attachment and feel the light entering your body as it dissolves them.

9. Wave to the child or adult as they walk away along a path bordered with beautiful flowers. You have given your offspring the gift of love and freedom to be themselves.

10. Imagine yourself washing all over, perhaps in the ocean, a stream or shower.

11. Thank Archangel Michael and the spirit of your child.

You may like to have a physical shower after this to cleanse away any emotions that are clinging to you. Then trust that an outcome for the highest good of all will transpire.

Health

Why do God and the angels let people get sick and suffer?

They don't. God and the angels witness human sickness and suffering. Souls have chosen to come to a plane of free will. You inflict all illness, pain and anguish on yourself.

It works like this. When your soul first contracts to incarnate on Earth, you understand that you have complete mastery over your physical body and it is your responsibility to look after it. You build your physicality like this: your core beliefs construct your skeleton and bone structure; your thoughts create your muscle and flesh; your emotions govern all the water systems in your body – urine, blood, lymph, tears. You attract accidents as well as happy or disastrous situations by your energy, made up of your thoughts, feelings and beliefs.

Your body is designed as a feedback system to mirror for you what is happening in your consciousness and how you are treating your physical vehicle. Perhaps your body is retaining fluid? This would be a signal to you to explore your withdrawn emotions and to cut down on certain foods. Maybe you are getting headaches, which indicate that you should examine your concerns about what others think of you and explore any allergies. Earache would be a trigger for you to be open to what you do not want to hear.

In your first few incarnations imbalances are easily rectified. Eventually people no longer maintain equilibrium, so they do not deal with the source of their physical problems during the lifetime in which it occurrs. This creates a backlog, their health karma, to heal in subsequent lives. When they reincarnate, the unresolved issues manifest as organ weakness, a tendency to an illness or in some other physical way. Gradually the origin of the problem is obscured by time, so it becomes increasingly more difficult to understand its cause.

As people have disassociated from responsibility for their own health, allopathic medicine has been developed. These powerful chemicals frequently mask the problem, for they can never heal the source of it. And so humans start to blame God, their parents, the doctors or hospitals for what they themselves have created.

There is a huge movement in current times for people to look within at the essence of their health problems. Medical intuitives are starting to draw attention to the correlation between different organs and diseases and their possible metaphysical cause. Natural methods of healing are returning.

We must also acknowledge that medical advances are offering grace to many who suffer.

Why don't angels always heal you?

Under spiritual law, angels cannot take away your free will, so they will not step in with healing if your soul has undertaken that ill health for a purpose. Nor can they heal you if you are not ready to accept the lesson offered by your illness. For example, you may develop Parkinson's disease because you hold a deep-seated fear of persecution as a result of something which happened in another life. If your soul is determined that you face the fear in this one, your angel must stand back and allow you to do so. In such a case the route to your healing is to explore your inner world. If you ask the Beings of Light for help, they will direct you to someone who can assist you, perhaps by enabling you to change your attitude, forgive, explore and release your past life traumas, deal with your emotions or alter your beliefs. When the mental and emotional are purified, a healing automatically takes place in your physical body.

When will angels heal you?

When you are ready to forgo hurt, anger, greed, pride, jealousy, envy or any other emotion that blocks your energy systems, your soul is very happy for you to receive a healing. Ask the healing angels or Archangel Raphael to help you. If you do this before you go to sleep, they can work with you at the appropriate level during the night.

Remember, too, that faith is a most powerful quality. When you have this, are ready to learn your lessons and hold the intention of forgiving everyone, including yourself, the angels will assist you in dissolving all health karma.

Why are some people dyslexic?

You live in a very left-brain society where children are pushed into developing reading, writing, logic and technology to the detriment of their right-brain creative gifts. Dyslexia is, of course, one of the choices a soul makes before birth and always involves a lesson. Very often it prevents the person focusing on left-brain options and forces them to take up work in which they can express themselves creatively and artistically. Sometimes it encourages an individual to find a different, more imaginative way to learn.

Jacob came from a family of solicitors and accountants, very left-brain indeed! As he was dyslexic, he could not follow in the family footsteps. Instead he became a successful cabinet maker. He also learnt to be modest, humble, contented, thrifty, caring and gentle, qualities that his parents and siblings lacked. The entire family thought he was inferior, but they gradually learned to value his special gifts and quiet personality.

*

Gwen's school days had been purgatory as, being dyslexic, she found learning very difficult. She regressed to a past life where she was a man in a very male-dominated society. She discovered that in that life she had autocratically and heartlessly prevented girls from being educated. Her regression helped her to come to an acceptance of her problem, as she recognised the karmic lessons involved.

What is the effect of morphine on someone when they are dying?

The consciousness is in the spirit, not in the physical body. If your mind is chemically affected, whether through alcohol, drugs or prescribed medication, it may be more difficult for you to pass easily. Your spirit, in a haze, may wander round, unable to find the light.

In these cases please be mindful that consistent prayer can help to direct the person on to their correct path, so that the angels can guide them home.

What is the spiritual perspective on organ transplants?

Your organs are created by your consciousness and contain your genetic and past-life memories. It is not just the physical body part that is being transplanted; the patient receives the mental, emotional and spiritual energy of the donor. The kidneys are filled with the fear and all the beliefs around survival of the person donating them. The liver contains the entire build-up of anger. The heart is more than a pump; it is imbued with the essence of love or lack of it. The recipient has to deal with it all.

It is time for humans to ask themselves whether they really want to transfer part of someone's soul to another, for it is an unconscious form of genetic engineering. The person who passes over without his body fully intact will also have difficulties with that missing part in his next incarnation.

However, angels do not judge. They watch as you impose the consciousness of someone else into a patient. And they remind you that death is but walking through the veil into the light.

Why do so many people have allergies now?

There are two reasons. Firstly, many sensitive or wise souls are repelled by modern society, feeling there is a better way to live. This rejection manifests as a physical allergy. Secondly, the toxicity of your air, water, food, household products and the emissions of your technology mean that you are living in a poisoned pool. People's immune systems are breaking down and allergies are one of the consequences. When this becomes too much, humans will seek a purer, healthier way of being.

I constantly get bitten by mosquitoes. What can I do?

First take the practical measure of covering your skin, then raise your consciousness.

I was told this story at a teacher trainers' meeting for the Diana Cooper Mystery School:

A man was in a canoe on the Amazon with three shamans when they were attacked by a cloud of mosquitoes. The visitor was stung all over and became absolutely furious when the wise men laughed hilariously.

'How dare you mock my misfortune,' he roared.

'We weren't getting at you,' they replied. 'We laughed to raise our vibrations, so that the mosquitoes would not bite us.'

No sooner had this story been told than one of the teachers yelped, 'I've been stung!'

They all collapsed with mirth, and for a moment she was furious with them. Then she got the point!

Do multiple vaccines cause autism?

Most babies can cope with the onslaught of multiple vaccines on their fragile immune systems. However, those who are high-frequency, sensitive souls simply cannot deal with the dark energy of the diseases being placed inside them. Their spirits partially vacate their physical bodies and find it difficult to return, often for that entire incarnation.

ALLOPATHIC AND NATURAL MEDICINES

How do the spiritual realms view herbs?

When your planet was first populated by humans and animals, God provided herbs which could keep every part of the physical, emotional, mental and spiritual body attuned to the Infinite.

Every organ of the body has a signature tune, and there is a herb to correspond to the vibration of each one. Imagine sickness in a part of the body. When the appropriate plant is ingested it will play within you the divine chord of that perfectly functioning body part. This enables the diseased organ or area to readjust itself gradually to the correct frequency again. Then the whole person will harmonise once more. If taken properly, the result is perfect health, with no side effects.

Medical herbs are complex structures which are impossible for humans to reproduce, for they contain a spiritual resonance which works on the subtle body. Those drugs which are created without spiritual considerations only work on the physical body and inevitably leave a toxic residue.

Human disease responds to herbs, love and rest.

What is the role of allopathic doctors?

Many allopathic doctors are healers. Their auras are blue with healing energy and they work with the angels without being aware of it. Such doctors are healing their patients at a mental, emotional, spiritual and physical level. However, they are currently limited by their training about medicines.

Some western doctors are technicians and may be brilliant at operations, setting breaking bones, diagnosing complicated ailments or prescribing powerful drugs when the whole body system is too fragile to respond to gentle natural remedies. Bless them for what they can do well.

Frieda was diagnosed with a brain tumour. She tried every holistic method to heal it, believing surgical intervention was bad. Eventually, in desperation, she accepted surgery, which worked for her. There is a time and place for everything.

Are we meant to have allopathic doctors?

Allopathic doctors are a response to left-brain, scientifically orientated societies who are seeking an instant cure for their own imbalances. While some are true healers, others are technicians who practise in strict adherence to their rational training. Remember that, in accordance with the spiritual laws of the universe, each individual patient attracts the appropriate doctor he is ready for, and until people are prepared to take responsibility for their own health, modern doctors will be needed.

Are allopathic medicines helpful?

Allopathic medicines often offer a person respite so that his own immune system can kick into action. Artificially produced drugs are very powerful. However, they can never deal with the cause of the disease, and in some cases are setting up long-term problems.

Natural medicines are much more subtle and gentler on the body. They support the body's own healing mechanisms and need to be supplemented holistically with good attitude, diet and rest. In these busy, stressful times, those who are out of equilibrium rarely allow themselves to be nurtured and rested back to health.

Does blessed water improve people's health?

When water or any food is blessed, its frequency rises and it becomes radiant and alive. The higher the vibration of any substance you ingest, the more easily it is absorbed and the more it increases the energy of your body. This, of course, impacts positively on your health.

CANCER AND ALZHEIMER'S DISEASE

What is the spiritual message of cancer?

The spiritual message of cancer is to remind you to treat your body as a pure temple and to live your life in joy, happiness and love.

Why do people get cancer?

Cells constantly break down, so cancer is present all the time. However, there are many reasons why a person develops it to a life-threatening extent.

At a physical level, the body is a delicate instrument which needs to be nourished and cared for in a pure way. Pollutants in the air, the chemicals that you ingest in food or through the skin in soap, shampoo, detergents etc. and radiation from mobile phones and electrical objects have a profoundly damaging effect on your physical sheath. They destroy the immune system and break down the cells, which can no longer protect themselves against invaders. A happy, deeply contented person rarely succumbs to this disease, which explains why it sometimes sets in after bereavement, divorce, redundancy or shock has left a person emotionally open and vulnerable. When the thoughts of the grieving person reject life, they send a depleting message to the body intelligence which weakens the life force.

It is important to do that which makes you feel full of energy, joy and vitality. If you give away your power to do what makes your heart sing, you tell your cells that life is a compromise, a burden or even not worth living. They react to your instructions by starting to close down, and this allows cancer in. Very often the person who is pleasing, compliant and popular has buried his or her true life aspiration in order to be liked and included. This compromises their soul satisfaction and ultimately their lives.

A number of people take on cancer as part of a family or individual karma. Others undertake the sickness as their method of exiting life because it enables their family to have some weeks or months in which to get used to the idea of their imminent departure.

Can the angels help a person with cancer?

The angels always attend the sick with love and compassion for they are ready and willing to help you release your illness if your soul allows it. However, you have to do your part. If your chemical and emotional imbalances or your mental rigidity are entrenched, the angels can only stand back and allow you to play out your painful destiny.

Of course, if it is the sufferer's preordained time to be ill or die, chosen by the soul before incarnation, the angels must heed the dictate of his higher will. If you ask, they will bring you all the love and caring you need to support you through your travail.

When a person purifies the physical, forgives and releases all emotional blocks and opens the mind to enlightenment and love, angels can heal you. Miracles happen constantly where there is love and pure intent.

Why is there so much prostate cancer now?

This is partly because of the levels of chemicals, hormones and radiation being ingested and bombarding you. But it is also because men feel disempowered and do not know how to express their sexuality, fatherhood and their manhood. Because the traditional roles of male and female have become blurred, deep unease and confusion exists in the consciousness of many. This weakens the immune systems of the sexual organs concerned.

Why is there so much breast cancer now?

As in the question about prostate cancer, this is partly because of the levels of chemicals, hormones and radiation being ingested and bombarding you. Women also feel disempowered and do not know how best to express their sexuality, femininity and motherhood. Their roles are out of balance. Some have placed themselves in competition with men. Many just want to be a mother, carer, nurturer and creator but feel compelled to go out to work, leaving their babies in someone else's care. Others want it all. These conflicts create disease. All attitudes other than joy and acceptance are detrimental to health.

What is the best prevention for cancer?

The greatest protection against cancer is happiness, contentment, self-worth, and good quality organic food and water. Then your immune system and all your cells are strong enough to repel any invaders.

What is Alzheimer's disease about?

Your body is designed to live in a healthy, vigorous way for hundreds of years, as was demonstrated in ancient times. However, humanity currently holds in the collective unconscious a belief that old age must be accompanied by a decrepit body and failing mind. This premise is untrue and does not serve you. Nevertheless, because so many people are open and sensitive to the power of the universal consciousness, they accept and absorb the lower understandings, which they then inevitably play out in their lives.

In addition, your planet has become a chemical factory. From babyhood chemicals in shampoos and soaps are lavished on your face and hair. As people become older colour dyes are added. Your food, cleaning materials and the air you breathe are full of toxins. All these chemicals close down or kill off the cells in the brain, as do the frequencies emitted by much of your technology. The epidemic of Alzheimer's in the world is not because people are living longer than they did twenty years ago. It is because they are ingesting and covering themselves with pernicious toxins and are bombarded with damaging pulsations.

When you learn what the pharmaceutical, food, beauty and technological industries are perpetrating on you, you will take responsibility for what you eat, put on your skin and have in your home. This will induce you to return to pure and healthy products and a simpler lifestyle. When you all take responsibility for your attitudes and your lives, you will find that Alzheimer's becomes rare.

Why does a person's personality change when they get Alzheimer's disease?

It doesn't. However, the control mechanisms and defences that the person has had in place for decades are no longer able to operate.

EXAMPLE

A woman may have been very angry with her father, mother or husband for many years but had to suppress it in order to be safe. Because her need for survival is so strong, her inner child has made sure that she pleases and is gracious to these people. However, when that survival control no longer works, the anger from her past is released and she will behave in what people consider to be an uncharacteristic way. In fact she is at last experiencing an opportunity to express her rage.

Is there hope for the future?

As people raise their consciousness and take responsibility for their feelings, learning to express themselves honestly, this backlog of suppressed emotions will no longer be locked inside, waiting like a time bomb to burst out inappropriately in old age. These last few years have been a huge time for clearance on the planet. As individuals, groups and sometimes even races or countries are taking responsibility for themselves and releasing the past, huge clouds of dark energy are streaming upwards to be transmuted by the angelic realms. This is a cause for rejoicing throughout the spiritual hierarchy and promises a healthier life and mentally alert senior years.

THE EFFECT OF MODIFYING FOOD

Why are so many people allergic to wheat?

Humans have genetically interfered with the pure strains of wheat originally provided by Source for your sustenance.

I talked to Cathie Welchman about this when she was attending one of my retreats. She has a B.Sc. in Biological Sciences and worked on data-processing in the food and chemical industries. For years she suffered from a devastating wheat allergy which was eventually healed through health kinesiology. This decided her to train in that discipline combined with nutrition and other therapies. She has devoted her life to promoting good health and is well known for her writing on these issues. She told me that the following information had emerged during her research work.

In the 1800s bread was made with mixed grains such as barley, rye and wheat. Rye, oats and barley have been left relatively unmodified. However, wheat was very expensive. Modern day wheat is the result of 150 years of hybridisation and genetic alteration, mostly to American, Canadian and British varieties. In the 1860s the original wheat, known as spelt wheat, was 'improved' by cross-breeding to increase the wheat germ size and double the amount of gluten within each grain. The more gluten there is the more elastic it becomes when yeast is added, so bread made with it rises more and decreases in density. In the digestive system, genetically modified bread expands when it comes into contact with yeast. It creates gas and causes bloating.

There is a particular kind of gluten present in wheat called gliardin which is proving to be especially irritative to human guts. Other grains also contain gluten, but not this particular type, which is difficult for the digestive system to break down because of its stickiness. In some people the gliardin and B vitamins present in yeast mix together and turn cooked wheat into a sticky glue-like substance in the gut. This lines the inside of the small intestine, thus preventing nutrient absorption. In others it is so irritating that it knocks the tops off the small villi that absorb food into the bloodstream.

It is not just the gluten content of wheat that has been altered. As the new high-gluten grains became increasingly more susceptible to attack by bugs and fungus, the toughness of the husk was increased. At the same time modifications were made to the outer shell and the stalk to combat wind and rain damage. The result is that the outer is now as tough as PVC. It passes through the small intestine into the colon undigested, but unlike other vegetable fibre, the bacteria are unable to break it down at all, and its sharp, spiky nature irritates the gut wall, causing inflammation, abdominal pain, cramps, haemorrhoids and diarrhoea as the body tries to eject it as quickly as possible.

Symptoms of intolerance to wheat gluten include bloating, gas, reflux, fluid retention, diabetes, acne, dandruff, itchiness, tightness in the chest, angina, allergies, ADDH, hormonal imbalances, cellulite, fatigue, headaches, irritability, and irregular bowel movements.

Most flour milling operations are now owned by one company. It is all bleached, and if brown bread is being made, the husks are minced up and some put back into the flour. For wholemeal bread most of it is returned. This is why, for many people in the West, wheat is interfering with their digestion.

(*Read more at* www.gaiaessences.com)

Action regarding GM food

If you choose to eat any wheat products, bless them.

Ask the angels to open and expand the consciousness of the scientists who genetically modified it, the governments who allowed it and the companies who profit from it. Bless all these people with higher understanding.

Visualise the angels touching all those affected by humanly altered grain.

Picture a six-pointed star with an ear of golden wheat in its centre, coming down from Source. This star consists of the interlinking of an upward star with a downward one, symbolising the bringing together of heaven and Earth and the return of pure and perfect food.

Surely genetically modified food takes the best genes, the most healthy and nutritious, and selectively breeds them into something better than the old? Isn't that what nature does all the time?

The angels weep to see what is happening in certain parts of your world. It is true that nature selectively and organically improves

179

itself. Humans were given the responsibility of co-creating with God, but those in charge are trying once more to manipulate creation for profit and control, not by selective breeding but by chemical engineering. In so doing they are hoodwinking their people. That is what caused the fall of Atlantis.

I understand that many GM crops are created by inserting a genetically modified virus or bacteria, which contains chemical herbicides or pesticide, into the chosen seed. When they grow into plants they contain the chemically tampered bacteria added to the DNA. A vicious circle is created as these need more toxic fertiliser. This in turn creates superweeds, which demand even more poisonous control. Throughout America and parts of Europe, people are ingesting this toxically contaminated food, usually without realising it.

Why are so many people suffering from diabetes now?

Throughout the western world people are feeling hungry for love and a sense of purpose. They are reaching for junk food and sugar-laden goodies to fill the hole. On an emotional level a sugar fix helps you when you feel disempowered or emotionally unsatisfied. On a spiritual level it clouds your aura and lowers your frequency. On a mental level it boosts your brain power temporarily, then makes your mind fuzzy. On a physical level it overloads and unbalances your systems, so that your pancreas can no longer function efficiently, creating diabetes.

After our conversation, Cathie Welchman emailed me this simple explanation about sugar and its link with cancer.

When you eat too much sugar, your pancreas produces the enzyme, insulin, to neutralise the excess. The body must rid itself quickly of too much acidity caused by sugar in the bloodstream because an acid environment cannot absorb oxygen efficiently and carry it to the cells.

If your overworked pancreas cannot produce adequate insulin or you have an enzyme missing, the body pushes sugar into storage organs such as the breast, or into those that deal with waste such as the liver, bladder or colon. The intracellular environment may then become too acid to absorb oxygen, so that either cells die or cancerous ones develop.

Because you do not get deoxygenated blood in the heart, it never gets cancer. The reason smoking is harmful is because nicotine acidifies the body, so the lungs are vulnerable to disease.

What is the healthiest balance of acid and alkaline foods?

When you eat eighty per cent alkaline and twenty per cent acid-forming foods, no germ or virus can gain a foothold in your system. Alkaline foods include most vegetables, fruits, herbs, seeds, nuts and some vegetable oils. Acid-forming foods include meat, dairy products, sweets and chocolates, bread and some oils.

Marriage

What is the spiritual purpose of marriage?

Originally marriage was intended as a sacred commitment between a man and a woman. The purpose was to live together and provide a loving home in which to bring up children with a balanced masculine and feminine influence. Marriage was a spiritual contract which was only undertaken if the couple were spiritually and emotionally compatible.

Can you be married in the eyes of spirit without a legal contract?

Indeed yes. Many couples who are not legally married are wed in the eyes of spirit. And there are those who have been husband and wife for many years who are not deemed spiritual partners.

The angels see only the depth and quality of the love between two people.

What is the purpose of a marriage ceremony?

Ceremonies are sacred occasions during which the higher powers are invoked to bless the couple concerned. An angel, who endeavours to keep the marriage together, is appointed to watch over them.

Please note the angels cannot force humans to listen to their spiritual guidance!

Is a marriage in a registry office blessed by spirit?

All marriages are blessed by spirit and an angel is always in attendance.

Is a handfast or similar non-legal ceremony blessed by the angels?

Yes. The love, intention and power of the invocations and ritual call in angels to bless the couple.

A handfast is a pagan or Celtic blessing ceremony in which a couple's hands are bound together to symbolise their allegiance to one another for a year and a day. After that they reaffirm their vows. These marriage rituals are returning to popularity but they are not recognised by the State.

Do angels bless the marriages of couples whatever their religion?

All marriages have the potential to be pathways to God. Religions are considered equal and sacred, simply offering different learning, so the colour, race or creed of the partners is immaterial to the angels.

Do angels bless marriages of mixed races or religions?

Indeed they do.

What if the marriage is just a social contract?

In many cases marriage has been debased over the centuries into a social contract between families or dynasties. In these instances both partners are sacrificed for money, position or to cement families or countries. If the hearts of the couple are not happy, the angels weep for them.

Years ago I had a client whose parents arranged her marriage. He was gay and living with a partner. She was also in a relationship. Once a week all trace of her true loved one was removed as she and her 'husband' entertained both the families for lunch. This charade had been continuing for some years to placate the parents. Now, however, she and her true divine partner wanted to start a family. They all had to learn to be true to themselves, despite the pressure of their relations.

Is marriage still important in our current society?

As social structure is breaking down, couples have claimed freedom to marry or live together outside a legal framework. Angels are interested only in the quality of love. However, it is observed that a formal marriage vow can often help to cement commitment and therefore offer a more balanced environment in which to bring up children.

What if a couple gets married because the mother is pregnant?

When the couple love each other this is a blessed union, whether or not the mother is pregnant. If they are marrying without love, because of social pressure, the situation is different. Where parents do not care for each other, they offer a dark and troubled incarnation to a child. And they earn karma if they do not work together for the highest good of the baby.

Is it the divine right of every person to have a child?

No. It may not be their karma or higher choice. Their soul may have committed to a different pathway.

Is there any point in getting married if the couple know they cannot have children or do not want any?

Yes. Marriage offers the opportunity for mutual love, support and spiritual growth. It also presents many lessons.

Why are so many marriages failing?

Firstly, at one time society dictated that there was one marriage per lifetime, so there was no let-out clause, however unhappy they were. This forced a couple to compromise and to accommodate one other. Two things have happened since those times: the consciousness has started to rise, and women in the West are claiming their power, so it is no longer spiritually acceptable for partners to live in such a heart-limiting way.

Secondly, a number of marriages are failing because many couples marry for unconscious reasons. They may be driven by a number of factors including neediness, desire for safety, lust or a need to heal their childhood. Such hidden drives offer an insecure foundation for lifelong commitment. When people do not know themselves, their expectations of a partner and even children are unrealistic, so it is not possible to relate maturely and compassionately to those close to them.

Thirdly, because it is now acceptable to have several partners in a lifetime, more relationship karma can be undertaken during an incarnation.

What do the angels think about failed marriages?

In spiritual terms the dissolution of a marriage is not failure. It just is. And it is an opportunity to open the door to a new experience.

But what about the children of the failed marriages?

The angels weep tears of compassion for many of the young souls torn by their parents' selfishness during marriage disintegration. However, at a spiritual level, the soul of the child has chosen to undergo this harsh experience, even though its heart may be broken. It is part of destiny and learning and it may strengthen the child for future work. The parents do, of course, bear karma if the separation is handled without consideration for the highest good of the offspring.

Is it true that couples who pray together stay together?

A good foundation of spiritual practice can help couples with their relationship.

My friend's marriage broke up. She was such a lovely person and it was all her bullying husband's fault. Why did it happen to her?

All relationships are collusions, so there is no such thing as one person being one hundred per cent to blame. There are only patterns that people act out until they learn. Your friend felt weak and powerless and so, because victims are automatically attracted to bullies and vice versa, she and her husband were drawn to each other to work on their issues. When your friend started to stand up for herself, the marriage was no longer sustainable. She has learnt from the experience and will not be attracted to another bully. But her husband has not accepted his lesson and will magnetise more similar relationships until he is ready to change.

Pollution

Why do people drop litter?

The dropping of litter is akin to fouling your nest. It suggests that people no longer care for their environment or feel a sense of pride in their surroundings and indicates a social malaise. It accompanies a lack of sense of community and belonging. At an inner level a refuse problem means that people have lost their sense of self-worth and dignity.

Rubbish attracts vermin which spread disease and this is connected to the closing of the heart centre. When your heart chakra is healthy, it creates a strong immune system which can overcome or repel germs. When it shuts down you become vulnerable to sickness. It is the same with society.

So when you see litter, do not judge the person who dropped it. Instead send them love and blessings. When you pick up someone else's litter, do it as an act of grace. Ultimately, when more people take responsibility for opening their own hearts, a sense of communal pride in the environment will return and you will see the reflection in a clean world.

I have a friend who found herself in a beauty spot which was spoilt by litter. As she thought judgemental thoughts about the people who dropped it, she heard an angel voice saying, 'And what about the psychic pollution you are leaving here with your judgemental thoughts?'

Action regarding pollution

If you are in a place which is polluted by litter or see it on television, call in the angels and visualise them holding the energy while people carefully pick up all the waste. Imagine the entire area pristine again.

～ Prayer to regenerate a damaged place ～

Angels of light, thank you for entering this scene and shedding your light and love on all those who live or pass by here. Enfold them in love and help them to feel their magnificence and worth. Fill this area with peace. It is done.

What is the higher perspective on chemical pollution?

Everywhere on Earth there are vehicles, aeroplanes and businesses pouring out chemical fumes. You are killing the trees, rivers, animals and your fellow humans and are causing a chain reaction that has an impact beyond Earth into the universe. It is imperative that you take measures to stop this.

Your body is a divinely designed chemical factory. However, it is being damaged insidiously by the world you have created, which is slowly impacting on the genetic structure of your cells. Many of you do not know what it is to breathe clean, pure air. The driving force for this pollution is greed and thoughtlessness. And yet no material possession can bring you peace; no drive for success can satisfy your longing to find God. Make your life simpler in order to clear your mind and heart.

～ Visualisation for a clean, pure world ～

- ～ When you are walking or sitting quietly, centre yourself by focusing on your breathing.
- ～ Picture the entire planet clean.
- ～ Visualise the rivers and oceans clear and full of healthy fish and pure water.
- ～ See the flowers and trees covering the earth in a beautiful mantle of green leaves and coloured petals.
- ～ Hold a vision of people worldwide working together, laughing, co-operating and living simply and happily.
- ～ Be aware of nature's energy – wind, water, sun and plants – being harnessed harmlessly for the benefit of all.
- ～ Pray to the Principalities to bring this into being.

Can you offer an overview on oil tanker leaks?

Water is a cosmic energy which purifies, absolves and cleanses at the deepest levels. The waters of the oceans are reservoirs of spirit. Fish incarnated for many reasons, one of which was to keep the oceans clear and clean. Religions which have an esoteric understanding of this use a fish as a symbol to represent the energy of unconditional cosmic love.

The many oil leaks that there have been at sea demonstrate, literally, that spirit is being suffocated and polluted. Your prayers as well as practical action are needed now to clean up the oceans.

Why are polythene bags so bad?

Polythene constantly emits low doses of toxic chemicals, which you breathe in. Where it is wrapped round food, fatty food in particular, the toxins are absorbed and you ingest them. Furthermore, polythene bags suffocate. They cause the agonising deaths of countless animals and fish, including turtles, when they are mistaken for food and eaten, blocking the creature's gut.

It is heartening that some countries have started to ban the use of polythene bags. If you wish to help the planet, one small action you can take is to carry your own shopping bag and buy as much unwrapped produce as possible.

Are nuclear fuels safe?

Because the level of consciousness of those in charge of your countries is so low, nuclear energy is one of the most dangerous hazards on Earth at this time. You are not ready to use the power wisely. You also have no safe way to store the ash and are currently setting up problems for future generations.

Is it better to use coal, gas or electricity?

Fuels that are extracted by digging into Gaia damage the planet. All your needs were provided by Source in a perfect way. Seek other energies.

What is the best form of energy for us to use?

Wind, sun and water power is freely available for the use of humanity without damaging the Earth. If every building was fitted with solar panels and a small wind generator it would considerably cut down the use of fossil fuels. There are already vehicles which operate by using natural materials, and it is time for new technology to be accessed for the highest good.

In spiritually inclined ages the people understood how to use crystals to provide heat, light and energy. You have already tapped into this possibility by using silicone chips in your computers, and soon you will learn to access greater powers. However, before you do this you must all raise your consciousness and learn to exercise responsibility and integrity.

How can I best help the planet spiritually and physically?

Everything that you can do to cut down on your use of water or fossil-fuel energy helps Mother Earth. When enough people do this it will make a difference. It will also automatically enhance your spiritual light and mark you as a caretaker of the planet.

Walk or cycle rather than take the car; this also serves your health.

Turn off the tap when you are not using the water.

Have a water butt to collect rainwater.

Grow your own organic vegetables and fruit or buy organic, locally grown produce in your shops.

Garden organically.

Avoid genetically modified food.

Clean your home with the minimum of chemicals.

Recycle all you can and pass things you no longer need to others who can use them.

Lady Gaia also takes in your energy, so smile often, keep your thoughts positive, act with honesty and integrity and be warm to others.

Be kind to animals and birds. Honour all life forms.

Forgive everyone, including yourself.
Constantly look for the best in others.
Pray and meditate for angelic help.
Visualise heaven on Earth and act as if it is already in place.

Can the planet clear all the pollution?

Gaia is a self-healing organism. The question is not whether she can clear all the pollution, but how she will decide to detoxify herself. Flood, fire, hurricane or earthquake are methods that Earth can use to throw off and transmute psychic and physical pollution. If you as an individual decide to clean up your mess *now*, and every country, big or small, does its part, the planet can move more easily into the future.

What are the effects of preservatives in food?

They pollute the body, depress the immune system and open you up to long-term poor health.

What are the effects of pesticides on the body?

They poison the systems and ultimately cause ill health. You are setting up a poor inheritance for your children, grandchildren and great-grandchildren. The more you can eat organically, clean yourselves and your homes without chemicals and dress naturally, the stronger your organs will be.

Relationships

My friend and her husband are both lovely people, but she subtly puts him down all the time. I learnt recently that he had an affair but came back to her, and I worry that he will go again. Should I say something?

Your friend is not ready to hear about her shadow from an outside source. Her soul was cut to the depth by her husband's earlier betrayal and it undermined her sense of worth. Reflect back to her the beauty you see in her, all her good qualities, and take every opportunity to remind her of her worth. In that way the light within her may grow and dissolve her fear. At the same time, look at your own relationship and make it as supportive, loving and happy as you can so that you demonstrate higher possibilities to her.

A friend I love dearly is drinking too much and has gone into depression since he was made redundant. How can I help him?

This man is very evolved and sensitive, and he has some very high and pure spirit guides, angels and loved ones who he used to meet in the inner planes during his sleep time. They were his true spiritual family, so he often woke feeling a sense of loss but with the sustenance and strength to live his Earth life. When he was made redundant his sense of worth was knocked and he started to drink to drown the feelings. The alcohol lowered his vibrations and he could no longer connect to his high-frequency links in his dreams. The spiritual refreshment that he used to receive at night is no longer available. That is the true cause of his depression.

Because he is not consciously aware of his dream life, the greatest help you can give him is to enter his inner world and assist him from that space. So when you meditate, shine light on to him and visualise him climbing up a golden staircase to reconnect with his spiritual links. Your energy and focused intention can help him to reach the higher levels again.

I get on with most people, but my brother-in-law makes me so angry. Why?

This is known as 'pressing your buttons'. Most people reflect back to you what you like about yourself. However, your brother-in-law is reminding you of an aspect of yourself that you do not like. He is a great friend in the spirit world, for your most diffi-cult links are often your greatest champions at a soul level. They volunteer to teach you.

EXAMPLE

If you consider yourself to be a very generous person but your brother-in-law infers that you are tight or mean, you will feel angry. The angrier, more hurt or fearful you are, the bigger the 'button' or issue you need to address. The lesson is to look within to find the source of your anger. Then you can heal the underlying fear.

The more triggers you have, the more difficult your life becomes emotionally.

Frederick liked to be popular, was really generous with presents and was always the first to pay his round for everything, but he had his limits. He disliked squandering money on what he considered to be wasteful luxury. A friend of his was always badgering him to buy vintage bottles of wine or splurge out on expensive restaurants, saying, 'Don't be so mean,' when he demurred. This pressed two of Frederick's buttons – that of not being good enough as well as his fear of being taken for a ride – until he realised what was happening inside him. Then he was able to remind himself that it was fine to be sensible with finance. After that he could laugh at his friend's efforts at persuasion. He was able to respond that they had different values around money and he was buying what felt right for him. It was only then that the friend acknowledged to himself that he was a complete spendthrift, overspent his income and often had financial problems. His friend never again had the power to upset him.

When someone presses your buttons and you feel a spurt of anger, guilt, hurt or really dislike the person, find a place to be quiet. Close your eyes and bring back the feeling. Then imagine how old you were when you first felt like that. You may have been a very small, vulner-able child. At that age you could not defend yourself. You wanted only to be loved, appreciated and kept safe. If an adult made you feel not lovable enough, not safe enough or not good enough, the feeling remains inside you. From time to time others will inevitably remind you of it. That stuck emotion will unconsciously drive your reactions and responses to people and situations until you release or understand it.

Visualisation to heal your inner child
1. Imagine that you are holding yourself as a small child when you first had the bad feeling.
2. Reassure your inner child that you love it and will always care for it. Tell it that it is very special and you are proud of it. Give it whatever it needs.
3. Feel yourself hugging your tiny self.
4. Make a decision that you will connect with the vulnerable little part of you every day until he or she truly trusts and believes you.

You will know when this has happened because you will feel happier and no longer react to the same comments.

I try to be a really good mother, but my mother-in-law constantly says what a wonderful mother her daughter is and never praises me. What am I learning from this?

You are a great mother! You strive for excellence but you do not one hundred per cent believe you are! This is not surprising for of course it is not possible to be a perfect parent. Your mother-in-law has found the chink in your self-belief and is reminding you of it.

Remember, the more you believe in yourself as a mother the less anyone else can upset you! Your first lesson is to quit trying too hard and accept that you are human. The second part of the lesson is this. By constantly building up her daughter, your mother-in-law is inferring that she feels she was not good enough as a mother so, if you want praise from your mother-in-law, let yourself be vulnerable about your defects.

Thirdly, you must praise her and her daughter – genuinely.

Vikki told me this story:

'I worked in a big office where one of the girls called Philippa was always unpleasant and aggressive. Although I like to think I am a nice person, I found myself being sarcastic and snide back to her. One day I mentioned this to the company psychologist and he said, "Find something to praise in her." Philippa was actually a very good worker, so I started commenting whenever she did something well. In a surprisingly short time she responded by being really nice to me. Her aggression simply disappeared. She needed to be valued and validated, and when she was, her defences tumbled down. Eventually we became really good friends.'

Exercise to open your heart to someone
1. Find a quiet moment where you can close your eyes.
2. Picture the person who has been nasty to you.
3. Their comment or action has come from fear, not hate. See him or her as a small child who feels so vulnerable that they have to keep you at a distance or justify themselves.
4. Imagine you are opening your heart to that scared little child and helping it to feel safe and loved.
5. You may need to do this several times, but it will start to shift the energy between you.

If I forgive someone for behaving badly, won't they think I'm a pushover and do it all over again?

When you genuinely forgive someone for an action perpetrated against you, the imprint in your consciousness is wiped clear. It has no energy. Therefore you cannot attract the same situation again.

If you falsely forgive, however, the original action still holds energy within you. Then two things happen. The act of suppressing the remaining anger, hurt or fear takes energy so you feel tired, and, secondly, you are vulnerable to drawing the same behaviour to you again.

194

One key is to do things that nourish you and make you feel so happy and satisfied that there is no room for anger.

Action to release anger
Ask yourself how long are you prepared to hold on to this anger which is damaging your health and your happiness. One year? One lifetime? Ten lifetimes? Remember that one day, eventually, you will forgive. Why not make it sooner rather than later?

I have had heart problems since my husband left me. I want to forgive him in order to feel better myself, but I still feel angry. What have I got to learn from this and how can I forgive?

You feel so deeply hurt and betrayed that your emotions are squeezing your physical heart. Forgiveness cannot be prematurely forced because then it is false, but your husband is still corded to you, holding you both in thrall.

The anger you feel comes from a closed heart. When a heart is fully open, it is so flowing with love that there is no room for anything else. And, of course, then you cannot attract hurt or betrayal, for love only attracts love.

Your lessons are about opening up and loving, which is the one thing you are afraid to do. Ask the angels to help you to open your heart.

Here are some exercises and affirmations which may help:

~ **Affirmations to open to love** ~

~ It is safe to love.
~ I am surrounded by love.
~ It is easy to love.
~ People respond to my love.

∼ Visualisation to uncord a person ∼

∼ Relax.

∼ Ask Archangel Michael, the angel of courage and strength, to help you.

∼ Picture the person you wish to release sitting in front of you. If this feels impossible, ask Archangel Michael to protect you.

∼ Explain to the person that you wish to release all attachments and set both of you free.

∼ If you can, sense or picture where the cords are and what they are like. For example, you may have a thick rope round your neck or a chain between your solar plexus and the other person's.

∼ Cut the cord or ask Archangel Michael to do it with his sword.

∼ Pull out all the cords and imagine yourself burning them.

∼ Thank the other person for coming into your life and offering you lessons. This may be difficult, but remember your soul has called him in to teach, test or strengthen you.

∼ Watch him leave your inner scene and walk over the horizon.

∼ Visualisation to heal your heart ∼

∼ Relax.

∼ Ask Archangel Chamuel, the angel of love, to help you.

∼ Imagine your heart, in a symbolic way, placed in front of you.

∼ Check what it looks like. It may be scarred, covered in pus, torn with barbed wire, bruised or damaged in some other way.

∼ Visualise yourself healing it. Soothe it with ointment, pull

out any barbs, sew up any tears or do whatever is necessary.
~ Then open the door into your heart and check what it is like inside. You may be surprised or shocked. Clear out anything dark or hurting and fill it with love.
~ Leave doors and windows open and welcoming, so that the sun can pour in and love can pour out.
~ The more often and the more deeply you do this visualisation, the more quickly your feelings will heal.

Love breathing exercise

Take a little time and space for yourself.

As you breathe in, imagine love flowing into your lungs.

As you breathe out, sense peace surrounding you.

Breathing love to the other person

Take a little time and space for yourself.

As you breathe in, feel love flowing into you.

As you breathe out, sense the love going to the other person.

~ **Prayer for healing your heart** ~

I give thanks for all the love I have ever received. I now ask for help to release all pain, so that I can fully open my heart. So be it. It is done.

Royalty

What is the spiritual purpose of a royal family?

In earlier times, certain evolved souls incarnated into positions of power to act as an example and lead with wisdom. They had titles such as King, Queen, Prince, Princess, Duke, Duchess, Earl,

Lord or Lady, each of which indicated the spiritual level they had attained. They were revered and admired, for they dedicated their lives and wisdom to help everyone.

In time, as the consciousness diminished, high-frequency souls withdrew from those roles. Their places were taken by those of lower understanding who wanted an opportunity to experience a life of royalty with all the glamour it offered. There were also many lessons involved about handling power, money, prestige, influence and hard work or indulgence.

Surely Queen Elizabeth II is very a dedicated person?

Indeed she has served well in her chosen role, especially as her soul has had very little experience of life on Earth. She has demonstrated discipline and devotion and acted as an example to all. It is highly unusual for someone with so few incarnations to be allowed to undertake such a position.

(For more information on soul ages and experience, see SOCIETY – Soul Ages p.219.)

Was Princess Diana murdered?

From a spiritual perspective, Princess Diana was murdered by many people. Everyone who sent her angry thoughts was responsible. Some very dark thoughts, like poisoned arrows, were directed towards her from those with vested interests in her removal. This energy all came together to become a physical force on that fated night and caused the car to crash. Never underestimate the power of energy when it is focused on a target. Each of those who sent dark emotions towards her bears some of the karma, which will play out for them in this life or another.

Why didn't Princess Diana's angel save her from dying so young?

It was her time, a fated death. Her soul knew she could do more by her untimely and dramatic demise than by remaining in a physical body. And indeed her passing raised great light. Her work was done and she fulfilled her mission.

What was Princess Diana's life purpose?

Princess Diana and Sarah Ferguson undertook a joint spiritual mission in this lifetime. This was to shake up the Royal Family, as it has served its purpose, and to draw the attention of the world to its secrets. Indeed they played a royal soap opera across a huge world stage.

Diana had a complex personality reflecting many past life threads, so her life purpose was not simple. However, she called herself the Queen of Hearts, and this was her second purpose – to touch the hearts of millions. Her soul chose to do this by allowing her innocence to be cynically manipulated by those whose hearts were closed. Then she claimed her power and became a true martyr. In this way people everywhere identified with her. She touched the hearts of sick people, those who were homeless, lonely or starving, suffered from AIDS, had unhappy childhoods, felt unloved, rejected, powerless or had eating problems. Then, when she had the attention of the world, she used her power to focus it on evils such as landmines.

What purpose did Princess Diana's death serve?

She touched so many people's lives that there was a huge outpouring of grief when she passed. People were able to release their own blocked sadness, hurt, loss and other emotions and a huge cloud of dark energy was then cleared from the astral planes by the prayers and intercession of the masses.

(See DEATH AND DYING, Can your funeral help others, p.158?)

What is Prince Charles' life purpose?

Prince Charles is an evolved soul from another star system, where he failed an initiation. The consequences of undertaking and failing such a test are dire indeed, in this case incarnation into Earth, which is a low-frequency planet. He was born with advanced understanding but with his power clipped, so he has been unable to influence others in the way he wishes. In addition, his soul has never before experienced a plane of existence with emotions and sexuality. He has had to learn about, experience and handle these with very difficult family links.

His life purpose was to come to your planet as a sensitive spirit into a situation where he was not understood and maintain his integrity. Camilla, a soul more au fait with life on Earth, chose to incarnate with him to support him through a very crucifying lifetime.

Are Prince Charles and Camilla twin souls?

No, they are not two halves of the original divine spark, but they are soulmates. This means they are on the same vibration and can support each other.

Is it spiritually correct for Prince Charles and Camilla to be married?

In the eyes of spirit they were married long before any legal marriage took place. The angels see that a couple is married by the love link between them.

Surely an evolved soul does not hunt foxes or shoot birds?

You are quite right, but one such soul who is powerless to express his truth may do so.

Will Prince Charles become king?

This is not yet written.

Sex and Sexuality

Why do humans and animals have different sexes?

The Lemurians, the race which preceded Atlantis, were androgynous, in other words they were male and female in one body. They petitioned Source to be allowed to experience full physicality. When this was permitted they naturally had to split into two separate identities, one half male and one half female, which was the origin of the quest to find your 'other half', your twin soul.

Have there always been homosexuals?

When humans first split into two genders there were only a very few who were confused about their sexual identity, but there were always some. The number increased as people experienced more incarnations.

Were homosexuals accepted in the past?

In times of higher consciousness, homosexuals were loved and accepted exactly as they were. During dark times of human consciousness they were persecuted, and in those periods most hid their gender preferences.

What about Sodom and Gomorrah?

They were destroyed, not because same-sex people loved each other but because of their hedonistic, lust- and greed-filled lifestyle.

Why is homosexuality so common now?

There are a number of reasons.

Firstly, as certain souls undertook more incarnations, they sometimes chose several consecutive lifetimes in a male body or as a female. When they finally agreed to be born into the opposite sex body, there was a feeling of strangeness and a longing for the familiar gender. Occasionally this emotion was so strong that they wanted to express their sexuality in a way they understood.

However, when homosexuality was persecuted, these feelings were suppressed, for only a very brave soul would dare to admit such inclinations. Those who denied their sexuality or who were mistreated often returned to spirit with unresolved issues. Inevitably they then had to reincarnate on Earth to resolve them.

Not surprisingly, most of these beings did not wish to return as homosexuals in times of repression. They preferred to wait until same-sex liaisons were considered socially acceptable. On your planet now, in certain societies there is a climate of understanding. As a result, many who wish to experience homosexuality have taken this opportunity to flock to cultures where this is possible.

Secondly and more importantly, for centuries the planet has been ruled by the masculine principle with its left-brain predominance. Males have controlled and ruled the religious orders, governments, financial houses and the domestic scene. The denial of the feminine wisdom has led to unhappiness and a loss of divine connection. In general, gay men are more right-brain orientated than heterosexual males. Therefore they are usually more creative, spiritual, gentle, caring – and less testosterone-fuelled. They are incarnating now to help with the balance of masculine and feminine energies on the planet.

Lesbians often have more masculine attributes than the average heterosexual woman, so they are helping to fight for the rights of women. However, there are also many warrior women incarnating who are heterosexual, and who are also advancing the equality of the female sex.

Thirdly some people are at last finding their twin flame or other half. If they have incarnated into the same sex, love usually proves stronger than social prejudice.

What is the spiritual purpose of sex?

Originally the purpose of sex was to offer a beautiful, transcendent experience which would enrich and enhance the lives of a couple and cement their love as they brought children into the world and raised them. When the sacred feminine was devalued, sex was used in ways that were never envisaged by the spiritual hierarchy – as a manipulation, as a love substitute, for power and control, for lust and sensual gratification.

The Church inculcated guilt into people by telling them that sex was bad and that babies were born sinful because they were conceived as a result of sexual union. From the angelic standpoint, sex with love is a divine expression.

Is same-sex marriage spiritually permissible?

The legality of marriage is made by humans, not God. From the angelic realms it is observed that a number of same-sex couples marry for love and with a deep and true commitment to honour and cherish their partner, just as many heterosexual couples do. Spirit never condemns love.

Others have more confused and selfish reasons for wishing to make a legal contract, which have nothing to do with unconditional love. Nevertheless, marriage offers an opportunity to experience commitment. In fearful times it helps two people to feel safer and gives them legal and financial safeguards within your worldly framework. In any marriage an angel is with the parties, blessing them and pouring love on to them. Spirit does not judge whether they are man and woman or the same sex. It is dedicated to helping all couples during their time together.

Is celibacy spiritually important?

Certain spiritually evolved people, both male and female, have been able to raise their sexual energy and use it in service to the divine. It is a relatively rare gift and usually a true celibate has been trained in the spiritual planes before he or she enters incarnation. They then need further training during their lifetimes. For most men it is such a difficult attainment that only those who have a vocation are able to fulfil the aspiration.

For those who aspire and fail, there is no judgement. They may retrain in the inner planes and recommit themselves for their next incarnation.

What happens if a vow of celibacy has been abused?

If a vow of celibacy has been abused, as has widely happened in certain religions where weak and sometimes evil men have misused their power, their soul reincarnates with very difficult karma.

Sexual abuse that has been perpetrated is now starting to be revealed. It is rising to the surface to be healed and ultimately forgiven and released.

Why do some people sexually abuse their victims?

As with any form of violation, sexual abuse is a form of ego gratification. Its source is the deepest lack of self-worth which leads to a desire to have power over or control another. In the case of sexual abuse of children, there may also be such a self-loathing that the abuser seeks to take the purity of an innocent child into its own soul.

From a spiritual perspective, the healing of both abuser and abused is about purification, forgiveness and self-forgiveness. Angels weep to see such terrible things happening and are waiting with compassion to help those who are ready to release the past.

What if someone wants to change his or her sex?

Before conception, the soul discusses with guides and angels the gender that would best serve his or her spiritual growth in that lifetime. There are no accidents. The sex of the baby is a decision taken at soul level. Once in a physical body, the personality may not be happy about the decision he or she has made. Take, for instance, the example of a man who has experienced several incarnations in a female body. Recognising that it could be very difficult, his soul has, nevertheless, decided it is now time to experience life in a male body. When he is born as a boy, he may find it uncomfortable, even traumatic, to live in what feels an alien shape and gender.

Until recent advances in medicine, there was no way out of a 'wrong' choice. Now some people can decide that the soul choice they made was untenable and they are prepared to undertake pain and hardship to get back into what their personality considers to be the right body. This then becomes a spiritual choice, and the challenges they face constitute their soul growth during that particular lifetime.

The angels watch and witness. They do not judge. They empathise and enfold you in love.

If a girl is provocatively dressed and is raped, is it her fault?

Rape is always a terrible violation, regardless of the circumstances. Every individual attracts his or her experiences, and this is not to do with fault or blame, but it is about responsibility. What energy is the provocatively dressed girl emitting? What messages was she giving out consciously or unconsciously? These attract circumstances to her.

What about the old woman who is violated while asleep in her bed?

Again, this is about energy. Only deeply held and often unconscious fears can call in such a horrific circumstance. The desire of the soul to clear karma is another reason.

Ultimately there is only one way to be totally safe, and that is to release fear and to forgive all things so that your aura is pure. Here is a forgiveness decree which also helps to dissolve fears.

～ Forgiveness decree ～

Say this twice a day.
～ I forgive everyone who has ever hurt or harmed me, consciously or unconsciously, in this lifetime or any other, in this universe, plane or level of existence, or any other. I offer them grace.

~ I ask forgiveness for everything I have ever done to hurt or harm another, consciously or unconsciously, in this lifetime or any other, in this universe, dimension, plane or level of existence, or any other. I ask for grace.

~ I forgive myself for everything I have ever done to hurt or harm another, consciously or unconsciously, in this lifetime or any other, in this universe, dimension, plane or level of existence, or any other. I accept grace.

~ I am free. All chains and restrictions fall from me. I stand in my full power as a Master.

If someone attacks while under the influence of drugs or drink, are they responsible and do the Laws of Attraction still apply?

Yes to both these questions.

You are ultimately karmically responsible for your conscious and unconscious actions and all that you attract into your auric field.

Why does pornography persist?

If you are emotionally and sexually healthy, pornography will not interest you. Your energy centres or chakras will be flowing with energy and light. The higher aim is to raise your consciousness from your base chakra, through your sacral or sexual chakra, up through the solar plexus and heart, throat, third eye and finally to the crown chakra.

However, if someone's thoughts get too focused on one area, the related chakra either gets clogged or becomes overactive, unbalancing the whole system. With the current focus on sexuality in the media, many people have sexual chakras that are stuck and which they unconsciously seek to stimulate by pornography. Others have overactive sexual chakras so that they focus increasingly on lewd subjects, becoming ever more out of equilibrium.

With the rising of the frequency of the planet, it is time to shine the light of pure spirit and innocence on to all sexual areas, so that the glorious energy of love and creation can be used appropriately.

What do the angels think of masturbation?

Angels do not think of it. Sex is a human activity. The body was designed for joy and pleasure. Sex was originally intended to bring two people together in such a way as to raise both their frequencies. When the planet was at a higher vibration, single people learnt to express their sexuality through creation and divine worship. No other option was considered. In your current world most people do not understand this higher use of energy.

In the majority of cases, occasional self-pleasure only temporarily affects the vibration of a person's sacral chakra. However, the powerful thoughts humans often direct to others while so engaged can penetrate the aura of the other person. This is very damaging, for it can deplete or make holes in the recipient's energy field. Inevitably this attracts karma.

Excess masturbation can clog the sacral chakra, causing it to become sluggish and sticky, in which case more sexual activity is sought to quicken it. Alternatively it makes the sacral chakra whirl round too quickly, unbalancing the energy field.

How can you clear your sexual chakra of imbalances?

Lust, fear, anger at the opposite sex, deep sense of inadequacy or desire to control are some of the emotions that cause sexual imbalances. Qualities such as love, serenity, self-worth and acceptance start to bring this chakra into alignment.

⌒ Visualisation to clear your sexual chakra ⌒

⌒ Close your eyes and breathe into your stomach with long, slow out-breaths until you feel relaxed.

207

- Ask your angel to help you clear and cleanse your sexual chakra.
- Imagine there are steps in front of you going down. Count the steps down to 20 as you descend with your guardian angel. You feel totally safe.
- You find yourself in a cellar.
- Turn on the light and look round.
- Take time to examine everything in the cellar. If it is flooded, dry it out. Take off any dust cloths to expose what lies underneath. If something needs to be washed, find the sink and clean it.
- You may find a person or people down there to whom you need to talk.
- When you have explored every corner of the cellar, take a broom and sweep the whole place clean.
- Then paint the walls whatever colour feels appropriate.
- Make the cellar into a warm, welcoming place. You may want to put in objects that represent love, warmth, closeness and caring. Do whatever is needed to make it comfortable, for you have the power to create what you want.
- Return up the steps to the light.
- Thank your angel.

Why are paedophiles sexually attracted to children?

Usually because the paedophile has dark, clogged sexual energy and is drawn to the pure innocent light of the child in an effort to purify his own sickness. To defile or tarnish innocence attracts a heavy karmic debt, and the spiritual forces watch with dismay at what has taken place on Earth.

Society

Why is society breaking down now?

Here are three of many reasons.

First, your leaders lack integrity. They are ruled by ego and serve their own needs rather than working for the highest good of their people. This has led to lack of trust so that the citizens no longer wish to contribute to the common good.

Second, people have lost their sense of belonging. They feel anonymous and helpless in an impersonal and unwelcoming world.

The third reason is this. At last the balance of male and female energy on the planet is being brought into equilibrium. However, men want to hold on to their old ways, fearing their authority and control is being undermined. They also feel confused and unsure of their roles. Women are trying to prove they are capable of being wives, mothers, homemakers as well as earners. They are also going out to work, driven by a need to provide a home or a desire to buy more material possessions. As a result many are too busy and stressed to provide a nurturing space and meet the needs of their families.

Both men and women are struggling to meet the changing expectations of society while their familiar base changes. However, as individuals seek to balance their own yin and yang, a new balance will be found. Then harmony will begin to reign and, as each gender honours and respects the other, the consciousness of society will rise.

Action to help society

Ask yourself what you can do to help your society. Small acts, like helping someone with their shopping or gardening or sharing the car ride to work, make a difference.

Positive actions, like volunteering to help in a charity shop or standing for your local council, all contribute to the cohesion of your local community.

209

Work on your own masculine-feminine balance.

Remember that your happiness is directly related to your level of integrity. Make sure you are acting from an honest centre.

Why are there so many aggressive women out in the world?

Some women are trying to prove that they are as good as men. They are using masculine energy because that is the way they imagine success should be. The masculine-feminine pendulum is seeking equilibrium, but in some cases it has swung too far, which is why aggressive women are appearing in business.

What is the best way to take society forward?

Bring back trust. The ultimate vision is to have an equal society, where everyone willingly shares, co-operates and helps each other. In such a community all are valued and honoured and there are no poor or vulnerable. As a result, science and technology move forward spiritually, for the two are totally compatible.

For this to happen, a change in levels of communication is needed, but the first thing is to re-establish your faith in each other.

Because consciousness is catching, your greatest contribution is to change yourself.

Open your heart and think, speak and act with integrity, kindness and in a trustworthy way. Use your intuition, not just your rational brain. Quit striving and relax more. Take all decisions with loving kindness. When enough people do this, the whole world will embrace a higher way of being.

Action to increase personal integrity
Each morning light a candle and ask the angels to help you to think, speak and act with integrity and loving kindness for the highest good throughout the day.

Is there an advantage to initiatory societies?

Initiation for boys is designed as a rite of passage to enable them to move into manhood. This does not simply involve tests of physical courage, though those are important. By understanding the myths, history and stories of his country, or culture, a sense of pride and belonging is inculcated. He is taught to honour female wisdom. When the initiate is ready, esoteric spiritual secrets are revealed to him. He then claims his adulthood, becoming a strong, wise and fearless supporter of women, children and those weaker than himself. Societies which develop men such as these are more peaceful than softer communities, and the people tend to feel safer, happier, more trusting and enjoy a better sense of self-worth.

Females do not need such initiation processes for theirs is internal. The three stages of womanhood are menstruation, child-birth and menopause. In initiatory societies, these passages are marked with rituals which give a female a sense of pride and joy in herself. Such women are not seeking to compete with males, for they feel whole.

From an angelic perspective, initiatory societies develop self-worth, belonging, wisdom, peace and caring, which are divine qualities.

Why are all structures, such as hospitals, government offices and supermarkets, now so large?

They are all edifices to the ego of those in charge and have nothing to do with the needs of the people.

How are social changes brought in?

The spiritual hierarchy watches the energy of places and people. As soon as they see that an individual has a particular light, the angels are sent to help that person to develop his or her vision. If the aim is to bring change to the world and help many people, the unicorns support the individual's integrity, pure intention and

211

determination. This is how Gandhi maintained his great vision of non-violence in the face of oppression and aggression. You have no idea how often the Illumined Beings are watching, waiting and pouring strength into people of great aspirations to help them activate their power for good.

If the angels see that a wave of energy is rising within a community, country, religion or the financial world to create change for the better, they will assist that movement. Where there is a chink of light in the minds of humanity to better the conditions of their fellows or animals to bring peace, to educate, to bring equality or to promote fairness, the Beings of Light are at hand.

Why are men so angry?

For centuries, the only power that women had was through their sons, so they learnt to manipulate their boys in many ways, some subtle, some blatant. In that way, when the child grew up, the mother maintained control of the next generation. These mothers made sure they were indispensable. Anyone who is manipulated feels angry and, at some level, bad. They may not be sure where to direct these feelings, but it is unconsciously driving them.

Now, suddenly, the pendulum is starting to swing and women are claiming their independence and freedom, so men do not know where they are. They feel wrong-footed and confused.

Of course, as soon as men take responsibility for their past actions and emotions and take mastery of their lives, the confusion disappears. When they forgive and release their past history, they will feel good about themselves and reclaim their true power. Then all anger dissolves and they can accept their manhood with integrity.

I am afraid to go out as I keep reading about attack and violence.

Everything you read or watch on television is drawn into your energy field and attracts like to it, so be careful of what you read and watch. The only way to be totally safe is to be harmless, so watch your thoughts and make sure they are peaceful, loving and inclusive towards others. Then your energy field will automatically dissolve any harm coming towards you. Know that a person in a pure aura is invisible to a person of evil intent.

∼ Visualisation for protection ∼

- ∼ Breathe peace into your aura.
- ∼ Ask Archangel Michael to place his deep blue cloak of protection over you. Sense it being put over your shoulders and the hood pulled over your head and down over your third eye. Imagine it being zipped up from your feet to your chin. Do this every morning and evening and ask that it remain in place all day or all night.
- ∼ Do the same for your children and loved ones.
- ∼ Ask the angels of protection to walk beside you and know that they are there.

Action to protect yourself
Wherever you go today, imagine your aura is golden and you are surrounded by pure light.

How can I keep my children safe?

On a physical level be sensible!

On a spiritual level, fear attracts harm. Whenever you worry about your children, you are penetrating their auras with your fears and may cause something to happen. If you ask the spiritual hierarchy to look after them but continue to be concerned for them, you are negating your request. Make sure that you constantly picture those close to you well, safe and happy. Ask the angels to protect each member of your family. Give thanks for their safety and trust that it is done.

∼ Visualisation for peace ∼

∼ Ask the angels to help you to see the best in everyone and every situation.
∼ Breathe a wonderful sense of peace into your aura.
∼ Picture a golden ball of light surrounding each of your loved ones and fill it with love and peace from your heart.

∼ Affirmations for safety ∼

∼ I am totally safe.
∼ My angels protect me at all times.
∼ I am held in the Christ Light.
∼ I radiate only peace and love.

If a harmless person is safe, why was Gandhi shot?

This was an offering by his soul to help bring about peace between Muslim and Hindu. He dedicated his life to non-violence, and when he was killed by violence, the shock made many people realise the wisdom of his teachings.

Why is identity-theft taking place?

The universe has a wonderful way of reminding you of your lessons. Many people now have forgotten their purpose. They are confused and no longer know who they are. They have metaphorically lost their identity, and to draw this to their attention, it is literally stolen.

Of course, on a physical level, this is a result of misuse of technology, and in the fullness of time those who steal from another will repay their due in karma.

214

Why are so many neighbours in conflict?

At this time, more souls are incarnating on Earth than ever before. It is overcrowded and people no longer have space to be. Where there is greenery, nature absorbs and dissolves negative energy, but you are now living in concrete towns, where the Earth Mother cannot perform her soothing, healing work.

Also, people no longer feel they belong. Their neighbours are often strangers with whom they have no communication. Where people know and talk to those living in their vicinity, it is much harder to act in selfish and angry ways towards them.

Action for neighbourhood harmony

Walk out in nature or in a park as often as possible, so that Mother Earth can draw the negative energy out of you and start to replace it with peace.

Light a candle and ask the angels to help you to relate well with your neighbours.

Also pray that people everywhere open their hearts and make friends with each other.

Visualise a pink ball of light surrounding you and those who live near you. If you live in crowded conditions, picture the pink ball surrounding the block of apartments or cluster of houses.

Most important of all, smile at your neighbours. Make eye contact. Talk to them about anything, however trivial.

Pete and Sally had a very grumpy old man living next door to them. No one in the road liked him and he was quite disagreeable. They decided to start a charm offensive on him. Every single time they saw him, they greeted him as if he was their greatest friend. They smiled or called greetings to him. They asked him how he was and genuinely listened to his replies. Before long he was treating them as if he was a good friend. He was still surly to everyone else, but his face beamed with pleasure when he saw them.

215

Why do nice people attract terrible neighbours?

The spiritual laws say, like attracts like. So if you are really warm, kind and loving, yet you attract a difficult neighbour, look within to check that they are not reminding you of something negative buried within you, and heal it. Suppressed anger attracts angry people. Belief in betrayal attracts someone who is untrustworthy. Look at the buttons your neighbour presses; then console and empower your upset inner child.

If your self-examination reveals nothing or you truly feel you have learnt the lesson your neighbour's behaviour has offered you, the universe may be telling you it is time to move!

Roy and Janice were the nicest, kindest couple with two charming, cheerful children and a well-behaved dog. They had lived in the same close for some time and got on really well with all their neighbours, until a new family with three boys moved in next door. The boys shouted abuse at them when they left the house, constantly kicked their football against Roy's car and battered their front door. They threw rubbish over the fence and the father parked his car across their driveway so they could not go out. When they remonstrated, the boys and their parents swore loudly at them. Although Roy and Janice both meditated for understanding and to bring peace to the situation, it just escalated. Their children and the dog were frightened to go into the garden.

As they discussed the situation with me on one occasion, they said that they had always wanted to live in the country with some land for lots of animals, but couldn't really afford to do so. Their wish seemed even more appealing now! They decided to talk it over with their families. Immediately one set of parents said they would gladly pool their resources so they could buy a big house in the country. Once the decision was taken, the universe followed through. Quickly their house was sold and a perfect house with land came on to the market.

Now they are living in peace and harmony in the life they always wanted. But it took the terrible neighbours to winkle them out of their comfortable home into the new and better. Darkness serves your growth.

Why does God let people behave so badly to each other?

When God gave humans free will, the divine role was to stand back and witness what people did with it. Would they maintain their spiritual understanding or would ego cause them to separate from Source and each other? Could they work together in co-operation and oneness, loving and serving each other, or would they try to control their fellow humans? Would they use their freedom to share the bounty provided on Earth or would they greedily amass material objects for their personal gratification and to feel superior to others? It is these choices made by individuals and collectively that have caused the inhumanity on Earth, not God.

And you are now rising up again to higher levels of caring and interdependence.

Every time you share, help those weaker than yourself or co-operate in a vision greater than yourself, you are greatly assisting the pendulum to swing towards goodness.

Why are old people so badly treated in many cultures?

The Spiritual Law of reflection causes your beliefs to be mirrored back to you. In these times of technology and speed, old people themselves believe they are useless. As a result they often act stupidly, complain, become cantankerous or difficult and this is reflected to them in the lack of respect and caring they receive.

In societies where technology and material goods have become the gods, many old ones are treated as anachronisms, stupid, a burden and a drain on resources because that is what they themselves feel. The young close their hearts to the needs of their elders and their minds to their accumulated wisdom because the elderly undervalue their own assets, so they think they have no role. This is why so many retreat into senility.

The angels see that old people are a font of wisdom and knowledge. They hold the ancestral understandings for the younger generations. In cultures where this is acknowledged and honoured, the Wise Ones have a place and feel happy and useful. It is time for the senior citizens to reclaim their status by acting with wisdom, dignity and sense so that youth responds to these higher qualities once more.

Action to help old people

Every time you see an old person or think of someone old, picture them surrounded in a golden flame of light. Bless that person and affirm that he or she is loved, valued and respected.

Your energy will transfer to the old person and start to make a difference.

Can I do anything to influence my old age?

Yes. You can decide what sort of old age you want. Do you wish to be surrounded by your children and grandchildren? Would you prefer to live independently in your own home, would you like to live in a community with like-minded people, or would you love to travel round the world until your death? Make your choice and then be clear about it.

Exercise to light up your old age

1. Focus on your intention. Talk about it and don't allow anyone to scoff or put your hopes down.
2. Picture what you wish to create and be sure that you never let a negative thought creep in to diminish your vision.
3. Make an affirmation around it, for example:

I am surrounded by love in my old age.
I am healthy and strong and independent until the day I die.

I am valued and respected by my peers and the younger generations.

In her youth, Evelyn was beautiful and charming and everyone wanted to be friends with her. She married a rich man and they were very happy, though they had no children. However, she had nieces and nephews and felt close to them. When she was widowed her life closed in. She kept saying she just wanted to be looked after. Her money bought her help in the house, a cook, a gardener and people to do odd jobs for her. But she would continue to reiterate, 'I want someone to look after me all the time.' As she became frailer she became totally senile and was placed in an expensive care home where she was very well looked after. This was in fact exactly what she had asked for all her life. She set up that scenario for her old age.

*

Robert was a yoga teacher who lived until his late eighties. He rode his bicycle, drove his car and taught yoga to the day he died. There were always people around him, listening to the information he imparted and hanging on to his wise words. He constantly affirmed that he intended to be active to the end. And he was.

Why is there so much unrest throughout the world?

Massive unrest is the outworking of divine discontent as people collectively insist on fairness against unjust laws.

SOUL AGES

Please explain what 'soul age' means?

Each time your soul incarnates on Earth you become more familiar with physicality, emotions, sexuality and the ways of your world. During your first few lives you are akin to a baby in that you need to be looked after. As you visit your planet more often and your 'soul age' increases, you become more knowledgeable and worldly-wise. If you have become highly evolved in other planetary systems, you may serve society and demonstrate much wisdom, but earthly ways will seem unfamiliar and you will probably have some traits of a younger being.

What are new young souls?

Souls incarnate to experience. New young souls are those who are not very evolved in other planetary systems and have only been to Earth a few times. They have to learn to manage emotions as well as the physicality of life in a body. Like babies, they need to be looked after and cared for. They will unquestioningly do what an authority figure tells them to do, for security is of paramount importance to them, and as a result many are found in dictatorships. They tend to gather in regions for safety, preferring to choose simple cultures. These souls find economically and technologically advanced societies difficult. In general new souls are not incarnating on your planet, which is changing too rapidly for them.

Are there souls who are evolved in other planetary systems but are young on earth?

Yes, they often reach positions of responsibility, for they have a mature understanding of nature and Oneness. However, they may stumble sexually or emotionally.

Could you please explain 'toddler' souls?

These souls can make their voice felt and can also be very destructive and careless of the feelings of others to the point of cruelty. They need firm boundaries and often congregate in fundamentalist religions. They hate change and try to prevent progress with their rigid, often judgemental views. They tend to be anti-abortion, anti-gay rights, pro-marriage and strong family ties, pro-Church, prison, hanging and, conversely, sustaining life at all costs if someone is in a vegetative state. They are accumulating karma.

What are 'teenage' souls?

These people have been to Earth many times. They are pioneers, entrepreneurs, those who want to make money regardless of the consequences, and they are full of energy. They often display selfish qualities, caring little about the feelings of those less fortunate. They will push out the boundaries of technology without due regard to those they harm or to world ecology. They will be found making money in stock markets, heading companies with a desire to expand regardless of the feelings of the employees. They are those gun-toting soldiers who enjoy the feeling of power. At the other end of the scale they believe in the sanctity of life, however painful or untenable for the victim. Naturally they are earning much karma.

What are the characteristics of 'middle-aged' or 'mature' souls?

These are people who have learnt about Earth. They have grown and evolved through the younger phases and now see life from a wider perspective. They want to care for those less fortunate, end starvation and poverty. They offer sensible peaceful solutions to war and seek economic and social answers that will benefit everyone, are liberal and democratic. These are the creative, artistic souls and those who try to conserve nature. They have a global consciousness. Many are repaying karma that they have earned in their past lives and seem to have difficult lives. Many of the European countries have predominately mature soul populations who are inclusive and opening up their boundaries to those less fortunate.

What are 'wise old' souls?

These are often wise, philosophical, retiring souls who wish to use their influence for good. They may be world-weary and want a quiet life but will radiate a benign influence. People will sense their higher qualities and be drawn to them, for they offer a voice of hope and sanity. They seek neither riches nor fame but work for the highest good of all.

Many are to be found in the Himalayas and other places of great spiritual light. Others are the wise leaders of the native cultures who understand the healing power of nature and human responsibility towards it. They are sprinkled everywhere throughout every continent, acting as teachers, healers, shamans and holders of the ancient stories and traditions.

Are there 'special' souls?

There are many entering incarnation now who have trained in the universities of light in other star systems, galaxies or universes. They have often had no lives on Earth, or very few. Yet they are spiritually evolved and may take leading roles in helping to encourage the planet forward. These illumined souls have entered the planet to spread an understanding of Oneness.

Can you comment on trends in different countries?

AFRICA

The new young and toddler souls of Africa allowed those who were then teenage souls in Europe to pillage their country for many years. While the continent is mostly populated by vulnerable young souls, now teenage souls are incarnating here. Unfortunately they are currently using their fiery energy to fight civil wars and cause untold misery. However, as the rest of the world produces more mature souls, their conscience and sense of responsibility will hopefully extend a helping hand and health care to central Africa. Already in South Africa the overthrow of apartheid, imposed by teenage white souls on mature, responsible and mostly peace-loving black souls is a shining example of what is possible.

AMERICA

The bible belt of America is predominately made up of toddler souls, though their hold on fundamentalist beliefs is cracking as more teenage souls incarnate. These teenage souls are the thrusting businessmen who have refused for so long to make necessary ecological changes. Now there is a growing mature soul population too, which is bringing forward a sense of social and global responsibility.

ARAB COUNTRIES

The rigid beliefs of the toddler souls are giving way now as they are evolving into teenagers, kicking against the systems that held them in thrall to their leaders and the West. Rebellion is the hallmark of the teenage soul who is not focused on money or success.

AUSTRALIA

Many of those who were originally deported to Australia are now teenage souls and are moving the country forward. A large number now are sensible mature souls with a social conscience.

CHINA

China was filled with new and toddler souls, ruled and dominated by teenage ones. Now the country has evolved to a teenage phase and these expansive individuals are seeking more freedom and opportunity to make trade and money. They are fairly quickly pushing the old barriers aside and bringing China into the twenty-first century technologically and economically.

EUROPE

For the past few centuries the teenage souls of Europe tried to colonise and dominate other parts of the world, pillaging and stealing their lands and their wealth. That is what undisciplined teenage souls do. The English, Spanish, French and Portuguese became wealthy at the expense of others. Germany's teenage destructive time, the Nazi holocaust, was more recent. This cannot happen again, for all these countries have evolved and more mature souls are incarnating there. Throughout Europe and Scandinavia, large groups of middle-aged and old souls are ensuring that social change is evolving.

INDIA
The reason the starving masses of India were subdued for so long was because they were predominantly new young souls, unable to stand up for themselves. However, that karma has now ended and in the past twenty years more teenage souls have been born there. They will no longer put up with poverty and are throwing their energy into technology and business, thus moving India into a new phase. Other countries will find it more difficult to exploit this country in the future. In the Himalayas and throughout India there are wise old souls, doing their best to heal and soothe the transition and inspire the population spiritually.

ISRAEL
This is yet another country filled with teenage souls determined to fight for what they see as their rights no matter what the consequences, and they have been encouraged in this attitude by America. However, it is just starting to move into a more mature phase, so voices of reason, understanding, compassion and compromise will hopefully start to be heard.

JAPAN
This country is currently full of teenage souls polluting the environment and making money. However, wise old souls are beginning to have a slight influence here already.

RUSSIA
Because of the large number of mature and old souls, change has been relatively smooth for so vast a country. It lacks the energy and enthusiasm of teenage souls to push it forward. Furthermore,

its inability to set free developing regions will continue to cause problems.

SOUTH AMERICA
This country is populated by young and toddler souls, but this, too, is starting to change as more teenage souls enter and refuse to put up with the old conditions.

GOVERNMENT

Is there one social, economic and political form of government that would be right for all peoples and cultures?

There is a perfect worldwide system which is currently lodged etherically in the Hall of Records in the Sphinx and which will be accessed when the time is right. At present too many countries are self-interested. When the world consciousness is high enough for a spiritual world government, then heaven will return once more to Earth.

~ **Visualisation to heal the world** ~

~ Picture the world surrounded in white light and people linking hands everywhere across the planet.
~ See everyone free, well fed, educated, happy and working for the common good.
~ Ask the angels to take your vision and add their energy to it.

How do you see capitalism from a spiritual perspective?

Capitalism encourages selfishness and greed, so the gap between rich and poor widens. It is a system beloved by energetic teenage souls who will do anything to further their own ego-gratification and financial power base. Currently, beings from Sirius are incarnating in capitalistic countries with the purpose of turning the minds of people away from this economic system. Many rebels come from Sirius.

How do you see socialism from a spiritual perspective?

Socialism works in countries where there are many mature souls who are ready to help the old, sick and disadvantaged. They set up idealistic education and health systems to offer everyone equal opportunity. And this is a positive step. The disadvantage of this in your current state of consciousness is that it disempowers those who allow themselves to be looked after so they end up not giving their due return to the community. Unless everyone aims for excellence, currently applied socialism also tends to encourage mediocrity. The system founders if a number of impatient teenage souls incarnate into the country.

How do you see communism from a spiritual perspective?

Community-based societies where there are plenty of young souls with enough mature souls to look after them and maintain the vision work very well. Everyone benefits as long as they all work for the common good. However, there is usually a tendency to exploit the young souls. Communism fails when toddler souls incarnate who push the boundaries or teenage souls emerge who want to work for their own rewards. This is part of the evolution of countries and society.

How do angels define a spiritual government?

It is a government of integrity that seeks a political and economic system operating for the highest good of the people. It recognises that all souls are of equal value, whether rich or poor, old or young, sick or healthy, and fosters interdependence, self-responsibility and trust. A spiritual government allows democracy and freedom with discrimination.

226

What is the answer for the best progress for the world?

Currently the world needs mature and old souls with a social and global vision to step forward. They should inspire and direct those less evolved to work for the highest good of all. You need to vote for leaders with integrity and ecological ideals, understanding that this is common sense for the future safety and development of your planet.

What is your higher perspective on identity cards?

In the current state of consciousness throughout the world, they will be abused.

How do you view high levels of taxation from a spiritual perspective?

When there is high taxation combined with lack of respect for the government, people spend too much time and energy trying to avoid or cheat the system. Regulations then become punitive. Morale suffers and goodwill is lost. It accentuates the lack of trust between the populace and those who lead them.

What is the spiritually correct rate of taxation?

It is ten percent, but with your current level of selfish consciousness on Earth, this would not be viable. It is only possible where there is love, caring, charity, and selfless devotion, and when the peaceful world community works together for the highest good of all.

What is the angelic view of home and land ownership?

Humans can no more own land than they can own a tree or a flower. You are custodians of the land and your homes, whatever your local economic system dictates. The highest perspective is to look after and nurture those gardens and buildings in your care to the best of your ability until you are ready to pass them to the attention of another.

Is it important for countries to develop technology?

The development of technology expands human consciousness. More crucial is how you handle what you develop. Governments of integrity and wisdom who use the advances for the betterment of the quality of life are acting for the highest good.

How can countries develop technology with responsibility?

In your world, the development of technology is mostly a left-brain activity and this means it can be created without heart. When you learn to value the right brain and educate your future generations to open this part of their consciousness, you will bring forward visionary technology, much mightier than anything you have yet conceived. And you will use it with integrity.

What is the consequence of governments ruled by left-brain leaders who are focused on achievement and statistics?

Left-brain leaders create short-term governments which accentuate the differences between cultures and peoples. Because decisions are made with the mind not the heart, little harmony or trust develops. Such a society tries to enforce structure and order without common sense or sensitivity, so there is an emphasis on rules, and orders and the proliferation of red tape. Decisions are frequently heartless, so people strive for more material possessions as a substitute for security and the economy is often their most important focus. Advanced technology and science develops. Within these countries religions form that have a focus on limitation and exclusivity rather than a spiritual perspective. As a consequence the people often feel empty, lost, fearful and rebellious.

What happens if leaders of society are right-brain orientated?

Such societies value originality and creativity, imagination and artistic ability. The arts and music are fostered. Because the right brain governs the feminine qualities of sharing, trusting, nurturing, being open-hearted and inclusive, these societies develop a high degree of co-operation and peaceful, happy citizens. The emphasis will be on spirituality and mysticism. However, there will be a singular lack of economic growth, scientific development, forward-thrusting activity and influence in the world.

Traditional aborigine tribes are typical of such right-brain societies.

What is the result if a country honours right- and left-brain development equally?

Where the people and their leaders balance the logic and order of the left brain with the wisdom and love of the right, the country develops in a harmonious way. The masculine energy of the left brain builds a strong economy with developed technology. At the same time the feminine honours nature, tempers rules and discipline with wisdom and cares for the needs of the people, who are happy to co-operate for the highest good, working conscientiously without being stressed because they feel valued and free. Children are educated to be numerate and logical. At the same time their originality and creativity is honoured and developed. Because these people have an expanded mindset, they are open to the infinite wonder and guidance of the spiritual world.

How much freedom do citizens of western democracies really have?

Look back over the last ten years and see how your freedom has been eroded. The angelic perspective is that so-called democratic nations are sleepwalking into police states. Watch and zealously guard your right to self-expression, which is truly a divine way to live.

No sooner had I written the above than two friends visited me. They talked about 'cooking the frog'. Apparently, when a frog is put in water and the temperature is raised gradually, degree by degree, it does not realise it is being cooked, so it remains inert until it is too late. The expression 'cooking the frog' is being used by western politicians to describe the way they are gradually taking away the freedom of the people without them registering alarm.

~ **Visualisation for freedom** ~

Because your leaders are shackled, they bind and limit you too.

~ Breathe comfortably until you feel relaxed.
~ Picture the world leaders in their current shackles.
~ Ask the angels to cut the chains and watch them fall away.
~ See the freed leaders shaking hands with each other meaningfully.
~ Now they are setting all the people free.
~ Picture everyone responding to liberation by being happy, productive and working for the highest good of all.
~ See family units together. Children playing freely in their neighbourhoods.
~ Picture communities in harmony.
~ Feel a sense of good will.

War, Violence and Terrorism

What do terrorists want?

Their aim is to spread fear. This renders society unstable and they can then bring about the change they want. Fear arises only when you are separate from your divine essence.

Why do people become terrorists?

Long-term injustice plus a feeling of being helpless and devalued drives the anger underlying all acts of inhumanity.

Is violence ever justified?

It is never spiritually justified to kill, hurt or damage any of God's creation, including yourself.

Does the ultimate goal to attain freedom or to overthrow bad rulers justify war or terrorism?

Fighting and killing is never spiritually justified. Many terrorists are inappropriately expressing their past-life anger and have no spiritual vision.

There is another way. Inner serenity is the greatest power anyone can have, for it influences people around you in profound ways and soothes the underlying fears of oppressors.

If there is injustice, how can people achieve their desired ends without resorting to terrorism?

There are peaceful means to redress imbalances in society. When an individual claims his sense of self-worth and personal power, those surrounding him automatically respond with respect. It is an inevitable result of spiritual law in action. When people feel valued, their anger disappears and they act responsibly. This applies to all groups, races and religions. Address your consciousness.

How best can we combat terrorism?

On a physical level, first address all injustices and educate the people. Make sure their basic needs are met. Most important of all, value everyone and honour their understandings.

Terrorism is a form of manipulation, a control mechanism of the ego to force people to behave differently. Fear or anger underlie the desire to control. When you respond to threats, be clear about your boundaries. Then show that you can remain calm and centred, acting honourably and peacefully for the highest good whatever the provocation.

EXAMPLE

A toddler is not allowed the sweets it wants, which are bad for it, and has a tantrum. The wise parent lovingly explains and does not let the child's outburst of rage sway the decision. A firm boundary is offered and the adult remains calm and centred throughout. But if a toddler is having a tantrum because it is tired and hungry, the wise parent recognises that it should have responded earlier to the youngster's needs and offers love, comfort, rest and appropriate food.

What happens to suicide bombers when they die?

Initially they enter a plane where their expectations are met. Then they are shown the consequences of their actions. They feel the anguish of those they have killed or injured and their families. They experience the devastating long-term effects on the child without a parent, the mother without her baby. Then they receive healing and discuss with their guides and angels what the next part of their journey will be. Some reincarnate immediately to try to redress some of horror they have caused. Others remain in the inner planes for spiritual education before they return.

Is there a spiritual difference between war and terrorism?

No. The intention of both is to control other people or force them to change the way they behave.

Is it justified to treat prisoners of war badly?

No. It is never justified to treat anyone badly.

Why are humans so inhuman to each other?

In the glorious days of Golden Atlantis, at a time when the consciousness of the planet was at its height, all God's creatures were considered equal. The citizens loved, honoured and respected each other as well as plants and animals. Because their heart centres were fully open, they empathised with their fellow beings. That meant they felt and understood everyone's pain and suffering, so they could not possibly hurt or harm anyone or anything.

However, greed and desire for power and control set in as the frequency declined. The hearts of the populace closed and they could no longer feel their own pain or that of others. Then they stopped honouring that which they did not understand or considered inferior.

Some individuals thought that they were better than animals and even than their fellow humans, so they believed they had the right to own or abuse them. That is the moment when inhumanity began, stemming from ego and a closed heart. In many 'civilised' societies it is considered appropriate to smack a child, thus teaching it from an early age that violence is an acceptable way to control another human being. In fact the only spiritual way to lead is by example.

Exercise to begin the day well
1. Light a candle each morning and ask the angels to help you see the best in every person you meet during the day.

2. Open your arms and imagine your heart opening fully.
3. Set the intention to be a shining human so that others follow your example.

What are the spiritual effects of violence?

The abused person and the perpetrator are both spiritually diminished. The feelings of anger, guilt, helplessness or fear inevitably tie both together over lifetimes until the karma is redressed.

My parents used to hit me and it never did me any harm. What's wrong with caning a child?

It falsely demonstrates to the child that the use of violence is an acceptable way of getting your own way or of controlling someone weaker than yourself. Having assimilated the understanding that brute force is power, the child may well become an adult who continues to perpetrate this behaviour. It sets up a karmic cycle of abuse until the parent and his damaged offspring find self-respect, self-worth and forgiveness.

Why would a young child hurt an animal or another child?

Only a child whose heart is closed, so he does not feel the pain of the other, behaves in this way. Perhaps the parents have not heard its distress, demonstrating that it is OK to ignore another's hurt. Perhaps its heart was closed by past life experiences. It is, of course, the spiritual responsibility of parents to show love to their children, but many parents, too, have shut down their emotions. This may have repercussions for lifetimes on the souls who incarnate as their children. However, the time for change is now. Remember, as you heal yourself, you affect past and future generations.

Megan's daughter was covered in eczema. Even as a baby she scratched so badly that she had weeping sores all over her body. Megan was a heart-centred, loving, caring mother who took the child everywhere to try to find some healing and relief for her. A clairvoyant told Megan that her daughter had had several past lives with uncaring mothers and, at a soul level, she was so angry, frustrated and hurt that she created eczema. But in this lifetime she had elected to choose a loving mother and the eczema would eventually disappear. And that is what happened. The skin irritation gradually went. Megan's daughter is herself now the mother of a baby girl and neither of them has a skin problem.

Where does a predisposition to violence come from?

Feelings of suppressed anger that were not dealt with in one lifetime will be genetically encoded into the individual when they reincarnate. Everyone comes in with karmic predispositions, but the influences of your parents and, even more important, your own attitudes profoundly effect how you feel and behave.

Why are some people so serene?

Serenity indicates an evolved soul who has learnt balance and equilibrium through many lifetimes. However, you can consciously and continuously choose to respond to stress with calmness and ask the angels to help you to develop inner peace. If done with sufficient intent and dedication, you will soon radiate a calm and tranquil aura.

Exercise to achieve serenity
1. Sit quietly and breathe in love.
2. Think peace as you breathe out slowly.
3. After a few breaths, make your peaceful out-breath a golden colour until you feel yourself to be in an egg of serenity.
4. This is a good space from which to take decisions.

Why are some Muslims being so belligerent?

They feel dishonoured and they are trying to manipulate people to honour them, while expecting the rest of the world to accommodate them and their beliefs. At the same time they are not allowing others to express their own understandings. This does not work, for respect is something you earn by your behaviour and your energy. Their learning and healing is to acknowledge and accept the differences.

For how long should nations remember past wars and disputes?

Honour the dead. Remember the valour and bravery. Forgive and forget the causes and the horror of the dispute as soon as possible.

Whether individually or nationally, the longer you hold on to the bad memories, the betrayal, the dirty deeds, the pain and the suffering the longer you keep it alive in your psyche. By holding something in your consciousness, you repeatedly attract the same situation or circumstances. The quickest way to end war and dispute is to let it go.

Honour the good in a nation instead of blaming it for a past failure. Then the people will behave warmly towards you. That is the foundation for peace between all countries.

Can there be true peace between Israel and Palestine, and can the outside world help?

Those born into these two races carry seeds of hopelessness and despair, which is expressed as anger. They have been incarnating into the situation for generations, often on different sides in consecutive lives, in order to re-experience these fears until their hearts wish to live differently. Like all humans, they also carry sparks of love and peace within their beings.

The outside world can leave them to resolve their own dilemmas without supporting either side, which would force them to face

236

something deep within. Or it could impose restrictions. But no outside agency can impose change or peace on to another. It must come from within to be permanent.

There is a spiritual way. If each Palestinian who is ready for peace would daily bless the Israelis and each Israeli who is ready would daily do the same for the Palestinians, those blessings would spread as peace. At the same time, if the rest of the world quit all judgement and instead continuously blessed both sides, a higher solution could evolve.

Why did God allow the nuclear bomb to fall on Hiroshima?

God witnesses and only intervenes when petitioned by the angels as a result of human prayer. The energy on Earth had sunk into degradation and darkness and people had to learn their lesson. Indeed, when the nuclear bomb was detonated, the world saw a reflection of its own darkness and it shocked all the parties, forcing change. However, the price was enormous, for it shattered and scattered the physical, etheric, emotional, mental and spiritual bodies of those who died – a dire and terrible thing. Nothing like this had ever been experienced on the planet before and the consequences were unimaginable.

GENERAL
QUESTIONS

Abundance

Why does God allow some nations to be rich while others starve?

God has given everyone on Earth free will and therefore stands back to witness how humans handle this gift. For centuries, people have chosen to act with greed and control and the stronger have exploited the weak. As a result, some nations have become rich, careless of the fact that others are starving. This situation is caused by lack of human feeling, not by a higher power, for in the divine vision every individual is equal and abundant and always has been. It is time for individuals to use their power and influence to reinstate equality.

Why are some people born rich and others poor?

Every soul chooses its family, connections and circumstances before it is born in order to experience what it needs for growth. Some have to understand poverty and the challenges it offers, while others need to explore riches. Wealth or penury are outer manifestations of spiritual choices. They are merely lessons, for your divine core is totally abundant.

What are the lessons of poverty?

When you are poor, one of your lessons is to value yourself, recognising and accepting that you are a worthy being whatever your circumstances. Your learning may be to open to abundance consciousness by changing the way you think, believe and act. If experiencing a life of poverty makes you feel a victim, your lesson is to master the spiritual laws and transform your beliefs. Or to become independent, your soul may need to understand dependence. The angels delight as you grow through your challenges and set yourself free.

What are the lessons of wealth?

Material riches bring with them lessons of responsibility, for money can be used wisely or profligately. It can be dedicated for the higher good, lavished on self-indulgence or used to purchase personal power. Being financially advantaged often causes people to wonder if they are truly loved for themselves or for their wealth, so, like poverty, it offers lessons of self-worth. It places much temptation in the life path, for a rich person may consider himself superior to another, which contradicts the spiritual Laws of Oneness. The ultimate test of wealth is to maintain purity of heart.

Physical objects are called 'trappings' because they bind people to material wealth and prevent their souls from seeking spiritual truth.

Why would your soul choose for you to be poor? It doesn't make sense.

To choose to be born poor may seem strange to your personality, but your Higher Self judges what experience you need for your growth, and reviews the entire journey of your soul, including your past lives on Earth, before it makes such a choice.

Here are a few reasons for your oversoul to choose poverty:

You may have abused riches in other lives and need to experience the opposite.

Your soul may believe that money is the path to damnation, so it chooses lack.

In past lives you may have found that wealth brought you misery.

Perhaps you wondered whether people loved you only because of your material state.

You may have felt there was too much responsibility attached to finances and so determined to live a life without emphasis on gold.

Your soul may value love beyond possessions.

There are many reasons for such a choice, including the simple challenge – can you be poor and still maintain your divine connection?

Why would a baby choose to be born, only to die within days of poverty or starvation?

In these sad cases the soul only wishes to touch Earth for a short period, perhaps to experience a mother's embrace or briefly reconnect with a loved one. Sometimes these are new souls who have never before known a physical existence and can only cope with a few days in your material plane. Alternatively, some wise old souls briefly incarnate to bring hope to the suffering masses. Their auras shine like lights in the dark.

Is it really difficult for a rich person to go to heaven?

Those who handle their riches with responsibility, humanity, fairness, justice and caring will find the gates of heaven open and welcoming.

Those who handle their privileged circumstances by controlling or exploiting others, by hedonism, profligate waste or careless indulgence will pass into lower dimensions, where they can review the consequences of their actions. Then they will discuss the lessons their souls have not learnt and choose another incarnation, which either offers less temptation or the opportunity to face the same challenges again.

How do some people change from rich to poor or poor to rich?

They have changed their beliefs. Whatever you believe in you can create, in your life, for, moment by moment, you write your own drama. It is very simple. You must focus your thoughts, words and actions on what you do want at all times.

By holding their vision in this way, some poor people become rich, though they may not even be aware how they are doing it. As they activate the Spiritual Law of Abundance by aligning themselves with the feeling of plenty, they automatically attract the rewards. They believe, and so it is.

The vast majority of poor people remain in poverty consciousness by constantly reinforcing their status with a feeling of inevitability that it must always be so – and therefore it is. They think about lack and believe they are victims.

Those who were once wealthy only to lose their material possessions have an underlying fear of loss or a belief in their own unworthiness. They then unconsciously write this into their life experience.

It is so unfair. I work hard and have no money and my sister never does a thing and is rich. Why does God allow this?

God does not allow this situation. You do. Consciousness creates karma, and your sister has a belief that she deserves what she has. Change your beliefs, your thoughts and words. Make them abundant and generous. Act as if you are prosperous, bless your sister in her wealth and watch your life blossom.

What is abundance consciousness?

Abundance consciousness is a belief that you deserve a constant flow of good to come to you and are open to receiving it. You know that plenty already surrounds you and you draw it in.

What is poverty consciousness?

Poverty consciousness is a belief in lack, that there is not enough love, money, success, work or happiness for you and that you do not deserve it anyway. This illusion is holding too many people back. The truth is, abundance surrounds you. You merely have to welcome it into your life.

I have been told I was rich in a past life. Does this mean I have to be hard up now?

Not necessarily. But at the end of that rich life your soul evaluated the way you handled your wealth. If you accrued a karmic debt, your soul chose to repay it in another lifetime, perhaps this one.

The karma is genetically encoded into your DNA and you work it out in your life.

You have the power to change all this by right living, relaxation, positive focus and abundant thoughts and actions. Forgive yourself, resolve to handle your true divine abundance with responsibility and step on to a golden path now.

How can I become rich?

You can focus on your vision without doubt and deviation. Let your thoughts, words and actions all be abundant. Believe that you are already wealthy and it is so.

I don't want to struggle for a living. What can I do about it?

Quit your focus on struggle. Whatever you energise continues in your life, so because you are thinking of battle and hardship, that is what you have created. Remember times in your life when things flowed and bless those moments. Decide what makes your heart sing and constantly picture yourself attracting a prosperous living by doing what you love to do most. Your beautiful future is already held in the mind of God. Your task is to open the gate and walk through it and make it your own.

How does God choose who wins the lottery?

Source does not make this choice, but it is made by your own God-self. Usually it is a result of accumulated good karma from other lives, in which case your soul is ready to accept the bonus now. However, it may simply be that your Higher Self wishes to experience wealth during this lifetime.

I used to know a wonderful spiritual palmist who told me that a windfall or big win is karmic and would be indicated on the hand. He also said that I had no such mark, so I never indulged in a lottery ticket! However, abundance flows from many sources, like a lake waiting in the inner planes to be tapped.

When financial institutions are so corrupt, is it spiritually all right to cheat them?

No. Their karma is theirs. Yours is yours.

When people say money is just an energy, what do they mean?

Every object starts with a thought. You then direct this mind power, and add passion, communication, belief and appropriate action in order to manifest it. Coins, notes and bank balances are the tangible outcome of this process, which uses your vital force or *prana*. Hence money is the product of correctly expended energy.

I have always been poor. So has my family. We work hard, have no time for pleasure, all our clothes are cast-offs. Life is just a miserable grind. So what do the angels say to that?

Poverty consciousness is holding you and everyone else on the planet back. It is time to stop your concentration about what you do not like and accept the abundance that awaits you as soon as you welcome it into your life.

Animals

Do animals have souls?

Yes, they do. Animals incarnate just as humans do in order to learn and teach. Some belong to a group soul, so each individual is part of a much bigger energy. Flocks of small birds or shoals of little fish are examples of such a collective entity.

Do animals have angels?

Every creature has a being from the angelic realms designated to look after it.

Is it true that white animals are special?

Pure white animals, not albinos, incarnate to demonstrate the Christ consciousness. There are now white buffaloes, lions, tigers, peacocks and others among you, quietly showing the way to enlightenment.

What makes someone cruel to animals?

A closed heart. Send your prayers to the perpetrator as well as the suffering animals and visualise all being healed.

⌒ Prayer for animals ⌒

Help me to open my heart fully. Allow me by thought, word and example to be a beacon of love to others. Bless the animals that suffer from human cruelty and open the hearts of those who perpetrate such deeds.

⌒ **Visualisation to help animals** ⌒

⌒ Picture a group of cruel people with their hearts locked in chains held by a padlock.
⌒ Imagine all the animals they have mistreated and be aware of the darkness of the fear that surrounds them.
⌒ Then visualise angels coming to each person with a golden key and unlocking all the padlocks.
⌒ See their hearts opening, radiating pink love to the animals.
⌒ Watch this love dissolve all the darkness round them.
⌒ They are now surrounded with pink light.
⌒ Hold a vision of animals living happily and naturally among people, all loving, respecting and honouring each other.

If there was no intensive farming, would there be enough for everyone to eat?

Oh yes. When humans work with nature instead of trying to control it, there is enough for all. As an example, when chickens are appreciated and allowed freedom to roam and peck the earth, they lay more nutritious eggs, filled with an energy of love, which nourishes the consumer on many levels. The people then need fewer eggs for their sustenance.

Surely free-range hens are happy?

Humans have a strange definition of a free-range hen – that the poultry is kept in a cage with access to an outdoor run. In practice, the weaker chickens cannot get to the opening and never reach fresh air. In their frustration they try to harm themselves or each other, and so many of these beautiful creatures have their delicate beaks sliced off. Would you be happy in those conditions?

Remember that their fear and frustration transfers into their eggs and flesh, which is ingested by humans.

Why bless the flesh of any animal you eat or the product thereof?

Blessing and appreciating your food raises its frequency. It creates higher-energy nutrition. It also sends gratitude to the soul of the dead animal, speeding its spiritual journey.

The following prayer calls on the Christ consciousness, which is unconditional love, to bless your food. Of course, you can call forth a blessing in the name of any of the Illumined Ones of any of the religions.

～ Prayer to bless food ～

In the name of the Christ I ask that this food be blessed, so that the fruits of the Earth feed my physical body and the blessings my spiritual body. Amen.

What is the angelic perspective on fox hunting?

Any cruelty to animals is contrary to the spiritual laws. Put yourself in the fox's place. Would you like to be chased and torn to pieces? In the eyes of God, all creatures are different but equal.

Does God punish those who are cruel to animals?

Love never punishes. However, under the Spiritual Laws of Karma your soul will wish to experience what it metes out to others and repay it in some way. Depending on your level of spiritual growth, this may happen in this life or another. An evolved soul balances the karma instantly. For one who is less aware, it may be several lifetimes before he is ready to repay what he perpetrated on animals.

Remember, the person who hounds will be hounded. This may be emotionally, mentally, physically or spiritually and it does not necessarily come from the original source of the karma. The person who baits will, in some way, at some time, be baited. Those who set animals to fight each other will find themselves in conflict. Those who feed unsuitable foods will be poisoned. This may range from a tummy bug to chemical poisoning. Those who cage will in turn be imprisoned.

Humans and animals are aspects of God, of the Oneness. You cannot hurt or harm a creature without damaging yourself. And when you love, respect, care for or heal any of God's creatures, this energy will return to you multiplied.

Action to bless animals

Whenever you see an animal, on television or in reality, silently bless it with love and appreciation.

Do you earn karma if you put an animal down?

This depends on the intention of the person who takes the decision. If you put an animal down because you are bored with it or for financial reasons, you will be karmically indebted to that animal. Love never attracts karma, so if you take the awesome decision for the highest good of the animal, there is only harmony between your souls. In the future, you and your animal will meet on the inner planes or reincarnate together in a happy, beneficial relationship.

I am sure I have been with my cat before. Is this possible?

Yes. If you have a bond of love with an animal in one life, you may choose to be together in a subsequent incarnation.

Why does a normally loving dog suddenly attack its master?

There can be a number of reasons. One man had been drinking alcohol in a pub where an entity attached itself to him and the dog launched itself at the spectre, believing it was protecting its master. If the owner mistreated his animal cruelly in a former life the attack may be the return of karma. Where the canine has been bred and trained to guard and kill, it may be reverting to its true nature. The question then is, 'Why did that human choose to live with that particular breed?'

Why is bird flu entering humans now?

Winged ones are on Earth to teach about freedom and joy and to learn to express their wisdom and vitality within the confines of gravity and a physical body. The cruelty perpetrated on them by humankind was not an anticipated part of their curriculum. It is vital that humans recognise what they are doing to feathered creatures. Through this particular flu virus the birds are drawing both their plight and their importance to the attention of humanity.

Are animals affected by the vibrations of the planet rising?

Oh yes. They are raising their consciousness too. Some animals are beginning to claim their true divine place on Earth. They know at the deepest levels that all are one in the eyes of God.

Why do people treat the dolphins so badly?

Dolphins are Enlightened Ones. They demonstrate the art of joyful being, wisdom and love. To think about dolphins or be in their presence tunes you to their special qualities and you start to create them within yourself. This automatically raises your frequency.

Low-consciousness humans are ruled by fear which tries to destroy anything they do not understand. However, they cannot kill any creature without the permission of its Higher Self. These beautiful mammals allow themselves to be trapped and killed in order to draw the attention of the world to their situation and that of other sea dwellers. They hope humanity will reflect about what they are doing to the oceans and make changes.

In 2005 the world watched a whale die in the Thames?
Why did it come up the river?

It was sent as an emissary from the whales to draw attention to the sonar which humans are using underwater. This is disorientating sea creatures and causing them untold misery. They are unable to fulfil their soul purpose and destiny while humans are polluting their waters and jamming their navigation systems.

Throughout the world people opened their hearts to this whale, who offered its life as a sacrifice to raise the awareness of humanity.

What happens spiritually if a species dies out?

When a species withdraws, it leaves a spiritual vacuum on Earth which can never be filled. In cosmic terms it is considered a terrible thing.

I have heard that cows are leaving the planet. Is this true, and where would they go?

Cows come from Lakuma, an ascended planet near Sirius, currently vibrating beyond your range of vision. Their souls return there when they die.

Cows incarnated into a physical body to learn about being solid, reliable, gentle and steady. The bull was powerful and protective while the female was loving and nurturing. They originally served humans by offering milk and always demonstrated a great capacity for generous giving. In return humans loved and cared for them.

However, this changed and their good nature was exploited.

In recent times, cattle let mad cow disease enter their systems as a protest about the way they were being treated. Finally, they allowed themselves to be sacrificed on blazing funeral pyres to draw attention to their grievances. The flames also helped to purify some of the vibrations of pain and suffering you have inflicted on the herds over the years.

No, cows do not want to withdraw from Earth. This is where they made their spiritual contract to learn and develop, and they still have much to do. However, their oversoul is exploring the possibility of continuing their education on another planetary system that is more loving. If they take this decision it will be an incalculable loss to your planet.

～ Prayer for cattle ～

We offer love and thanks to all the cows who have ever incarnated for all that they have given us and the forbearance they have shown us. We ask that the angels of light touch the hearts and minds of all those who look after them or make money from them in any way, so that they are treated with love and respect.

Where do the souls of animals go when they die?

Like human souls, those of animals eventually return to their planet of origin to take back the learning they have absorbed during their incarnation on Earth and to help that planet develop. Before they do this, many spend time in the healing planes to recover from their ordeals or sicknesses. They may visit those they have loved who are now in spirit or even still alive. And, of course, their souls will assess their lives and decide on the next stage of their soul journey.

We had a sweet little kitten who was run over and killed. Thirty years later I looked out into the garden and watched him playing with my father-in-law's tabby. They were rolling about together and having a wonderful time. I heard later that day that the old man's cat had died the day before I saw them, and knew that they had come to show me they were all right.

253

WHERE DO ANIMALS COME FROM?

Like humans, they come from a variety of planets, star systems and universes in order to experience life in a physical body. The aim of their Higher Selves is to take their learning back to their place of origin.

ORION

Orion is the planet of enlightenment. Spirits who belong here or visit their training establishments are Enlightened Beings. To be in the vicinity of such a presence, whether human or animal, lights up the aura and opens people up to the higher frequencies of light.

These creatures originate from Orion:

Bears: Bears are here to demonstrate power. When they are baited or turned into a circus act, they illustrate poignantly how their authority and dignity can be emasculated.

The cat family: This entire family, including domestic cats, lions and tigers, brings lessons of enlightenment to Earth. They also psychically watch over its people. Even in the current times of low consciousness, domestic ones have the power to look after their families, protecting them from negative entities. In the days when people lived in the fifth-dimensional frequency, felines assisted with healings and held the energy for the higher vision of those with whom they worked.

Because the big cats have more power than smaller ones, more of them incarnate in times of turmoil to try to hold the light steady on Earth.

Goats: These often misunderstood creatures bring higher energy to the world. They demonstrate humility, ecology and waste disposal by eating dry twigs and left-over food.

Pan, the god of nature is seen with goat's horns, which represent enlightenment. Unfortunately the goat's horned head has been denigrated in your time to a devil's head.

Juliette de Bairacli-Levy, the enlightened herbalist, tells a story about her baby daughter, who she could not breastfeed. When a wet nurse could no longer supply the milk, a goat appeared. At feed times she would simply arrive and allow the child to suckle directly from her teats. What an offering of love!

Rabbits: Rabbits originally incarnated to demonstrate to children the feminine qualities of softness, caring and nurturing. They also taught them to have fun. They can heal the heart with their wisdom and love. The Higher Selves of the animals allowed myxamatosis to be introduced in order to draw the unconscious attention of humanity to the gentle qualities that were lacking in society and to try to engage their compassion.

Red squirrels: Red squirrels bring to humanity a wonderful sense of joy and vitality. They demonstrate freedom and happiness. These Enlightened Beings are slowly withdrawing from Earth as conditions become impossible for them, allowing lower-frequency animals to take over.

Giraffes: Giraffes offer gentleness, tenderness, dignity and grace. While they appear to be vulnerable as a result of these feminine characteristics, when they defend themselves or their young, their kick is like the iron fist in a velvet glove.

CANIS MAJOR
This is known as the dog star. Sirius is one of the stars of the constellation of Canis Major, and Lakuma is an ascended star around Sirius.

SIRIUS
Sirius is considered the planet of intellect and rationality. Many souls who bring in new technology or work with left-brain activities such as mathematics, the legal profession, science and some aspects of writing, will have visited Sirius for training before incarnation. The vibrations from this star also offer mind-

healing, which affects attitudes, thought patterns, beliefs and inherited miasmas, and helps to bring in the wisdom of the higher mind.

Dolphins: Dolphins, the High Priests and Priestesses of the oceans and keepers of wisdom, hold the sacred information of Atlantis for humanity. They are like living computers. These special ones have decided to enter a physical body to demonstrate to your world that there is a higher way of being. They also remind those arrogant ones who believe humans are the most evolved creatures on Earth that there are others much wiser. Many people who are swimming with the dolphins or linking into their energy are downloading the higher knowledge and receiving healing.

Birds: Birds have incarnated from Sirius to learn to express freedom and joy while trapped in a physical body. They are also demonstrating that it is possible to overcome gravity and are living examples of how to fly.

Albatrosses: These most powerful birds epitomise the power of serenity and confidence. Conserving their energy, they demonstrate going with the flow.

Eagles: The eagle symbolises power with majesty and the ability to judge from a higher and greater perspective.

Humming birds: With their constant activity, these birds teach about industry and work ethic without striving. They show humans the balanced use of energy.

Ostriches: These huge birds show the world that you can be what you believe yourself to be. They travel at enormous speeds and teach and illustrate the power of mind over matter.

Robins: Robins show us nature's beauty. They proclaim that it is possible to be territorial, accepting of humans and work in partnership. Co-operation and friendliness are their lessons.

Swans: These beautiful creatures offer a pure exposition of regality, majesty, dignity and faith.

Sparrows: Small but tough, sparrows show they have the self-belief to survive anywhere. They are teaching and learning about simplicity and the power of the group.

Vultures: Their office is waste disposal.

LAKUMA

Cows: Cows have incarnated from Lakuma, bringing humans an offering of milk. Originally, in times when cows were very high-frequency beings and the grass and herbs on which they fed were of a beautiful vibration, their milk was rich and perfect for humans. This is no longer so. They chose Earth on which to incarnate and develop their spiritual paths because of the love and respect in which they were held by the fifth-dimensional beings of Atlantis.

Horses: When horses first incarnated from Lakuma to be involved with the experiment of Golden Atlantis, they were ridden bareback and directed telepathically. No one dreamt of restricting their free spirit with a saddle or bridle until after the fall. They helped with transport and in the fields, but in those times were never taken for granted. They are a very high-frequency creature, learning and teaching lessons of love, and dignity as well as pride and worth.

Deer: Deer bring qualities of gentleness. They are learning lessons of trust and teaching you to trust.

Camels and dromedaries: These animals originate from Lakuma. They are learning and teaching about service with endurance and about using resources wisely.

Elephants: Elephants, those gentle giants, have come from Lakuma to learn and teach about family life and structure. They exhibit the seeming opposites of majesty and fun, intuition and masculine power.

MARS

Kangaroos: Kangaroos are powerhouses of wound-up energy. They are unpredictable, protective and energetic and demonstrate how to use, conserve and discharge feminine energy.

257

ANIMALS FROM OTHER PLANETS

Monkeys: Monkeys of all varieties come from many different planets, though they step their frequency down, like many humans, through the Pleiades. They incarnate to experience fun, family life and structure. They are here to learn about life on Earth, not with the intellect of a human, but with the right-brain qualities of unconditional love, acceptance, loyalty and trust.

Alligators, Crocodiles, Reptiles: All these creatures arrive from a planet not in this galaxy that has Plutonian energy. They are illustrating the human shadow-qualities, such as untrustworthiness, cold-blooded detachment, stealth and many others. They enable you to bring up your deepest fears. Because they help you to understand your hidden agendas, they appear in your life when you are ready to look at your shadow aspects. Then you will do so, whether or not you are conscious of it.

Co-Creation

What does co-creation mean?

Co-creation is the use of your will backed by universal energy.

As sons and daughters of God, you were given the free will and power to manifest with your thoughts, words and deeds. Whatever you chose to concentrate on would be backed by cosmic force and brought to life. It was anticipated that your aspirations would merge with the divine force to glorify and expand creation in a wondrous way. Then, as you progressed, spiritual technology would be channelled down and this would be used to improve and amplify the lives of all. Co-creation is a power that can be used for good or evil. Many have concentrated on dark, angry thoughts which co-create undesirable situations, relationships and creatures.

It is not too late to focus your hearts and minds on a vision for the highest good of the people and the planet. Remember, every single thought you energise creates. You have an immense opportunity to make something wonderful happen in your world. The divine force will support you.

How can I co-create with God a better life for myself?

The life your heart desires is already there, in the etheric, just waiting for you to manifest it, or any version of it that you choose, into physicality.

Listen to your inner promptings and, when you are clear what you really want, focus your thoughts, words and imaginings on it. Ask the angels to add their energy to it and take action when you receive their signals. Always add these words: 'Let this or something better now manifest for the highest good of all.' That is your safeguard, for, assuming you correctly heard the voice of your Higher Self, the angels will help you with your endeavour. If you did not hear properly and what you ask for is not for your highest good, these words will ensure it will not manifest.

Exercise to manifest for your highest good
1. Decide what you want your better life to be. If you find yourself thinking about what you don't want or that you do not deserve it, you are sending mixed messages to the universe and blocking your hopes.
2. Write down exactly what you wish to co-create. Make sure every word you use is positive and in the present tense. The more clarity you have, the better. Remember to add at the end, 'This or something better now manifests for the highest good of all.'
3. Then visualise it as if it has already come into your life. Remember, the universe is completely impartial. You can have

whatever you believe you deserve. The only thing that prevents you from receiving all the abundance of your heart's desire is your own self-worth.

4. Thank the angels for helping you to bring it about.
5. This activates the power of faith.
6. The more prepared you are mentally, emotionally, physically and spiritually to live your dream, the more quickly it will arrive in your life.

Drawing exercise to manifest for your highest good

Writing utilises the left brain. When you draw, you use the right brain, so if you illustrate in addition to writing as you do the exercise above, this ensures that your entire mind computer is helping you create your vision.

When you have completed your drawing in as much detail as you wish to, draw a pink balloon round it. Then imagine yourself releasing it, so that it can fly out into the universe. You must let go of your vision, so that the angels can energise it.

What if my desire does not manifest?

If it does not manifest, it was not for your highest good, or you were not ready, or you did not truly believe it would happen.

If humans were expected to expand God's creation, was it not perfect already?

God's creation is and always has been perfect. Everything is held in the divine mind at all times as whole and complete.

The expansion, divinely anticipated, was one of experience. Parents have children who go out into the world and bring back their new understandings to enrich and expand the family, just as each individual's life enhances Source. As above, so below.

Do humans have the right to interfere with God's creation?

You have free will to co-create. However, this does not give you the right to interfere with the divine genetic blueprint of your own or other life forms.

I have heard much talk of the cosmic ordering service. Is that co-creation?

Yes, that is another way of describing the power of manifestation with the divine.

Imagine that the cosmos is a huge warehouse. You can order whatever you want and it will be sent to you as long as you have the money to pay for it. The secret is to get the currency right, which, in the case of a cosmic order, is the vibration of your thoughts and emotions. You must ensure that you are emotionally prepared to receive what you have requested. Are your thoughts one hundred percent positive? Do you believe you deserve it? Can you imagine yourself having this in your life? Will it enhance you? Can you cope with it? Will your family and friends support you? Are you ready to make any changes to accommodate this? If the answers to these questions are affirmative, expect miracles.

I manifested a new car that I had dreamed of for ages, but it was stolen shortly afterwards. Why?

Your belief that you did not truly deserve this new car attracted the thief to steal it. It drew your limiting thoughts to your attention.

My grandmother had a plaque on her kitchen wall which said, 'It's no use having Rolls Royce ideas on a push-bike income.' In fact the daydreams start the process of manifestation. After that you must believe it can happen, which means changing your consciousness to that of someone

261

who owns a limousine. So think about having a special car, talk as if you have it and finally act as if you have it. Then watch the universe for hints about how it will come to you. As soon as you are psychically ready, it will be on its way.

We drew the house of our dreams and ordered it from the universe. It was quite uncanny for we found the exact house we envisaged and moved in two years ago. Now we are having a problem with meeting the mortgage payments. What has gone wrong?

You know you can manifest. Now you need to apply the same principles to your finances! Decide how much you need. Draw a picture of your bank statement as you wish it to be. Let the universe decide how it is to happen, for there are many streams of prosperity that you can bring into your life. Simply focus on the end result.

Remember that any doubts you have are particularly damaging. Any statements such as, 'We can't afford it!' will close down the channels of prosperity. You must at all times hold and affirm your vision. Then the full amount for your mortgage payment will always be there.

I want to co-create a healing centre and I have a clear picture of it in my mind. I have even seen the building I want to have for it, but how do I know it is really the right thing for me to do?

Your vision is too cloudy! The fact that you are asking this question suggests you are having doubts that it is your right next step. Meditate daily until you are really positive it is the correct thing for you. If it is not, let the concept go so that something new can emerge.

My life keeps changing. I decide something is really right for me and pursue it one hundred per cent. Then, after a few years, it no longer captivates me and something else excites me. Am I a rolling stone or is there a purpose in this?

Your soul has a vision for you. However, you need to gain varied experience and master several stages before you are ready. It is good that you are following your intuition. At present the universe is helping you co-create the situations from which you need to learn. When the time is right you will be encouraged on to your divine right path and then you will feel settled.

Disasters

Why does God allow disasters to happen?

God doesn't. Disasters are the natural result of collective human karma. Having given you free will to love or destroy, God stands back and witnesses your actions.

Why did 9/11, the Twin Towers, happen?

This horror was forecast hundreds of years ago by Nostradamus, if humanity did not change its ways. There are many reasons why this happened.

Humans have created a world where people are unequal, though you know in your hearts that everyone is equal in the sight of God. Human greed and desire to control has formed pockets of individuals who have material riches, often built on the labour of those who have nothing. The impoverished are inevitably angry and frustrated. This is particularly so if they perceive themselves as good and hard-working, while the wealthy few live self-indulgent and possibly hedonistic lives.

The anger of such victims is inflamed when they feel exploited, are forced to pay extortionate rates of interest or their livelihood is threatened by punitive restrictions on trade. When a human being or animal feels caged and powerless, it feels enraged, and this fury will be expressed violently by those of lower consciousness.

Of course, violence is never the true divine pathway and is not condoned by the spiritual hierarchy. However, the angels have enormous compassion for those who are downtrodden.

Is there another way to achieve equality, other than by violence?

Mahatma Gandhi incarnated to demonstrate to humanity that there is another way. Non-violence is a great spiritual aspiration. It takes time, but the respect it engenders ultimately creates change and mutual understanding.

Why did the Aberfan disaster take place in 1966?

This horrific disaster is still vividly remembered. Coal waste from the mountain above the village of Aberfan, in Wales, slid down the hillside, engulfing the local school. The physical cause was water from an underground spring and heavy rain, which loosened the coal waste. The spiritual reason was the violation of the resources of the Earth and careless disposal of the waste, together with the long-trapped emotions of the people of the region. It drew world attention to the importance of your children and your families, and it served as a warning to governments throughout the world to take care of the land and keep the people safe.

In this case the tragedy precipitated action and a law was passed in the UK to prevent disused tips being a danger to the public. All blessings to those children and their families.

Why did the Titanic sink?

The energy that went into the building and launching of the *Titanic* was that of arrogance. The intention was to conquer the oceans, without respect or humility. Water is a mighty power, and it is important that humans learn to honour it and work with it. Many souls gave their lives in order to draw this lesson to the attention of the world.

Why do people choose to live on fault lines of the Earth?

Some people like, consciously or unconsciously, to live on the edge and seek uncertainty, drama and adventure. Such souls are attracted to live on fault lines.

Why do shooting tragedies keep occurring?

These are a result of out-of-control human aggression and anger, combined with the lethal opportunity offered by weapons. A number of terrible tragedies have occurred in which several children have been slaughtered. Usually those souls have agreed that they will die in this way in order to focus people's minds on the danger of guns. At present, in certain parts of the world, the masses are not listening. They are choosing fear over peace.

Why did shootings happen in the Amish community, which believes in and preaches peace?

Quite simply they believed that the outside world is dangerous. This belief in evil drew it to them. Most importantly, talking of peace is not the same as feeling it. Fear and discontent open the doors to terror. This horrific shooting has a higher perspective, for the community wanted to test their faith and resolution about forgiveness. At the same time, focus on the tragedy drew the attention of the sophisticated world to a simpler way of life.

NATURAL DISASTERS

What is the metaphysical reason for floods?

Tears release grief and pain from the human system. Water, which is a cosmic purifier, washes the planet. A flood in your home indicates that it is time to deal with and release unresolved and possibly unrecognised emotional issues. A large flood suggests that there is much hurt and other forms of negativity in the area that needs to be cleansed and healed.

What is the spiritual reason for the New Orleans flood?

There were a number of spiritual reasons for this devastation.

In the deep south of America, New Orleans carries the scars of the violation, pain, inhumanity and hate of slavery. The lessons have never been learnt, so the flood served the purpose of drawing to the attention of the world that there were still poor blacks and rich whites living there.

It was a hedonistic city, where many seeking selfish gratification were attracted. The passion, joy, creativity and expression of the jazz the city was famed for were not enough to balance the karma created over centuries.

When an individual is powerful, self-centred and only gives help, never receiving anything, he is out of balance. So it is with countries and nations. It was time for the strong to experience vulnerability.

Finally, when children grow up they should no longer blindly rely on their impoverished parents for support, and so it is with bankrupt governments and their regions. Aim for self-sufficiency.

Why did the tsunami happen?

The Intergalactic Council started planning for this particular piece of purification a long time ago. They issued a cosmic invitation throughout the universes for souls to incarnate on a cleansing and healing mission on Earth. Thousands, recognising this great opportunity for service, responded and duly incarnated. For some it offered the chance to clear all earthly karma, for others a spiritual promotion, for a few the blessing of experiencing life on your planet for a short while. These special souls agreed to soak up into their energy fields the negativity of lust, greed, power struggle, poverty consciousness and so on held within the earth. At the predestined time of 26 December 2004, they gathered in specific places. And on that day a great wave, magnified by the full moon, rose from the oceans to create a major tsunami, taking all these people into the light together, carrying the toxins with them. Only those who were predestined to pass over in the disaster did so, and there were millions of angels waiting to welcome them.

Because many of them came from the richer nations, the entire world watched what was happening and hearts opened with compassion, love, empathy, co-operation, generosity or desire to help. Thousands more had their lives devastated as they experienced, learnt lessons, repaid karma and practised courage, selflessness and many good qualities.

Of course, the spiritual perspective does not diminish the horror, grief and loss felt by their loved ones and everyone on the planet, but the tsunami changed more than the people and countries directly affected. Because the victims came from so many countries, millions of heartfelt prayers were offered in every part of the world. They rose like a cloud, enabling intercession to come forth from the higher realms. You are asked to continue to pray for your planet, the people and the natural world as you have never done before, for Earth is still undergoing its healing crisis.

A similar situation occurred when Princess Diana died. The world focused on her loss and there was an outpouring of grief. As a result of the collective prayers and love directed towards her, her spirit was able to take a vast amount of negative energy with her into the light to be transmuted.

A course participant approached me to say that her son had been in Thailand with his buddy when the tsunami struck. He survived but his mate died. Her son spent five days combing the area for his companion and at last found him. Then he brought the dead body home to his parents.

A year later her son was ill and full of aches and pains. She wanted to know if this was likely to be connected and what she could say to him.

Of course, it is very likely to be connected. He underwent a terrible trauma and the emotional impact takes time to work through the physical body. However, it may help the boy to know that his comrade who died had a soul contract, entered into before birth, to die in the tsunami. He, on the other hand, had a soul contract to survive the tidal wave and serve his pal and his pal's family by bringing the body home. He fulfilled it admirably and there is no need for guilt. His friend is where he needs to be.

Were the animals part of the cleansing of the tsunami?

Most of the animals, who are still in tune with nature, heeded the subtle warning signs of the tsunami and disappeared to high ground, so only those ready to pass over did so. Animals were not part of the cleansing because they were not the perpetrators of the negative energy that was being transmuted.

Were the animals learning lessons too?

Some were, but many animals were serving or teaching you.

A story was reported from Phuket, Thailand about the action of some elephants who became very agitated and unruly about twenty minutes before the first tsunami wave hit. Four of them, who had just returned from a trip and had not yet been chained up, helped the other five tear free from their chains. Then they all climbed up a hill and started bellowing. Realising something was wrong, many people followed them so that they were out of danger when the waves hit. As soon as the water had subsided, the animals charged down from the height and started to pick up children with their trunks. They ran back up with them. Once all the children had been rescued, they started to help the adults. After saving forty-two people, the extraordinary creatures returned to the beach and carried up four bodies. They didn't allow their handlers to mount them until this task had been completed, and they then began moving wreckage.

Why are such devastating earthquakes happening?

When someone shivers, he releases fear from his core. Where fear is held within the soil and has penetrated deeply into the rocks and deeper strata of the planet, the earth literally quakes, releasing fear. At the same time this causes pain, havoc and destruction for all those in the area. On a spiritual level, only those souls who sign up to be affected by the disaster will be at that place at that time.

Some will be absorbing some of the fear into their essence and passing over with it in order to release the energy from the planet. This may be a karmic issue or spiritual service of the highest order. Others are also making brave choices: to experience bereavement and loss, homelessness, chaos, helplessness, vulnerablity and powerlessness. Some souls wish to test their faith, others to be offered an opportunity to show courage, compassion, empathy or offer healing.

Why do pit disasters occur?

Earth is your mother, and when you enter it you must honour and respect her. Humans have plundered the resources of Mother Earth for centuries. They have polluted her with chemicals and negativity. Where she feels violated or exhausted by the demands on her, she will collapse. That is the spiritual reason for pit disasters.

What is the spiritual reason for hurricanes?

The element of air is about communication. Out-of-control hurricanes, gales or tornadoes come as a reminder to humans everywhere to connect with each other and with nature. Wind blows away the cobwebs, clears the mind and allows a new thought process in. Destructive winds are a reminder to change your beliefs and purify your mind. Where a whole area is devastated by the power of air, the spiritual message is that a collective shift in attitude is needed.

Why do fires happen?

Fire is a cleanser which erupts where there is deeply held anger. It creates the space for transformation. From forest fires to those in houses or cars, they transmute negative energy. The horror and loss that results for the people and animals involved is tragic, but part of a karmic clearance for all concerned.

Is there a metaphysical reason for a volcano?

If a human has a boil, it erupts with pus and releases physical poisons as well as a build-up of the emotional toxin of anger. A volcano performs the same service for the planet. Fire is a cleanser, and it purifies the area on many levels.

What is the best thing the average person can do when they hear about a disaster?

If there is direct action you can take, such as giving your time, money or experience to help, do so.

If you do not have the means or do not feel called to take action, light a candle and pray for the souls of those affected. Visualise them passing over with ease. Prayer is incredibly powerful, much more so than most people realise. It can assist those passing over as it helps provide a wave of light, and it can draw in more angels to support and enfold those who need love or healing.

Prayers of gratitude for the special mission that the participants have been engaged in is also helpful, for it adds to their soul energy, and at the same time draws more abundance to Earth.

> ⌒ Visualisation to assist disaster victims ⌒
>
> ⌒ Light a candle.
> ⌒ Visualise a golden light streaming down into the affected area and see the souls of those passing, rising up through the light with their angels beside them.
> ⌒ Picture the angels enfolding, healing and helping everyone who is injured, traumatised or in need of material assistance.

The energy you are sending will enable more spiritual help to go to the region and people in need.

Do angels gather to help at the site of a disaster?

Many angels congregate at the site of big disasters to help the afflicted. They create a huge light to direct the spirits of the dead on their journey, and gather to prepare a welcome for them on the other side.

What are the lessons of a disaster?

There are many and varied lessons. You are on Earth to learn about all the various aspects of love, so a catastrophe offers opportunities for selfless service, courage, devotion, fortitude, generosity, compassion and many other qualities. It even allows people to use judgement and discernment about where to give money or who to help. Those who are bereaved have undertaken heartbreaking experiences of loss, which sometimes leads them into a spiritual quest or tests their faith.

One lesson is to detach from the emotion of the disaster. This is very difficult for some, but detachment allows you to transmit pure spiritual light into the scene, and this can help beyond your understandings.

Why do so many children die in disasters?

The souls of children volunteer to pass over in a disaster for a number of reasons. Physically, they are vulnerable and weak so less able to cope with the situations. More importantly, such tragedies are wake-up calls. The pure innocence of the children touches the hearts of the masses and forces change in a way that the death of an adult does not. When the soul of a child only needs a short experience on Earth, it may offer to be part of a collective happening which will so affect humanity that action is taken. The greatest way you can honour the life of such a child is to work for change if you can or, if you cannot, to use the power of your visualisations to see the defect made perfect.

Why me? Why did my home get damaged? Why was my loved one hurt? Why was I there to experience the horror?

Because your soul commanded that you have that experience and learn from it.

Why wasn't my neighbour, who is a bad person, affected?

Either it was not your neighbour's karma or it was not the right time for your neighbour to learn those lessons. Bless your neighbour.

Dreams

Is there a spiritual purpose to dreams?

Yes, dreams act as a bridge between your spirit life and your physical one. Some convey messages from your unconscious mind to your conscious awareness. Others allow connections with the angelic realms or other aspects of the higher planes, bringing you teachings, healing or comfort.

Are there different types of dreams?

Yes, but most dreams are coded messages from your soul to help you deal with your daily life. Nightmares and recurrent dreams come into this category. There are also psychic dreams, which are really astral journeys, when your spirit is flying free from your body. These include meetings on the inner planes, receiving information about the future and past life dreams. Then there are spiritual dreams. These include visions, meetings with angels or masters, the receiving of symbols or messages from Higher Beings.

How would I know if a dream was really a psychic dream?

A psychic dream is usually very vivid and you wake feeling it really happened. It does not fade like a normal dream.

How do I recognise a spiritual dream?

You just know it. You are in no doubt whatsoever.

Why is the message in a dream coded?

The information from your soul is often about emotions. Humans suppress or deny their feelings because they cannot or do not want to deal with them at the time. They push them down into the unconscious mind, which is sealed from the conscious by the critical censor. When your Higher Self wants to draw your underlying state to your conscious awareness, it tries to bypass the censor by turning the message or feelings into a story, pun or metaphor, which you can later decode.

How can I translate my dreams?

Remember that every part of the dream is an aspect of you, with a message it wants you to hear. When you listen, hear and acknowledge each part, you will be on the road to self-under-standing and spiritual growth.

If you take a dream story in which a stone, a dog and a crying person have parts, they are all representing aspects of your person-ality. To understand the message, close your eyes and run the pictures through your mind. Then talk to yourself as if you are each of the images. Be the stone and express how you feel and what you need as the stone. You may say, 'I feel as if everyone is stepping on me without noticing me. It hurts and I'm angry. I need to be acknowledged and noticed.' Or, 'I'm sharp and hard. I hurt people and I want to be softer. I need to be more gentle and caring to myself.' The dog may feel happy, sad, carefree, beaten or anxious and is expressing something important about you. And the crying person is upset, guilty, afraid, grieving, hurt, angry or one of a dozen emotions. Again, their deepest desires must be met.

As these are all different parts of you, only you can listen to the dream, acknowledge your feelings and fulfil your own long-ings. No one can do this for you. But as soon as you heal your-self, other people will behave more positively and affirmatively towards you. Dreams offer a wonderful way to learn about your-self and bring your different personalities into harmony and balance.

Can dreams help me resolve my inner conflicts?

Yes. As soon as your personality is ready to resolve an internal conflict, your unconscious mind will present a dream to you, which will enable you to find the answer.

Exercise to work with conflicting inner personalities:
1. When you wake, run the dream through your mind.
2. Set yourself as the mediator.

3. You may need your angel or a respected figure, such as Jesus, Mohammed or Buddha, to accompany you and keep the different personalities within you safe from each other.
4. As the mediator, talk to the people in your dream, find out what they need and what they want to say to each other.
5. Negotiate a contract of behaviour with them.
6. See them all shaking hands and smiling, ready to work in co-operation.

Can I receive the answers to my dilemmas in my dreams?

Yes. Ask the angels to give you a dream which contains a solution for the highest good of all. However, when you recall and translate the dream, you must act on the guidance. If you do not, the universe will presume you are not really serious about your spiritual aspirations.

I had rather foolishly lent a friend a lot of money over the years, which she had never been in a position to repay. As she was desperate, I then gave her money towards some work she was to do for me. She took the money, then said she did not have time or energy to do the work and was adding the sum to her debt! I felt angry and cheated and knew these feelings were cording me to her. My dilemma was, should I insist she repay it, which would be a great hardship to her, or should I uncord the whole ball and chain and release her from the debt? What was the spiritually correct thing to do? Which action would give the right message to the universe? I thought I was lending her the money out of compassion, but was I really creating a victim perpetrator situation?

I asked the angels to give me a dream containing the guidance I needed. In the morning, this was my dream: 'I have placed a pile of bricks in my neighbour's sitting room. I realise I must go round and remove them.'

I translated this as, 'I must take the burden of debt which I have placed on my friend away,' and I wrote to her that day setting her free. And I thanked the angels for bringing me this expensive lesson!

How can I remember my dreams?

As soon as you start to become interested in dreams and realise their true significance and importance, your dream recall will become stronger.

Sharing your dreams with others will enable you to remember them more often.

Write them down. Place a pen and paper by your bedside to tell your unconscious mind you wish to bring your dreams to awareness.

Clearly remind yourself that you intend to do so.

Water is the element of dreams. Drink a glass of water before you go to sleep.

Eat lightly, early in the evening. Heavy, late meals block spiritual aspirations.

As you put your head on your pillow, ask your angels to help you with your night work.

Can I translate someone else's dreams?

Yes and no. Some people are very gifted psychically and can tune into the meaning of others' dreams. While a number of them seem very clear and obvious, you all perceive things differently. Most people project their own ideas and beliefs on to the dreams that are presented to them. It is safer to encourage the dreamer to find his own message.

EXAMPLE

Two people dream a kangaroo is jumping across the desert. To one a kangaroo means being able to bound along quickly and enthusiastically, and the desert is a flat place with no impediments. This dream is a message that their life or work is moving fast, energetically and easily and nothing is blocking the way. To the other a kangaroo is an alien species and a desert is a bleak, empty place. To that person the dream is about feeling different, isolated and alone.

Only the individual can translate their own dreams.

Do some dream symbols have the same meaning for everyone?

Yes, some symbols have a universal meaning. At the same time, it is important to check internally what it means to you.

I know two therapists who work with dreams. How do I know which one to go to, as they both work very differently?

Let your intuition help you decide which one is right for you. But remember that your soul wants you to learn your lessons and grow spiritually, so it will give you perfect dreams of the kind that your chosen therapist can work with.

I only dream when I go on holiday. Why is this?

You dream every night, but you only remember them when your life, and particularly your mind, is more relaxed.

Whenever I go on holiday I have bad dreams. Why?

If your life is very busy and active, you probably do not remember your dreams or only remember those that relate to your daily situations. However, when you are relaxing on holiday and have time to examine them, your soul takes the opportunity to thrust your unresolved unconscious fears and beliefs into your awareness. These suppressed energies have been driving your reactions, often inappropriately, so it is vitally important that you write them down and explore their meaning.

What is the purpose of nightmares, and why do people have them? What can you do about it?

A nightmare reveals to the conscious mind fearful and unpleasant feelings which have often been suppressed for a long time. These emotions about an incident or situation which took place earlier in your adult life, in childhood or in a past life are locked inside you. At the original time, you were too vulnerable or powerless to deal with what was happening. However, whenever the blocked emotions are triggered they will express themselves through your bad dream. It is often helpful to replay it while imagining you have the power to face the situation. Then satisfy the feelings in a way that you could not when you were so vulnerable.

A recurrent nightmare indicates that an emotion has been suppressed inside you for a long time and is crying out to be released.

A terrifying dream can also be the consequence of a scary psychic meeting with another spirit in the astral planes. In this case, put very strong protection around yourself at night before you go to sleep. If you have small children who need to access your energy, specifically state that you are allowing them through your protection or they may feel bereft.

⌒ Visualisation for protection ⌒

- ⌒ Ask Archangel Michael to place his deep blue cloak of protection over you. Feel this happening and make sure you zip it up and put the hood over your head.
- ⌒ Invoke the Gold Ray of Christ three times and feel the light spreading over you.
- ⌒ Visualise a pure white ball of light all round you, bouncing off any attack.
- ⌒ Draw crosses, or any other symbol of protection that is meaningful to you, in front of you, behind you, to both sides, above and below.

DREAM MESSAGES

I dreamt there were two paths up a mountain. I was
struggling up a very difficult one strewn with boulders
and sharp stones. The other was sunny and easy, but in
order to reach it I had to cross a ravine. The message is
very clear and I feel it is important. My life does feel
burdensome, but how do I move to the sunny path? Help,
I have no idea what my true path is or how to get
there.

You have changes to make in order to find happiness. Your true
life path will be revealed to you when you have done this.

You are walking up the mountain, which symbolises a spiritual challenge,
revealing that you have a higher path to take. In order to access this new
way of life you have to cross the ravine, in other words move from one
state to another. While dreams are messages from your unconscious mind
to your conscious one, you can positively send instructions back to your
unconscious to reprogramme it. You do this with visualisations which
send instructions through your conscious mind back to your mind
computer.

Here is an exercise for you to do which will indicate to your soul that
you have listened to the dream message and are ready to do what it
takes to reach the sunny path. At this moment you do not need to
know what your true vocation is. Just accept that it is there waiting for
you.

Exercise to work with a dream
1. Shut your eyes and relax.
2. Imagine you are back in the dream climbing the difficult mountain.
3. Call in your guardian angel and picture yourself walking to the edge of the ravine.

4. Ask your angel to help you build a strong, sturdy bridge over the gap.
5. Use your imagination to give messages to your unconscious mind. There may be a wide plank lying around that you can use to cross the void. Or you may need to call in an expert bridge builder with heavy equipment to provide the help you need.
6. When the bridge is complete, thank your angel and cross to the easy path.
7. You may need to do this visualisation more than once in order to instruct your inner mind that you are ready for change.
8. Stay open to guidance from the universe about your next step.

I dreamt a strong woman was smothering me. What could this mean?

You are so cautious about your health that you cannot enjoy life.

A woman in a dream is a feminine aspect of yourself. In this case your inner nurturer has become too overprotective. The dream is warning you that this female aspect of your personality is not allowing you to be true to yourself. There is an additional message. Under the spiritual laws of Earth, whatever inner feelings you have are reflected back to you by your outer life. Therefore it is quite possible that a woman is stifling you in some way. If this is so, lighten up internally so that the outer reflection will automatically shift.

I woke up with a horrid feeling after this dream. A beautiful pink blossom fell on to a peaceful lake. It was just starting to open up when suddenly something dragged it down under the water. I have just got married and love my husband. Is something going to go wrong?

You are right that the pink blossom represents the blossoming of love, and your relationship is very peaceful. Be careful of your unconscious motivations, which could submerge you.

Pink is the colour of love, and the flower represents the blossoming of love. Water represents emotions, so watch carefully how you express your feelings, in case something unconscious emerges that could upset your marriage.

Exercise to explore a dream
1. Shut your eyes and relax.
2. Imagine you are back in the dream with your guardian angel protecting you.
3. You are shining a very strong light into the water, so that you can see exactly what is dragging the blossom down.
4. You may see something symbolic, like a fish or an octopus, in which case imagine you are able to communicate with it. Ask it how it feels, why it is doing this and what it needs in order to stop this behaviour.
5. Alternatively, you may see or think of a person, an aspect of yourself such as your inner child or your inner witch. Or your boss or a current or past situation may appear. Communicate with whoever or whatever it is and negotiate a solution in your inner world which can later translate into your life.

I dreamt I had two children. The older one was very bonny, but the younger one was ailing and sickly. It needed special care. In real life I have no children. I was always very healthy, but my younger brother was always ill. He's all right now that he is an adult. I run a thriving business but have just started a new project which is not doing so well. Does the dream refer to any of these things, and what should I do about it?

Give your attention to your new project. It has great promise, though it needs more help in the early years, and it will survive.

ANGEL ANSWERS

In dreams, children often represent new projects, ideas or businesses, so it may help if you imagine you are reliving the dream and find out what the ailing child needs. It is interesting that, when you sent me your dream, you remembered your younger brother was ill as a child but is healthy now he has grown up. Your Higher Self has produced a very clear parallel for you to consider. It has given you the same message twice, once in the dream about the ailing child and the second in the metaphor of your brother's health. Thank your unconscious processes for being so clear! Help the struggling business while it is new and it will be fine as it matures.

I dreamt that my husband and I are driving along. My mother is sitting in the back of the car with her hands on the steering wheel and we don't even realise it. I did not feel anything when I woke, but the images were very vivid. What is the message, and is there anything I should do?

Your mother is subtly influencing your marriage in an inappropriate way.

If your mother is driving your relationship, it may help you to uncord from her, and this would also enable you to connect with any suppressed feelings.

When you send a thought or emotion to someone, it creates a psychic cord from you to that person. He or she also sends cords to you which fasten into your energy systems if you are open to receiving them. You will unconsciously affect each other through these links. It is helpful to remove all cords that you sense or see, for unconditional love does not form attachments. You then free the other person to act with more integrity, and you too are released to become mature and empowered. See page 196 for an uncording visualisation.

I dreamt that I was swimming in a murky pool with crocodiles. It was horrible. What does this mean? What can I do?

You are in emotionally dangerous conditions. Move away from them and then clean up your life.

You are in a murky situation, so it is important to let go of some of the anger, hurt, fear and other negative emotions which taint your aura. When you purify yourself, many fears disappear. What does a crocodile mean to you? Is it frightening, underhand, dangerous, cunning or something else? If you pride yourself on being nice, you may not wish to look at your hidden crocodile tendencies, so you project them on to others, who behave meanly to you.

∼ Visualisation to purify yourself ∼

The Gold and Silver Violet Flame is a powerful trans-muting energy which helps to dissolve dark emotions and thoughts. Invoke it to come to you, then visualise it surrounding all the situations in your life as well as all parts of your body and the people around you.

I dreamt I was walking down the road with no clothes on. I woke feeling very embarrassed. Can you comment?

Yes, naked dreams are about feeling vulnerable and exposed.

Perhaps you have shared a secret with someone, told people about an intimate side of your life or been caught out in a lie. Your dream is drawing to your attention your feeling that your vulnerable inner self has been laid open.

I dreamt I was going to the toilet in a public place. What could such a dream possibly mean?

Toilet dreams are about releasing emotions or beliefs. In this case you feel you have revealed them publicly.

I have just started a new job, and on the second day I dreamt that there was a huge barrel of lovely apples, but one was bad.

Be very careful about what you say to your colleagues. One is not as honourable as you think.

Your unconscious picks up warning signs much more quickly than your conscious mind.

I had a dream which I felt was very important. I have worked on it in all the ways I know how, but I could not understand the meaning. What more can I do?

When you really cannot understand a significant dream you may, in sleep or meditation, climb the mountain of the Masters and ask for the meaning to be clearly revealed to you. Do this visualisation in meditation or before you go to sleep.

~ **Visualisation to ask the Masters for information** ~

~ Relax by breathing comfortably.
~ Imagine a tall mountain in front of you.
~ Climb to the top. Even if you are physically unable to do this, in your inner world you can.
~ At the top is a beautiful circular temple.
~ Enter with reverence, for inside is one the great Illumined Masters who can help you.

⌒ Ask him or her to give you a message in your next
    dream that is totally clear and obvious.
⌒ Say thank you.
⌒ Climb back down the mountain and rest.

That evening have paper and pen ready by your bed and expect
a clear message in response to your request.

PSYCHIC DREAMS

*I dreamt about my son who passed over last year. In the
dream he told me he was well and happy. Can you explain
this?*

Your son loved you very much and when he died he wanted to
reassure you that he was all right, so his spirit came to you. This
often happens, but it is less common for someone to remember the
meeting. It must have been very strongly impressed upon you.

*I often dream that my grandmother, who died several years
ago, is watching over me? Is she really doing so?*

Your grandmother is helping you from the spirit world.

*I never met my grandfather, who died before I was born,
but often feel he is around me? Is this possible?*

Yes. He often pops in to see that you are all right. The fact that
he never met you in the flesh is not important, for he has a strong
spiritual link with you and loves you.

*My friend dreamt that a choir of angels was singing over
her and she woke up feeling so happy and well. Did this
really happen?*

The angels often sing over people at night. It brings them comfort, helps to connect them to the angelic kingdoms and raises their frequency. She is so blessed to remember.

Five years ago I dreamt that I was in hospital with my leg in plaster. It was so vivid that I could remember all the details of the ward I was in. I was nervous that it might be a premonition, but relaxed after a few weeks. Three years later I found myself in the hospital I had dreamed of, with a broken leg. Isn't that bizarre?

In your sleep time you slipped into a possible future scenario, so it was a premonition. Your soul gave you three years in which to change your lifestyle so that you did not need to undergo that particular experience. However, your way of living and beliefs did not change sufficiently to alter the course of your future.

I dreamt of a plane crash in which many people died. I could very clearly see the wreckage. I woke feeling shaken and sick. To my shock, when I turned the television on next day, there was the crash exactly as I had seen in my dream. How could this happen?

In your dream state you can access other dimensions and times. You viewed a happening that had a huge amount of emotion attached to it, so you picked up some of the feelings of those involved. That is why you remembered it so clearly.

I often dream of earthquakes and disasters as they happen. When this occurs I wake feeling exhausted. Why?

You are able to tune psychically into these disasters. Your spirit goes out of your body on a rescue mission to help those who have died as well as comfort the survivors. You wake feeling exhausted because you have been working very hard.

When I was ill with a fever I dreamt my mother sat by my bed and stroked my hair. She said I would be all right. I felt very relieved but when I woke I realised that Mum was physically in another country. How could this happen?

The spirit is not bound by time or distance and your mother was only a thought away. On a psychic level she is very connected with you, so her spirit flew to you to comfort you as soon as she felt you were in danger. You remembered her presence and the way she stroked your hair as a dream.

When my children were small I occasionally dreamt that the house was on fire and I couldn't get them all out. I would wake in panic. This dream stopped as they grew older.

This actually happened to you in a past life and the feelings of panic have never been released. The unconscious memories rose to the surface while your children were young. A dream such as this also releases some of the stuck emotions and helps to free you from their thrall.

I have several friends who are intuitive. In the weeks before Kennedy was shot we all dreamt that he was assassinated. None of us could pinpoint a time or location. Could we have stopped it?

You all tuned into the energy which was building up before the dreadful event. However, it was a fated death and you could not have prevented it.

If I dream of a disaster or accident, what can I do?

You may be able to warn someone, but this may or may not be heeded. However, you can always pray for their safety and for help for the victims. Hold the scenario in the light and ask the angels to help those who die to pass over safely.

My son died when he was a baby. On what would have been his twelfth birthday I dreamed a young man came to me and smiled. He looked radiant and I felt it was him. He was telling me he was fine. Am I right?

Yes, your son in spirit has been growing up with you and your family. His soul chose to continue to experience and grow in this way rather than by living in a physical body. He did indeed meet you on his twelfth birthday to reassure you he was all right.

I have had an abortion and a miscarriage and I sometimes dream of two children playing happily in the garden. Could this be the spirits of the two I lost? If so, how best can I help them?

Yes, the spirits of the two children come to you in your dreams to remind you that they are fine. They are growing up with you in their spirit bodies and evolve as you and your family learn and experience. It really helps them when you acknowledge them. For example, putting a bauble on the tree for them at Christmas, or planting a flower in their name gives them a sense of belonging. The greatest help you can give them is to be happy yourself and to offer simple prayers for them.

⌒ Visualisation with prayer for the spirits of children ⌒

- ⌒ Light a candle for each spirit.
- ⌒ Thank them for touching your life.
- ⌒ Ask the angels to enfold them in love.
- ⌒ Say this prayer: Dear God, I ask you to bless and look after the spirits of these children.
- ⌒ Picture them whole, radiant, healthy and perfect.

When I was eight months pregnant I dreamt a little girl came to me and told me her name and that she was my daughter. Wasn't that wonderful? When she was born I called her by the name she gave me.

Yes, indeed it was. You must have been very open and receptive to enable her to connect so vividly and clearly with you. The vibration of a child's name is very important and calls many lessons to him or her. Usually it is transmitted telepathically from the child to the mother.

PUNS AND METAPHORS IN DREAMS

Why do some dreams contain puns or metaphors?

Dreams bring hidden feelings or situations to the awareness of the dreamer. In order to pass these through the critical censor, the unconscious cleverly disguises them as metaphors or puns.

I dreamt a hen was wearing pink glasses. What does this indicate?

The mother-hen part of you is looking at your family through rose-coloured lenses.

I'm putting on a pair of wellingtons but my feet are too big for them. What could this mean?

Metaphorically speaking you are too big for your boots. It behoves you to be more modest and humble.

I dreamt that my new boyfriend was eating a piece of cheese while I was scribbling with a piece of chalk. Is this significant?

Your soul is drawing to your attention that you and your boyfriend are as different as chalk and cheese. Because your Higher Self has your greatest interests at heart, it wishes you to be aware of this so that you consider the viability of your relationship.

In my dream a man I work with is outside flying a big red kite. Does this have a meaning?

Flying a kite can indicate having fun, but it also suggests that there is no foundation for his ideas, though they are full of energy, as indicated by the colour and size of the kite. It reminds you to be careful of exaggeration.

I dreamt that a man was walking out of the house fast asleep in pyjamas and about to cross a busy road.

The man in your dream is your masculine energy, representing your outgoing nature or your career. That aspect of you is sleep-walking you into a dangerous situation.

In my dream my sister is heavily pregnant and is jumping over the moon. In reality she is single and a journalist.

Being pregnant in a dream is about bringing a creative idea or project forward. This one is quite far advanced, as indicated by your sister being heavily pregnant. Being over the moon infers feeling delighted with what is happening. When you dream about someone else, it asks you to look at qualities you project on to that person. What adjectives do you use to describe your sibling? What does she represent? Those aspects of you are very pleased about something you are creating. This particular dream is not a psychic one, so it is about you and your internal processes.

My friend dreamt she could see a huge black cloud above me with a silver lining. I have been having a difficult time recently.

This is a psychic dream. Your friend has been very concerned about you and has received a message from the spiritual world that there will be good things coming to you soon.

My boyfriend was holding some leaves in my dream. I woke feeling anxious. Do the leaves represent anything important?

This is a pun. Your boyfriend is thinking about leaving and you have picked this up, which accounts for your anxiety.

RECURRING DREAMS

Why do dreams recur?

Dreams are a method of drawing something to your conscious attention. If you do nothing about the message but remain stuck in the same situation or feelings, your soul will continue to bring this to your notice until you deal with it.

Every six months or so, I dream that a little girl is lost and alone and no one can hear her cries for help. I wake up feeling quite tearful, with a lump in my throat. What does this mean, and what can I do about it?

Your adult self has devised coping mechanisms to deal with life. Your soul is using your dream to remind you that your inner child still feels lost and alone. When you were small, there were times when you believed no one was there for you and you were very sad and vulnerable. Each time this old feeling is triggered, the dream surfaces. As a youngster you could not do anything about it. However, your adult self can now listen to your inner child's feelings. It is certainly time to do this and heal your past.

Remember that, because your outer life reflects your inner, while this dream recurs you will attract to you people who are careless of your emotional needs.

In dreams like this, it does not matter whether you are a man or woman; the inner child can be a boy or a girl, reflecting your yang or yin energy.

Exercise to help your inner child
1. Find a space where you can be quiet and undisturbed.
2. Close your eyes and imagine yourself back in the dream.
3. This time your adult self finds the little girl who is lost and alone.
4. You hold her and tell her she is safe.
5. You ask her what she needs and listen to her without censure or interruption.
6. Use your creative imagination to satisfy her yearnings and reassure her fears.
7. Tell her you will always respond when she needs you. This commitment means redoing this exercise once a week for a time. Also watch your thoughts and feelings and start fulfilling your inner child's desires.
8. Open your eyes and give yourself a hug.

I smile when I remember the recurring dreams I used to have.

When I moved from seeing individual clients into group work, I ran workshops from my home, but clearly my soul wanted me to progress into bigger courses in the wider world. My first dream was of buffaloes running round my workroom trying to find a way out. The second was my garden full of wild animals all trying to escape into the wide world. The third was even clearer and more graphic. A large blue fish jumped out of a small pond and made its way across dry land towards a bigger pool! A fish is a spiritual symbol to me, and blue is the colour of communication. It was this dream that finally forced me to expand.

*I have consistently dreamt the same dream over the last
few years. I leave home on business and when I return I
find I have forgotten to feed my dog and cat, who are
skeletal and starving. I am working away from home a
great deal, but I don't have any animals. Is this relevant?
Please help me understand this.*

In your dream, working away from home indicates that you are
out of touch with your consciousness. In this case you have abandoned your need for nourishment, physical, emotional, mental
or spiritual. The cat represents feminine energy, the psychic,
nurturing, wise, loving part of you. The dog represents masculine energy, the way you support yourself by earning a living,
how you defend yourself and how you logically think things
through. You are feeding neither of these aspects. You will know
when you have dealt with the imbalance because the dreams will
not return.

When you have a dream about someone or something starving, the
questions to ask yourself are: How do I get my emotional needs fulfilled?
Do I eat the right foods? Am I mentally stimulated? Am I following a
spiritual practice?

*I often dream I can fly. I feel free and powerful, then I
wake up to ordinary life. Why do I keep having this
dream, and what does it mean?*

There are three possible ways to translate this dream.

Sometimes it is a psychic dream in which you are remem-
bering the experience of your spirit flying out of your body on
its night-time journey.

Secondly it can be a wish-fulfilment dream in which your
desire to be free and powerful is being metaphorically presented
to you. If this intuitively seems right decide what you need to

293

do in order to achieve this feeling, and start working towards it. Remember that situations and conditions do not imprison you. Only your mind can do that, and then your life follows suit.

Thirdly, it may be a past-life dream. Those who were Initiates in Atlantis had to learn to overcome gravity and fly in order to access the Temple of Poseidon. They also had enormous power. If this seems correct, meditate on Atlantis and practise visualisation and mind-control exercises to start bringing back your wisdom and higher powers.

I sometimes dream I am about to trip and fall over a cliff. What does this mean?

Please start looking where you are going. There are problems that you do not yet see, and the consequences would be very challenging. Your soul would like you to avoid these.

This is a classic fear of failure dream. When you have such a dream, the questions to ask yourself are: In what way can I trip myself up? Will the feared outcome be so dreadful? It reminds you to take stock of your life and decide what you can or cannot do. Look out for pitfalls. Meditate about success. Decide what you want to accomplish and visualise this positively in a relaxed and happy way.

Graham rarely remembered his dreams, so when he was woken one night by this very vivid one for the third time in as many months, he was bemused. He was about to trip over and bang his nose.

We discussed where he could fall over in his life, and what his nose meant to him. A nose traditionally represents intuition or being nosy. He flushed when I told him this.

'Oh,' he said. 'I've been worried about my wife and I've been looking in her diary to check what she's doing when she's late home. Would that be the nose bit, do you think?'

I nodded and asked, 'And what does your intuition tell you she is doing?'

He responded promptly. 'I think she's seeing someone, and that really would trip me up.' He looked agonised for a moment.

He decided his dream was a warning that his suspicious attitude was putting his marriage in danger. He matured and started to consider and care for his wife. Their relationship survived, possibly thanks to him listening to his recurring dream warning.

My recurring dream has the following elements. I am always locked up or chained, and there is a cruel guard outside my door. He refuses to let me out and I feel so frustrated. What does this mean, and how can I stop having it? I wake feeling very stressed and tense.

Discipline in your life is out of balance and has become control. Your soul is asking you to relax and enjoy life.

This is the dream of a workaholic who gives himself no freedom to have fun; or the person who feels he cannot get away from a situation that he himself has perpetrated. Whichever it is, it is not helping your spiritual journey, so take decisions to give yourself space and fun. Enjoy your life.

In my most frequent dream I am driving a sports car too fast and am out of control. Would it help me to understand this dream?

You are racing through life too fast. It is a warning to slow down while you can. Take life more easily before something happens to you that you cannot do anything about.

Moving too fast and out of control in a dream is a warning. It may be that you are taking decisions which are too hasty, working too hard, pursuing a relationship too quickly or burning the candle at both ends. It indicates it is time to put on the brakes.

SPIRITUAL DREAMS

I have had a bad shoulder for years and have been
praying for help for a long time. After reading Angel
Inspiration *by Diana Cooper I asked to go to Archangel*
Raphael for healing in my sleep. That night I dreamt
golden hands were stroking my neck. When I woke the
pain was gone and it has been fine every since. Was this
really an angel healing?

Your prayers were answered. Your spirit visited Archangel Raphael
during the night and received grace. This healed your physical
symptoms.

When my father died I felt overwhelmed with grief. I
prayed for help and dreamt that a choir of angels was
singing over my bed. I felt as if all the pain was being
lifted from my heart.

Angels were indeed singing over you. They heard your prayers,
felt your grief and responded with divine compassion. Their love
and the vibration of their music dissolved your pain.

I dreamt I was riding on a beautiful white unicorn and it
felt wonderful. Was it really happening at some level?

Like the angels, unicorns are etheric beings, which you cannot
normally see or hear unless you are psychic. In your dreams,
however, you can meet them. Your unicorn has visited you to
take you beyond the bounds of limited understandings and
to remind you of the magic and mystery of life. This divine
creature will help you to aspire to a higher vision with courage
and dignity.

I dreamt I was swimming with a pod of dolphins. One of
them looked at me with such love that I thought my
heart was melting. Then I felt as if codes were being

placed in my third eye. Is it possible that this really happened at another level?

Yes. You have a great affinity with dolphins, who are the keepers of the oceans and hold much ancient wisdom. Some of this was being downloaded to you. At the same time your heart was open to their love.

I dreamt an old crone was handing me an amethyst. Does this have any significance?

The crones were the wise women. An amethyst is the stone containing the power of transmutation and ability to rise to higher spiritual levels. During your sleep your wisdom is being triggered and your gifts are being returned to you.

My mother was senile and quite nasty to me. I did not like her. Then one night I had a very vivid dream that she was a beautiful, radiant young woman and was looking at me with such love. I woke feeling that her higher self had visited me. It felt so very special.

Yes, your mother's Higher Self is a beautiful being, very different from the personality she is currently displaying on Earth. She cannot physically express her love for you, so her visit was to help you understand how very much she does love you.

I dreamt I was being shown a symbol by St Germain. Could this have been real and what shall I do with it?

Yes, St Germain is an Illumined One. You were with him during your sleep and he was teaching you. The symbol is a key to open part of your mind. Draw a picture of it if you can, and look at it frequently, so that it can do its work unconsciously.

Some years ago I woke from a very vivid dream in which a young man comes across a Tibetan monk, who gives him an Atlantean scroll as he dies. He tells Marcus it is his destiny to get it translated and spread round the world. The dream takes place in the Himalayas.

I wrote it down carefully because I knew without doubt that I was being given the first part of a spiritual novel. It was also interesting that I was born in the Himalayas. A year later I met my daughter in India for a holiday and we found ourselves in the scene of the dream. It took another year and many travels before the remainder of the story was revealed to me. Eventually it became *The Silent Stones*, the first novel in my trilogy.

I dreamt I walked to the tree at the end of my garden and there were fairies dancing round it. They did not see me but I stayed and watched entranced for some time. Then I woke up. Were they real?

So you have seen the fairies at the bottom of your garden. In your dream state you were able to tune into their world. Now you know that they are really there, vibrating at a frequency that most of you cannot see. Make your garden chemical-free and inviting for them and they will respond by making your space beautiful.

A Last Word

I hope *Angel Answers* has helped you to look at life from a higher and more benevolent perspective. It may have answered some of your queries, but I am sure there are many more. Your guardian angel is very close to you and is ready and willing to respond to your questions. Please remember to ask, then still your mind so that your angel can impress information into you.

Your angels can help you in every area of your life, so tune into their energy and know they will support you. It is time now to move forward with confidence.

List of Exercises, Visualisations and Prayers